MY SPIN
ON
CRICKET

MY SPIN ON CRICKET

Richie Benaud

H
HODDER &
STOUGHTON

Copyright © 2005 by Richie Benaud

First published in Great Britain in 2005 by Hodder and Stoughton
A division of Hodder Headline

The right of Richie Benaud to be identified as the Author
of the Work has been asserted by him in accordance with the
Copyright, Designs and Patents Act 1988.

A Hodder and Stoughton Book

3

A CIP catalogue record for this title is available from the British Library

ISBN 0340 833939

Typeset in Stone Serif by Hewer Text UK Ltd, Edinburgh
Printed and bound by
Mackays of Chatham Ltd, Chatham, Kent

Hodder Headline's policy is to use papers that are natural, renewable
and recyclable products and made from wood grown in sustainable forests.
The logging and manufacturing processes are expected to conform to
the environmental regulations of the country of origin.

Hodder and Stoughton Ltd
A division of Hodder Headline
338 Euston Road
London NW1 3BH

Sometimes dedicating a book can run to pages, almost a small book in itself. This is simply to say thanks to all those who, for me, in the short space of 75 years, have made cricket a game of such character, full of so many characters. I've raised a glass to Colin Cowdrey, Ted Dexter and others who have provided a reminder that it should be no hardship to embrace the Spirit of Cricket as well as the winning of the game. Subtly, they have also posed the question of whether it really is impossible to win a cricket match without what, in these modern times, is known as sledging.

CONTENTS

Acknowledgments   ix

Introduction   1

1   Time to Say Goodbye   3

2   Some Cricket Joy   18

3   A Fleeting Regret   32

4   Say What You Think   45

5   Raised Fingers   58

6   Offbeat Television   78

7   Technology – a Problem?   93

8   Being a Selector   103

9   'Tiger'   126

10   Illusions Abound   139

11   The Season   161

12   Well Bowled   168

13   Three Greats   178

14   Six Australian Innings   193

15   Australian Hall of Fame   216

16   The Entertainers – West Indies   229

17   Admin – Take It or Leave It   239

18   One-day Cricket   253

19   Two Young Guns   263

20   Potpourri   271

Something for administrators to ponder

At the Double – over the years

Richie Benaud Biography

Epilogue – people cricket can't do without

Index   280

ACKNOWLEDGMENTS

One of the great joys of being associated with cricket is that it is such a diverse game and one which never stands still. Like the players who take part, the game itself is always evolving with new playing conditions and the method of taking it to the watching, reading and viewing world changes almost day by day. Television provides a constant challenge, not so much in the sense of talking a great deal, but more in what to avoid saying. Book writing is a big challenge, so it was no wonder Daphne calmly looked at me for some considerable time when I mentioned casually that, after eight years, we were about to write another one. She mentioned, just as casually, that my 100-year-old mother had said a few days earlier that she was pleased we had decided not to write another book. Daphne's knowledge of the English language, sub-editing, cricket, television and the ability to work twenty hours a day has made a very difficult job considerably easier. Our assistants, Cathy Mycock in Coogee, and Clare Oldridge in London, as well as Vivienne Schuster of Curtis Brown, have provided great assistance. John Benaud, with his calm editorial eye and common sense approach has again provided valuable help. There is no doubt cricket is still the most controversial game of all and there are always things we can do without, but the game certainly remains a reflection of life. Roddy Bloomfield continues to be the bravest publisher we know; the extra grey hairs and the ice-packs haven't dimmed his enthusiasm and we are extremely grateful to him.

Richie Benaud
Coogee, Australia
February 2005

Photographic acknowledgments

The author and publisher would like to thank the following for permission to reproduce photographs:

Patrick Eagar, Empics, Allsport Hulton Archive/Getty Images, Popperfoto.com

All other photographs are from private collections.

INTRODUCTION

O NE of the most pleasant times we've had in recent years was when Daphne and I went with an ITC-organised trip to watch England play West Indies in Barbados and Antigua. This was as a preface to the 2004 English summer where I was due to cover for Channel Four and *News of the World* the two series, seven Tests in all, between England, New Zealand and West Indies. As New Zealand were due to tour Australia in October, and then West Indies were going to be there for the triangular series, there was plenty of information to be gained from watching at Kensington Oval, Bridgetown, Barbados and then at the Recreation Ground, St John's, Antigua.

In addition there was the good fortune of having Tony and Joan Lewis and David and Thorunn Gower on the ship and also Laurence and Val Parry from Sarasota, Florida, where I am the Patron of the cricket club which they started many years ago.

The organisation was brilliant, as is always the case with Drew Foster, who was responsible for a splendid piece of advice at the pool-deck bar when we were having a rum punch or two made to the bartender's special recipe. The subject was cricket and Drew asked me a question which I couldn't answer without checking some records. I said to him that he should ask Daphne who was further along the bar chatting to Val Parry. He did that, received the answer, came back and asked me another question and I said Daph would have the answer. He came back happy with the second answer and asked me a third question. Again I said Daph would definitely know because she had checked the particular Test match only a couple of days ago.

Drew said, 'I'll catch up with everyone at lunch' and turned to go down the stairs. Then he stopped, walked slowly back to the group at the bar, looked hard at me and said, 'Rich, do you mind if I offer just a small piece of advice? *Don't leave home without Daphne* . . .' It was a nice throwaway line and brought a roar of approval from the rum punch group, so good that one day it could be on a bookshelf sitting alongside *Anything but . . . an Autobiography*!

The fifty-seven years I have been playing, watching or commentating on cricket have been a mixture where the good things have far outweighed those that have been disappointing. It's a good lesson for everyone; that a youngster who throws a tennis ball up against a wall in a country town can still go on to captain his country at cricket, watch more than 500 Test matches, see cricket played in daylight and, as well, at night. It's been a fortunate life and one which has been very much enjoyed.

1

TIME TO SAY GOODBYE

S ARAH BRIGHTMAN and Andrea Bocelli sing one of the most beautiful duets ever produced in the world of music and listening. '*Time to say Goodbye*' has about it all the qualities needed to finish off a day of wonderful cricket at Lord's or the Sydney Cricket Ground. It's a case of the cut and thrust and sheer brilliance of the day's play at those grounds leaving me wanting to raise a celebratory glass at The Montcalm or Coogee a few minutes after the close of play, then another in anticipation of the morrow. Four minutes and four seconds of pure sound. There may be better voices than Bocelli's but I haven't been lucky enough to hear them. Brightman is at her poignant best with 'I'll go with you . . .'

Their short duet has always provided a connection for me with my early days, experiences which gradually disappeared and were never able to be reclaimed by a young cricketer.

> *I'll go with you*
> *Upon ships across the seas*
> *Seas that exist no more*
> *I'll revive them with you.*

When I was first chosen in the 1953 Australian touring team under Lindsay Hassett's captaincy, we boarded a ship at Fremantle and sailed to England. I was a Parramatta boy and, because I had been lucky enough to play cricket, I had been outside New South Wales, but being on a ship was something else. My father had been on a small steam-ship in 1917 when his family moved from Coraki to

Grafton in northern NSW. Neither of my parents had ever been on an aeroplane at any stage of their lifetimes. I travelled by plane early in my cricket career, now, in 1953, I was about to travel first-class to England, second-sitting dinner at the ship's captain's table, dress: dinner jacket. I did the same as a player in 1956 and 1961, the latter year I was captain. The next time by aeroplane, 1963, was my first tour undertaken for free-to-air BBC Television and that retainer continued until 1999, then the last six English summers have all been for Channel Four. As well, there has been Australian commercial free-to-air television with Channel Nine from 1977 to the current time.

In those early 'fifties and 'sixties, television was slightly primitive compared with today. Television didn't begin in Australia until 1956, Channel Nine was the first to go to air and the first presenter on Sunday, 16 September, 1956, was Bruce Gyngell. This was on the day after the Australian cricket tour of England finished with the match against Scotland at Aberdeen. We had all been given a three-week break at the end of the tour of England and each player had made his own decision on what he would do during that break. The team travelled by train from Aberdeen to London to pack and on Monday, 17 September, I moved from the Kensington Palace Hotel to the Royal Automobile Club. The team during the tour had been honorary members of that club and I had organised my accommodation in a tiny room on the lower ground floor which was going to suit me as I was paying all my own expenses for that three-week period. My decision of what to do in the break was to attend a specially-arranged BBC Television training course organised for me by Tom Sloan, BBC's Head of Light Entertainment. He set up for me a comprehensive list ranging through sports events, drama and comedy, and alternating between directors' boxes, sitting at the side of the audience, standing at the back of the director's van and many other aspects which I found fascinating.

There was a small story in a couple of London newspapers stating that television had begun in Sydney, but it was of no real importance in London because the medium had been going there for a considerable number of years.

If I hadn't done the BBC course in 1956 my life would have been very different. It was a most fortunate experience, even though I had to wait seven years for my chance actually to find any work on television as a sports commentator. In 1960 I worked on BBC Radio but up to the First Test, England v West Indies at Lord's in 1963, I had never done anything on television other than be interviewed. This was when I was captain of the Australian team and during that 1960 English summer I was several times interviewed by Brian Johnston and Peter West. It was great experience.

I had watched and listened to Henry Longhurst and Dan Maskell in the 1953, 1956, 1960 and 1961 English summers and had trailed around behind Peter O'Sullevan at Newbury for two days during the 1956 BBC course. The key feature with all of them seemed to be economy of words, even Peter, who had to describe the races with a running commentary. It was natural for me to follow the same path, at least until I was shown, or told, this was not the way to go. It isn't easy being a summariser on television and at the same time being economical with words but, on BBC, it was mandatory there would be comments made at the end of each over, even if nothing much had happened. It was important to be able sensibly to fill that gap between overs.

I knew none of the work I had done in the BBC training course would be of direct use to me on arrival back in Australia. I looked on it though as a form of insurance if I were, for example, to be interviewed on television. At least I would know what was going on. With TV in its infancy in Australia, the two channels available for viewing had their own schedules worked out, as well as their own commentators and stars. Any work coming my way would be well in the future, if at all, and I was more concerned with doing well in the Australian summer with bat and ball and then making it into the Australian team for the short and unofficial tour of New Zealand, also the major one against South Africa which was scheduled to start at the beginning of October 1957.

Lord's 1956 was a turning point for me in my cricket career. I didn't know it then but I was approximately half way through the 16-year span of breaking into first-class cricket in 1948–49 and retiring in 1963–64. If Lord's was a turning point, then the South African tour was vital because it was there I managed to make a mark as a Test match cricketer, in the main due to the extra responsibility I was given.

Scheduling of Australian tours of England was strange in those days. The sequence was 1948–1953–1956 and then 1961. That was one reason it was such a good idea to begin what might be termed a proper job at the newspaper and try to build a career in writing, which I enjoyed anyway. It was around this time that television networks and the Australian Board of Control started talking about the televising of cricket, albeit in an extremely low-key manner. No one at this stage had the slightest idea of the impact television would have on sport, or sport on television, almost 50 years on.

One of the great ironies of the administrators' dipping-a-toe-in-the-water approach around this time was that the first match they allowed to be televised was sensibly chosen because they decided the two strongest teams in Sheffield Shield Cricket, New South Wales and Victoria, should provide the entertainment. And it was played at the suburban St Kilda ground in Melbourne in 1956–57 because the MCG was out of action for cricket, being listed as the main stadium for the 1956 Olympic Games which were to be held from 27 November to 8 December. The television people didn't properly realise the significance of the match, they were far too busy putting together all their outside broadcast equipment and making certain a signal was getting as far as the city of Melbourne up the road and possibly to the whole of the metropolitan area.

What made it even more unusual was that the game was played

over six days, though only four of them were actual playing days. It started on Saturday, 22 December. There was no cricket then on Sundays, so that took out the 23rd, we played on the 24th, but not on Christmas Day, the 25th. The game then continued on Boxing Day and came to its gripping climax late in the afternoon of Thursday, the 27th. The crowd paying their money on the last day totalled 7,092 through the turnstiles, but quite a few of them had gone home to watch on television by the time the final wicket was taken by Ian Meckiff for the match to be tied.

It was the beginning of what for me is a rather unusual record in that I have seen three ties in Australian cricket, that one at St Kilda, then the Tied Test at the 'Gabba when I was captain against the West Indies in 1960, and the one in Adelaide, South Australia v Queensland in early February 1977, just before the Centenary Test at the MCG. There were three run-outs in the final over of the Queensland second innings, Phil Carlson, Malcolm Francke and Col Cooke. It was not dissimilar to the final over Australia had gone through 17 years earlier at the 'Gabba. One thing we did know after the Victoria v NSW match in 1956 was that the television people went home happy because there had been some excitement to show the viewers. At least it showed both cricket administrators and television networks that there might be something in this cricket business, though the general feeling in Australia was that it was all a bit too drawn out to be able to hold the attention of viewers over four or five days.

The good news for them was that it didn't cost much. The television network had to pay £50 apiece to the NSW Cricket Association and the Victorian Cricket Association.

Later relaying cricket telecasts became very important. When, on 9 January 1959, Australia played England at the SCG in the third match of the Ashes battle, the final two hours of play each day were relayed from Sydney to Melbourne. This in a sense was an experiment, but it worked, and it was the basis of more televised cricket when the West Indian side came to Australia under Frank Worrell's captaincy in 1960–61. In fact, that Tied Test series was the catalyst for televised sport in Australia, so exciting were the matches and so captivating the thought for viewers that they would be able to watch the action at no cost from an armchair in their living-room. Television had only been a factor in Australian life for a relatively short time at this stage, something around four years, and it was only the linking of ground-based relay stations between Melbourne and Sydney that allowed a complete telecast of the final Test in Melbourne in February 1961. The series at that stage stood at 1–1 following the 'Gabba tie. Between the first and last matches of the series Sydney viewers had been able to watch the last couple of hours of Australia winning the Second Test played in Melbourne. Additionally, at the end of the Adelaide Test, the Fourth, one of the biggest viewing audiences to watch television to that time in Australia tuned in to see 'Slasher' Mackay and Lindsay Kline save the match for Australia in dramatic fashion. It was the kind of audience that in 1961 could only ever be obtained by an extra-ordinary prime-time evening show or a special event.

The introduction of satellite technology meant that in 1970–71, when Ray Illingworth brought the England team to Australia, the whole of the country was able to watch the Test series on televi-sion. This, purely by coincidence, turned out to be one of the more important happenings for cricket because, when the first three days of the 1970–71 Melbourne Test were completely washed out on 31 December and 1 and 2 January, the cricket authorities from both countries tried to find something to interest an irritated and frustrated Melbourne cricket public and they arranged a one-day match with a maximum of 40 eight-ball overs each side. This was slightly more than the 50 overs of six balls that apply to all one-day Internationals these days. It was an instant success. No one had really bothered to tell the players what was going on, or what was about to go on, nor had anyone asked them if they wanted to play a one-day match. There was some one-day cricket being played between the Australian states at that time and I had watched and been part of television in England one-day cricket for the previous ten years. That began in England with Rothmans Sunday matches, then the 'Cup' started in England in 1963 with 65 overs maximum for each team, and, extraordinarily, with no sponsor, though later Gillette came in as the first sponsor of that facet of the game.

The match at the MCG in 1971 drew a crowd of 46,000. It was a splendid game and ABC Television had great ratings, though in those days they spurned ratings as being something invented by the devils of commercial television. How times change! In 1972 the whole of the final day of The Oval Test was telecast by satellite to Australia on the ABC and then the introduction of colour television on 5 March, 1975 further lifted audience interest. Hundreds of thousands stayed up through the night to watch the 1975 World Cup final telecast from Lord's and this match also alerted the minds of Australian government ministers to the fact that legislation was necessary to ensure the type of programmes which would be shown at certain times during a 24-hour period.

The Australian Broadcasting Control Board decreed that from six o'clock in the morning through to midnight at least half the programmes shown had to be Australian in origin. Until this legislation was enforced, most sports broadcasts were handled by the Australian Broadcasting Commission, serving not only the capital cities but also far-flung country areas. It was certainly free-to-air. The attention of commercial networks was drawn to the possibility of covering cricket once colour was introduced and it was the following year that Channel Nine lodged with the Australian Board of Control a bid for the exclusive rights to televise cricket.

The bid was something that should have caught the attention of the Australian cricket authorities because it was A$500,000 a season for three seasons, compared with the A\$70,000 a season being offered by the Australian Broadcasting Commission. The Cricket Board at that time had Bob Parish as chairman and Kerry Packer had been trying for several months to arrange a meeting with him to discuss the matter of exclusive rights. At the 1977 High Court hearing before Mr Justice Slade, Mr Packer testified that he had failed to organise that meeting and then later was very quickly told, when he walked into the board's meeting, that they were declining his offer because the rights had already been granted to the ABC. Mr Packer in the witness box added his opinion that the board's lament that they weren't able to pay the cricketers more money could have been solved instantly by accepting Channel Nine's bid. The board's miserly payment of players was quickly to be a factor in the greatest change ever to take place in cricket.

When Channel Nine decided on their tactics regarding ratings in the year of 1977 it was a coincidence that one of the people Mr Packer talked to on a personal basis was John Cornell, who was the manager of Australian television star Paul Hogan. At the same time, one of John Cornell's friends, Austin Robertson, a former Australian Rules footballer, talked to him about his knowledge of serious player unrest over the fact that the Australian Cricket Board were paying the players as little as possible in match fees. Also that there were similar difficulties in other countries over the fact that administrators wouldn't listen to the players on the subject of higher payments.

From that came World Series Cricket and for two years Channel Nine televised their own matches while the ABC televised the Australian board matches. It was Mr Packer who tabled the idea of playing day-night games with the grounds floodlit for the second half of the matches, as in American baseball, with spectators able to leave their place of work and go to the grounds to see a result. Television coverage also changed. To that time a cricket match had been covered with the minimum number of cameras, now Channel Nine started using eight cameras and coverage in WSC matches was from both ends so that viewers would no longer see the backside of the wicket-keeper, just in front of that the backside of the batsman, then the bowler in the distance running towards the camera and therefore the front of both the above-mentioned players.

One of the reasons commercial television began to be interested in cricket coverage was certainly the Australian content provision for programming, but equally the fact that the Australian population was increasingly interested in buying television sets.

The advent of colour TV made a big impact on sales in various retail outlets and although, in that, there was no direct benefit to the television networks, there definitely was the dramatic indirect benefit that more television sets around the country meant the possibility of more advertising and a vastly expanded market. This market involved an increase in television being watched in homes around Australia from 58% to 80%. As is the case with all sport from the moment television took hold, the watching audience paying their money at the turnstiles was a small number compared with those who might choose to watch it in their own homes. A Test at the SCG for example could cater in a day for 35,000 to 40,000 paying spectators, whereas the same play could be televised throughout the country to more than two million people.

The aim over the past 28 years in Australia, as far as Channel Nine are concerned, has been and remains to provide viewers with the best seat in the house. Mr Packer and David Hill, the producer, revolutionised the way cricket was telecast and things which were innovative in the early years are now regarded as commonplace. When Hill and Brian Morelli, the senior director, at a cricket match in Perth in the early 1980s invented the moving scorecard, the 'ticker' in the top left-hand corner of the screen, it was regarded as an extraordinary breakthrough. Now it is taken for granted, no sports telecast would be without it and it is being adapted in new ways every year.

Australian sports television certainly became far more innovative in the late 1970s when Channel Nine showed the way through World Series Cricket. Those innovations continued and were extended from 1 December, 1979 when Channel Nine telecast the first match after the return to official cricket of World Series players. Everything was and is geared to providing the best possible pictures and as much information as possible for viewers at home or in whichever place they might be watching the match.

There have been many changes in cricket watching and television over the past 50 years, some of them seemingly grand at the time, later received with a wave of the hand. All of them noted below had a significant effect on the way Australians watched their sport, not least the fact that those going to the grounds these days have the benefit of a large colour electronic scoreboard which allows spectators to see replays of various incidents. In the tied Sheffield Shield match at St Kilda, the scoreboard at the ground for that historic match was of the same type as any other at a suburban cricket ground where cricket and football would be played. On the larger grounds where Sheffield Shield was regularly played, the best scoreboards, and the envy of cricket visitors to Australia, were at Sydney, Melbourne and Adelaide.

There have been many important dates in the history of Australian TV and cricket, none more important than 21 June, 1975, the first time Australian audiences saw a full day's play from a match played overseas. It was that Prudential World Cup final played at Lord's, won by the West Indies over Australia by 17 runs. The extraordinary match finished at 8.42 p.m. London time (7.42 a.m. on the east coast of Australia). It featured for the Australian audience colour television and action-replays and was one of the highlights of my media career. What the Australian audience saw was the BBC production, with David Kenning and Bill Taylor the producers, and a commentary team led by Peter West as presenter, Jim Laker, Ted Dexter and me as commentators. Laker and I were the lead commentators, Ted was the expert summariser. The match was 60 overs a side maximum and we were each commentating over a nine-hour stretch. It sounds a lot, and it was, but it was also one of the great experiences of my life and one where I was extremely grateful for having decided to do that BBC course almost 20 years earlier.

Also very important was 28 November, 1978, the first televised day-night match ever played at the Sydney Cricket Ground, World Series Cricket Australia v West Indies.

One feature of Australian sports watching is the excellent grounds and facilities for spectators where both cricket watchers and football enthusiasts are very well catered for. As regards television it has always been a part of the Australian sporting landscape that certain events, if being shown live, will be on an anti-siphoning list and restricted to free-to-air television which could be the Australian Broadcasting Commission or commercial networks, but it is definitely *not* Pay Television.

Fewer than one in four households in Australia had access to Pay Television in 2004 and the aim of the anti-siphoning legislation is to ensure that as many viewers as possible are able to access important events without having to pay.

The latest list was published on 7 April, 2004 and this took account of the fact that some smaller sports on the old list were receiving no television air-time. On the new list are sports like Rugby League and Rugby Union, horseracing with the Melbourne Cup, the England FA Cup Final, Wimbledon, the Open Championship, the Olympic Games and the Commonwealth Games. The list is in force until 31 December, 2010. The full list for cricket remaining on free-to-air television is:

- Each Test match played in either Australia or the United Kingdom involving the senior Australian representative team selected by Cricket Australia.
- Each one-day cricket match played in Australia or the United Kingdom involving the senior Australian representative team selected by Cricket Australia.
- Each one-day cricket match played as part of a series in which at least one match of the series is played in Australia involving the senior Australian representative team selected by Cricket Australia.
- Each one-day World Cup cricket match.

There was criticism in the Australian Federal Parliament of one aspect of the April 2004 legislation not going far enough to address an anomaly. This had allowed Australia's Premier Media, formerly Fox Sports, to use a loophole in the government's rules to buy the rights to the 2005 Ashes series in the UK. These then were sold on to Pay Television.

It can be said correctly that, because of free-to-air TV, I've had the best of both worlds for a long time in my working life. The BBC course was undertaken with an eye to the future, although I had no idea where that future might take me, if indeed it would take me anywhere at all. The fact is when I started working in television it was in England and for the BBC, all of which merely underlines that cricket and its appendages often are a game of chance.

When I started with the BBC at the beginning of that England v West Indies series in 1963, it was with Ray Lakeland and Phil Lewis as producers, Brian Johnston, Robert Hudson and then Peter West leading the commentary, Denis Compton and I were the summarisers. After the Lord's Test, where he was injured and played no more in the series, Colin Cowdrey came in as an extra summariser. Up until 1967 Jim Swanton also did a considerable amount of work on TV as well as on radio. He was the one summing up at the close of play and he was outstanding, always with perfect timing to close the programme to the right second. To say 1963 and the following summers were interesting would be something of an understatement!

I was also a journalist and had been through the experience of working with Noel Bailey on *The Sun* Police Rounds where it was pointless writing more than you had been asked to write because, no matter how brilliant the extra words might be in your own mind, they would never see the light of day in the chief sub-editor's mind.

When, in 1972, Ian Chappell's team toured England, the established rostering was that Peter West would be presenter, Jim Laker and I would be the commentators and Denis Compton and Ted Dexter the summarisers, with David Kenning and Nick Hunter the regular producer/directors. It worked very well, we were pleased with it and apparently the BBC found the new method very much to their liking as well. The working situation is different in England when compared with Australia. In Australia there is always a producer seated in the commentary box and he will be responsible for the content of the programme whereas, in England with the BBC, it was a case of the producer/director being in charge of everything from the van. It all works well, no matter which method is being used and it is a case of the commentator adjusting to the situation. When I joined Channel Four though, Gary Franses, an outstanding executive producer as well as director, preferred to work with the Channel Nine method.

One thing never changes for the commentator. Before he opens his mouth he must put his brain into gear. You can phrase it as you wish but that stricture, or gentle advice, has never basically changed since the time cricket television began in England in 1938. When Brian Johnston was asked to start work on television on 22 June, 1946, when the Indian team toured England, he was seated alongside Aidan Crawley for the First Test at Lord's. For the final

Test of the three-match series he had with him Percy Fender, Jim Swanton, Dudley Vernon and R.C. 'Crusoe' Robertson-Glasgow. Seymour de Lotbiniere was Head of Outside Broadcasts and he set down for Brian what was known as a Pyramid method of commentating, the most important part of which, in relation solely to television, said: *'Don't speak unless you can add to the picture.'*

You can't put it more clearly than that and it has certainly stood the test of time over the past 60 years. It has the great advantage of keeping things simple and, at the same time, having right at the forefront of a commentator's mind that on television the pictures tell a story, though not necessarily the full story.

That is completed by the commentator who needs to remember he is on his own with that microphone in his hand. No one can save him because whatever he utters goes to air and to millions of viewers. The other aspect is how the commentator goes about telling the audience what has happened if the audience already knows because they are watching the action on their television set at home. I was very lucky to have started television with the BBC when I did. 1963 was a quarter of a century after the first televised cricket match in England which was at Lord's when Bradman brought his team to the old country in 1938. It was then nothing more than a hopeful experiment. Three cameras were used, two of them at the Nursery End and the third was on the roof of the old Tavern. The first commentator, and the only commentator, was Teddy Wakelam who quickly realised that radio commentary, which he had already done, was, in every sense, completely different from what the television commentator needed to achieve.

His view all those years ago was that the television commentator would be in the position of helping and explaining what was occurring. He was before his time in understanding that a radio commentary providing a brilliant, exciting description of stroke-play, fielding, bowling, and other aspects of action on the field, might run into trouble if people sitting back in their armchairs at home could see precisely what was happening.

Television can undo some people because it does enable everyone to see precisely what is going on. The flowery phrase on radio and the cleverly-sculpted paragraph in the newspaper also need to be accurate because television leaves no margin for error or exaggeration. A commentator on live television must always remember that he has no fairy godmother looking after him in the guise of a sub-editor.

Free-to-air television is all I have ever worked on and Bocelli and Brightman have perfectly summed up my life with their magnificent voices in their beautiful and aptly-titled song.

2

SOME CRICKET JOY

CRICKET is very much a reflection of life. What you see happening on a cricket field can invariably be related to what is going on in the real world, sometimes joy, sometimes warts and all. Cricket is an unusual sport, in some quarters people call it quaint. It began all those hundreds of years ago and unlike football, which is still basically played in the same fashion in which it started throughout the world, cricket now has various styles. While there is more publicity and exposure for the international game at Test and Limited-overs level, the fact remains that, without grass-roots cricket played at club level, there could be no international cricket. Recently the theory was advanced to me that it would be quite possible to do away with competitions like the Sheffield Shield, which in Australia is now named the Pura Cup, and the County Championship in the United Kingdom, and simply play limited-overs cricket as the level below Test matches.

This might sound attractive in theory because those first-class competitions are great money loss-makers. Just to break even for the Pura Cup in Australia, Cricket Australia need a million dollars a year in sponsorship. But a country's strength at Test level is directly associated with the strength of its four-day domestic competition, that's one of the reasons why Australia have been doing well on the international scene in recent years and have done well over the past 129 years. A six-team first-class competition, and a strong club level set-up below that, forms the basis of success. There is no way cricket authorities could successfully organise Test match competitions without such a structure and it is why countries like Bangladesh and Zimbabwe have struggled so much. That will continue to be the case for them until they have a proper structure in place and it's not the slightest use other countries closing their eyes to that fact.

When the fracas erupted in Zimbabwe in 2003, there followed the stupid and appalling situation where Zimbabwe were represented by a team no better than a second-grade club side and international teams visiting there were presented with false and ridiculous results. ICC then removed Zimbabwe from the Test calendar but, astonishingly, allowed them to play in Limited-overs Internationals which was one of the more bizarre decisions ever made in the history of cricket. Outside Zimbabwe some international players only ever play at limited-overs level. They were forced to take part in rubbish matches where their own performances were exaggerated because they were up against a substandard team. I've never met any cricketer who could gain the slightest pleasure from something of that kind. It was a shameful situation.

What should have been done was to remove Zimbabwe from both the Test and one-day International circuit until they had satisfied other countries that their structure was in place and that their playing strength was up to international standard. The whole process which took place certainly cannot be thought of in any way, no matter how vivid or kindly one's imagination, to be anything by way of a celebration of cricket. It was a farce.

That was my view as an observer. The man on the spot, Australian captain Ricky Ponting, was constructive with his thoughts on the game, and on Zimbabwe in particular. After he had led the Australians on their short tour there he said, in part, that if Zimbabwe continued to play international cricket it would cheapen the game. Batsmen and bowlers would be scoring runs and taking wickets against players who were not good enough to be playing at that level. The credibility of the international game would continue to suffer because one-sided spectacles would turn people off watching the game.

Ponting said: 'It really is difficult to see a way forward for Zimbabwe cricket at the moment. The problems with Zimbabwe, as in Bangladesh, need to be addressed from the grass roots up with coaching and development programmes, a proper domestic structure and decent facilities. It is clear the ZCU need to get their affairs in order. Ideally, they first need to resolve the players' dispute; until that happens, I would favour a total ban on Tests and one-day International cricket.'

On the matter of football and the manner of playing it over the years, whether we are thinking of the round ball game or Rugby, there has been no great amount of change in each era of football. With soccer football it was a case of finding a field of play, putting up goalposts and crossbar and scoring by putting the ball between the uprights and under the bar. Rugby involved handling the ball, running with it and scoring over the try-line. Goal-kicking came later.

Cricket was different. I like the thought that the earliest proper games of cricket were played between villages. Equally, it seems likely that those villages were in Kent and Sussex, in the south-east of England, where it is possible the game was referred to as 'stool-ball' in some areas because, in that part of the country, the stump of a tree was known as 'a stool' and those tree-stumps available, because of land clearance, were used as the first wickets. In other areas the entrance to sheep-pens consisted of two uprights and a movable crossbar. The crossbar was called a bail and the uprights and the bail were known as a wicket. In the Weald area in England the stool went out of favour and the uprights and bail became the preferred wicket because the ball gently brushing a tree stump might have simply produced arguments, no such chance when the bail was dislodged.

The inventive nature of those playing the game in the very early days has never ceased to surprise me. The old measurements, before we became immersed in metrics, were such that a 22-yard pitch was a perfectly logical length when you took into account a 'gad, or goad', 'a nail' and a 'cloth-yard or ell'. The original method of scoring a run seems to have been to make one's ground at the wicket which was one foot high and two feet wide with, between the two uprights, a hole in the ground into which the ball had to be 'popped' in order to run out the batsman. Popping crease has lasted through the centuries, though not the specific manner of making the dismissal which in 1727 moved to 'the wicket must be put down with ball in hand.' In the *New Cricket Umpiring and Scoring* (Tom Smith, 2004), 'the wicket is down if the fielder with the ball in hand removes a bail, or the arm (shoulder to fingertips) may be used to remove a bail, providing the ball is in the hand of that arm.' Quite a dramatic change. When the first code of Laws was produced the batsmen, to make a run, needed to touch the umpire's stick. This, from photographs, seems to have been a bat carried by each umpire, one standing at the bowler's end, the other at the batsman's end in a position which these days would equate to a backward short-leg for a slow bowler.

The game evolved quickly enough, including the styles of bowling. They began bowling under-arm, with the same action as a lawn bowler trying to take out the 'jack' at the other end of the green, fast and under-arm. The changeover, or 'over', would then come after four balls. Also there was the occasion when John Willes's sister Christine, because of her voluminous hooped skirts, found it impossible to bowl under-arm to her brothers, so bowled side-arm. Over-arm bowling was not quite instantaneous but, looking back to those times, it was certainly inevitable!

The first Test match ever played between England and Australia was, in fact, only an ordinary contest in 1877 between two teams captained by James Lillywhite of Sussex and Dave Gregory of New

South Wales. It was, at the time, listed as a game between an All-England XI and a Combined XI of New South Wales and Victoria. Australia won by 45 runs, but it was another 12 years before Adelaide cricket historian Clarence Moody's list of matches in *Australian Cricket and Cricketers* was accepted as the definitive guide to Test matches, covering games until then played between the two countries. By far the most important match was the single game at The Oval in 1882 when Australia, having already played 31 matches on their tour, arrived back in London from Bristol on the evening of Saturday, 26 August to prepare themselves for the game against England, a two-day fixture at Kennington Oval on 28 and 29 August.

Bell's Life (England) covered what was known as *The Tour of the Australian Eleven* and they then produced a book containing all the articles written by their three distinguished correspondents, Sydney H. Pardon, Edgar S. Pardon and C. Stewart Caine.

After the Preface of the book penned by Charles F. Pardon, there were two Letters of Approval. One was written by the very popular Australian team manager Charlie Beal, whose forte was administrative skill and a love of cricket, rather than batting or bowling ability. Beal played in three matches on the tour, batting at number eleven for scores of nought, five and seven, the latter innings against Gentlemen of Scotland where, in his first over, he bowled what was described as a 'best on record'. This was the widest wide ever seen by anyone present, the ball going between point and cover after leaving his hand.

The other letter was written by the Hon. Ivo Bligh who was captain of the England team about to tour Australia, a team of eight amateurs and four professionals, quite different from the one which had been beaten by Australia at The Oval at the end of August 1882.

That two-day Oval match was listed in the *Bell's Life* book as Australia v England, covers 12 pages in the book and is a restrained but also wonderfully graphic account of the great victory achieved by the Australians by seven runs. The match finished on the Tuesday afternoon.

In the *Sporting Times* the following Saturday, the writer Reginald Brooks, eldest son of Shirley Brooks, a previous Editor of *Punch*, prepared the mock obituary notice to the effect that *'English cricket had died at The Oval on 29th August 1882 and the body will be cremated and the ashes taken to Australia.'*

The legend of the Ashes came into being from the moment the Hon. Ivo Bligh captained the England team to Australia and, at Rupertswood, a property outside Melbourne, was presented with a small urn containing ashes. There are still arguments as to what kind of ashes. The favourite seems to be that they may be the ashes of a bail or perhaps ashes taken from the fireplace at Cobham Hall, the home of Lord Darnley, who was formerly the Hon. Ivo Bligh.

At that time cremation was a very controversial subject in the United Kingdom and one of the reasons the urn was not on public display was that had it been it would have provided a great deal of criticism of Bligh, even though his views on the subject had never been published.

Cricket 123 years later is a contradiction of itself, in a sense remaining as it always has been, yet at the same time totally different. Much of this difference has occurred in the period from 1977 when World Series Cricket started, to the present day, five years into the new century. Up to World Series Cricket the game had consisted of Test matches at the highest level, first-class cricket below that and some one-day matches. To make one's way into first-class cricket you needed to be good at club level and, before that, almost invariably, a schoolboy star.

The same applied in all countries. Every time you were sitting in a dressing-room after a day's play, the conversation would drift between what your team-mate or opponent had done to start off in cricket, how they had made their way in the game and what their ambitions had been at the start of their playing days.

In Sydney, it was a perfectly simple chain of events, the biggest problem was that not many could make the cut. Schools cricket was the nursery in those days and, in the period 1938–40, I went to Burnside School at North Parramatta and went through fifth class and sixth class, the latter being the stage where I then sat for an examination which would tell the examiners and the Education Department to which school I might advance. It could be a High School and there were only eight of those in the Sydney metropolitan area, one of which, at Parramatta, was a co-educational school. Or it could be an Intermediate High School of which there were scores, but certainly not hundreds as is the case today.

I sat the exam, passed it and was listed to go to Parramatta High School, which was something that pleased me and also pleased my parents. It was the school, in the area of Central Cumberland, my father had attended in 1923–24 after his mother and father had moved from Grafton, on the north coast of NSW, to Penrith where I was born. My father had attended Grafton High School and was a very good schoolboy cricketer.

While at Parramatta High, he played on Saturdays with a club team and became the first bowler ever to take all 20 wickets in a match. This was in the Penrith area where he was living and he was playing for Penrith Waratah against St Mary's. The arrangement in that Saturday competition 80 years ago was that the matches were played over two Saturday afternoons, the first day on the home ground of one team, a week later the second afternoon on the home ground of the other. It was perceived that this would negate any advantage to the home team and it seemed to work well. If there were to be an advantage, my father certainly seized it the first afternoon at Penrith Showground where he took all ten wickets for 30. Six were bowled, one lbw and three caught. The following week he bowled five of the opposition, had three caught and two stumped and finished with 10/35.

24

Twenty wickets in a match – the scoreboard
Penrith Waratah v St Mary's

Penrith Waratah

L. Reddan	b R. Morrison	2	b A. Morrison		23
G. Gow	b M. Bennett	0	b M. Bennett		0
F. Knight	b M. Bennett	2	c and b M. Bennett		16
H. Wright	b R. Morrison	14	b R. Morrison		16
L. Benaud	c G. Bennett b R. Morrison	9	c G. Bennett b M. Bennett		1
T. Glassock	not out	49	c and b A. Morrison		30
A. Edwards	b M. Bennett	6	c Beacroft b R. Morrison		0
R. Burns	c G. Bennett b Moore	0	absent		8
C. Thorndike	c Dollin b M. Bennett	0	c Ward b Dougherty		8
L. Moore	run out	5	run out		2
N. Greaves	b Moore	3	not out		3
Sundries		8			9
Total:		98			116

First innings bowling: M. Bennett 4/31, R. Morrison 3/25, G. Bennett 0/21, Moore 2/13

Second innings bowling: M. Bennett 3/29, R. Morrison 2/24, Dougherty 1/15, Moore 0/18, G. Bennett 0/10, H. Dollin 0/6, A. Morrison 2/5.

St Mary's

H. Dollin	b Benaud	4	st Greaves b Benaud		10
R. Morrison	b Benaud	1	c Wright b Benaud		24
E. Dougherty	c Glassock b Benaud	10	c Wright b Benaud		4
M. Bennett	c Gow b Benaud	4	c Reddan b Benaud		0
A. Morrison	c Wright b Benaud	10	b Benaud		0
J. Beacroft	b Benaud	16	b Benaud		3
G. Bennett	b Benaud	0	st Greaves b Benaud		4
D. Turner	b Benaud	0	b Benaud		0
W. Dollin	b Benaud	0	b Benaud		18
W. Ward	lbw Benaud	0	not out		11
G. Moore	not out	0	b Benaud		0
Sundries		7			5
Total:		52			79

First innings bowling: Benaud 10/30 (including hat-trick), Wright 0/15

Second innings bowling: Benaud 10/35, Edwards 0/21, Wright 0/8, Reddan 0/10

Penrith Waratah won outright by 83 runs.

Central Cumberland Club representatives, impressed with the publicity generated by this bowling feat, went to see my father's parents and asked that he be allowed to play with the club. He played almost all the season in the Cumberland second grade and then a telegram received on 4 February, 1925 at Penrith told him he was promoted to first grade for the last match of the season, the game to be played at the SCG. This was a great thrill for him because it was at the SCG three years earlier that he had watched Charlie Macartney hit 170 off the England bowling attack.

When eventually the family moved from Jugiong to Parramatta in late 1937 and my father went to teach at Burnside School, he had thoughts of retiring from cricket, reasoning that at 33 years of age it was probably too late to be making any further progress in the game. His Burnside headmaster, 'Banna' Edwards, persuaded him to go to the pre-season practices at Lidcombe Oval and he was immediately named in the first grade team. Later in the summer he played two games in second grade, taking 11 wickets in 28 overs, was promoted to first grade again and, in the final match, took 6/47 to conclude an excellent return to the club for which he had last played 14 years earlier.

Having started at Parramatta High in 1942, I played fourth grade school cricket for two years and there were times where my interest in cricket was greater than in the scholastic side of things. So much so that my marks in mathematics in the final examinations at the end of the year were a disgrace, something that was not so gently pointed out to me. The mathematics master of the time was a very nice chap but we weren't quite on the same teacher-pupil wave-length. He also taught music and neither aspect of life was on the same plane for me as cricket, although in later years I developed a great love of music. Mathematics played a greater part in my life when a new schoolteacher came to Parramatta. He was a master called Ted Roxby, known also at PHS by the nickname 'Bob', who had been teaching at Gosford High where a young left-hand cricketer, Alan Davidson, was making a big name for himself in schools cricket as a hard-hitting batsman and left-arm over-the-wrist spin bowler. Cricketing fate was to bring the two of us together for NSW and Australia later in our lives but at this time it was, for me, far more a case of looking up to 'Bob' Roxby because he was a cricket lover and would stay behind to coach the fourth grade team after lessons finished. I returned the compliment by studying mathematics so hard that in second and third year I passed the examinations with flying colours and did the same with the Intermediate Certificate in third year.

This was typical of the way young cricketers were brought along in those days more than 50 years ago. It was a time when schools were the nursery of the game but all that has changed now, with school-teachers in the main forced to work to rigid rosters, and so many rules and regulations negating the chance of old-style coaching. Now it is local clubs and systems put into action by the state associations, often age competitions, that shape the manner in which young cricketers will become part of the game. That is in no way to downgrade in the slightest the wonderful work many enthusiastic schoolteachers still do in schools these days as regards coaching and nurturing young sportspeople. It's just that the system has dramatically changed and unfortunately it has shackled them beyond measure.

A celebration of cricket can be a misnomer. For all the celebrations and good things, if you keep a balanced view of the game, there will be times where there is precious little to celebrate. The cause might be something to do with the game itself, something connected with the players or just that we could all be going through a bad patch. I was asked recently if, because I had seen more than 500 Test matches in one way or another, I would care to nominate the best time I had gone through over that period of 50 years. Possibly a season, a summer perhaps, a two or three-year period? Possibly ten years? Oh, and while I was about it, when was I going to retire from the commentary box?

As it happened the two questions were interwoven. I was able to say the 20 months from May 2003 up to the conclusion of the Test series between South Africa and England at the end of January 2005 was certainly the best time I had known. This all started with the 2003 Test series in England against South Africa, where Graeme Smith hit two brilliant double-centuries, 277 and 259, South Africa won both matches in handsome fashion, then England won at Trent Bridge and Headingley with flair and courage, and the series was eventually drawn.

Then I had a combination of watching on television in Australia brilliant cricket between Sri Lanka and Australia and then, on the spot, the last two Tests in the Caribbean in 2004 where, in Barbados, England clinched the series 3–0 and in Antigua Brian Lara again became the holder of the record for making the highest individual score in Tests. Over a 46-year period that record had been held by Garry Sobers 365, Brian Lara 375, Matthew Hayden 380 and now Lara again with 400. If that all sounds as though it was nothing but a batting bonanza in Antigua, it is far from what actually happened.

At the same time as I was watching Lara and the record, I was also seeing the emergence of a splendid England bowling attack and an Australian team with back-up bowlers temporarily replacing Shane Warne and Glenn McGrath. A fine job they did too for Adam Gilchrist who deputised brilliantly for Australian captain Ricky Ponting in the first three Tests in India in late 2004.

There was also in 2003–04 the wonderful Test series between Australia and India, in Australia, where Rahul Dravid and V.V.S. Laxman turned on such entertainment that Australian audiences were marvelling at their skills, and this at a time where there had been a question-mark against India's ability to win in Australia. In the end they didn't win, it was a drawn series with excitement up to the final overs when Steve Waugh walked off the Test stage for the last time.

The three Australian Tests in Sri Lanka mentioned above were quite extraordinary and provided superb entertainment for those in Australia watching on television. Three times early in each Test Australia seemed to have received a knockout punch; three times they came back and won matches where, after a day and a half, it seemed to me they had little chance of victory. On all three occasions Sri Lanka batted last, so Ponting had made a good start to his captaincy career by winning three valuable tosses and Shane Warne, back after suspension, bowled superbly, one of his spells in the Kandy Test was as good as anything I've seen from him.

You need to bear in mind there is more cricket played these days so there is, theoretically, more chance of having a lot of good cricket. But that period May 2003 to the conclusion of the Centurion Park Test, South Africa v England, at the end of January 2005 is tops for me.

There is a tendency these days for touring sides to Sri Lanka, India and Pakistan not to have as a mandatory policy the use of two over-the-wrist spin bowlers. Selectors now think along the lines of including a fast-medium, or medium-fast bowler who is more of an allrounder, and who is able to use reverse swing with a ball which becomes well roughened on one side. Or they will use as their second spinner an orthodox rather than over-the-wrist spinner. At any rate, Australia won that series in Sri Lanka 3–0 and provided a reminder for England's players and cricket followers that they would need to lift their game even more in 2005 if another Ashes battle were not to go the same way as had been the case since 1989.

In the summer of 2004 England certainly took note of that reminder. They began by beating New Zealand in three successive Test matches at Lord's, Headingley and Trent Bridge and then won the next four against West Indies to provide the statisticians with something they hadn't seen for 76 years, England winning seven successive Test matches. Michael Vaughan was the skipper through this period of brilliance for six of those, with Marcus Trescothick captaining the opening Test against New Zealand because of injury to Vaughan. This aspect of the 18 months simply added to the excitement of the cricket I was watching.

The real excitement though was to see an England bowling attack able to dominate matches and make clear that opposing batsmen were no longer able to relax at the crease. Steve Harmison, Matthew Hoggard and Andrew Flintoff had a sharp edge to their bowling and, when you added one of Simon Jones or James Anderson and used Ashley Giles as the one spinner bowling to a tight, pre-conceived plan, England suddenly started to look a real Test team.

It is something of a cliché, particularly if you are to ask batsmen their opinion of the phrase, but *bowlers do win Test matches*. You only win a game if you take 20 opposition wickets and suddenly, in that period of which I'm talking, England started to do that. In addition, Ashley Giles began to bowl well. He was at that time the best spin bowler in England but, such was the pressure on him, there were stories bandied about in the print media that he was consulting psychologists concerning the best way to control his nerves and start taking more wickets.

Statistics are always part of cricket and one of the more interesting is that in 2004, at Newlands in Cape Town, Giles became only the ninth England cricketer to do the traditional double of 1,000 runs and 100 wickets in Test cricket. In the same match Andrew Flintoff became the tenth. Those England players who had previously achieved the double were Wilfred Rhodes, who was the first to reach the mark against South Africa in 1913–14, Maurice Tate v South Africa in 1930–31, Trevor Bailey v South Africa 1956–57, Fred Titmus v Australia 1965–66, Ray Illingworth v Pakistan 1971, Tony Greig v New Zealand 1974–75, Ian Botham v India 1979 and John Emburey v Pakistan 1987.

Then there was the Australian tour of India when Australia, with Adam Gilchrist standing in for the injured Ricky Ponting, won two of the first three Tests and therefore the series. The victory was great for Ponting but the fact that he couldn't be part of it must have been one of the worst times of his cricketing life. He broke his left thumb in the Champions' Trophy one-day series played in England in September 2004 and was immediately sent home to Australia to have the injury assessed. Brad Hodge, the outstanding Victorian batsman, was drafted into the Australian team and Gilchrist was the automatic choice as captain. The final twist of the Test series in India was that the last day of the Second Test in Chennai was unfortunately washed out, then victory at Nagpur left the Australians two up with one to play. It was a great series win where the touring party showed skill and courage but, more important, made certain their planning had been clear and focused in approaching the two very difficult months in India. India then won the Fourth Test in Mumbai, a match played on what looked, and was, a very unusual surface. There were two things I liked about the match. The first was that Michael Clarke, a fine young batsman, put the pitch into proper perspective by taking six for nine in the Indian second innings. The other was that Jason Gillespie, who has a dry sense of humour, in a radio interview refused point-blank to say anything about the pitch because Cricket Australia's contract strictures did not permit players to comment in that way. Quite straight-faced though he said he had just had a phone call from a mate of his who was watching the match on television in Australia and the mate had said, 'That's a disgraceful track, "Dizzy" . . .'

Twenty months of magnificent cricket and I count myself as one of the luckiest people to have seen it either first or second hand.

3

A FLEETING REGRET

I NEVER met Hansie Cronje.
There are other cricket players around the world I haven't met, thousands of them at all levels of the game, but Cronje is one to whom I would have liked to say hello. There are others of eras outside my own who would certainly be on a list where I would have regarded sitting down to discuss cricket as an interesting exercise, sometimes as a real treat.

Cronje was in a different category. The circumstances of not meeting him were unique, in that at the time he was captain of the very strong South African cricket team when they toured Australia in the season of 1997–98. The Test match at the Adelaide Oval was the last game of the tour. The First Test of the series had been drawn; the Second was a resounding victory for Australia by an innings and 21 runs with Mark Waugh making a brilliant century. The manager of the South African team was Alan Jordaan and he came around to the Channel Nine commentary box to have a look at the way the network operated, the upstairs part of it anyway. When he was on his way out of the box he stopped for a chat and said he understood I had never met Hansie. I said that was correct although I had seen him play in a considerable number of matches, something around thirty, but because I was either presenting or hosting cricket telecasts in Australia, or England, it meant that before the match and during the intervals I was almost always required to be in the studio.

In the various cities we were never staying in the same hotel as home or touring teams. Ian Chappell, who presented the toss in the centre of the ground, and Tony Greig who did the pitch reports, were always in a better position to chat to members of the two teams or captains if, that is, the players wanted to chat to anyone.

Alan said that Hansie would like to meet me and I replied with what is something of a standard answer, 'That's fine, I'll be very happy to buy him a drink at the hotel at some stage.' I hadn't done my homework well enough at that time to understand a glass of chardonnay might be out of the question, but the contents didn't really matter, a glass of something liquid and a chat would be fine.

In the end nothing came of the invitation and the acceptance of it because this turned out to be a very awkward match with umpiring controversy and the touring party livid at one last-day decision they believed cost them the match. The decision involved Mark Waugh who again was standing in their way with an impressive batting performance. In their first innings Cronje's team made 517, a consistent performance all the way through with no centuries and a top score of 87 not out from Brian McMillan. The story then was that Mark Taylor played one of the greatest innings of his career in making 169 not out to avoid the follow-on for his team. It was, as well, one of the most unlikely follow-on saves I had ever seen. The sequence was that the ninth Australian wicket fell at 317 when Jacques Kallis had Michael Kasprowicz caught by Pat Symcox. Taylor and Stuart MacGill then added 33 for the last wicket in very clever fashion. Their tactics were that MacGill would stay at the end so he would face Symcox's offspin, Taylor would take the pace at the other end. It worked perfectly until Stuart became over-confident and Symcox bowled him as he was aiming for 'Cow Corner'. South Africa declared their second innings and Mark Waugh made his century to deny South Africa a victory in the final Test of this three-match series. South Africa missed ten chances in the match.

There was however an incident concerning Waugh on the final day which indirectly meant the South African team members were unlikely to want to drink with anyone but themselves that evening. Waugh was struck on the forearm in playing defensively and was wandering around in pain when his bat came into contact with the stumps, removing the bails. The South Africans appealed for Hit Wicket and the umpire at the bowler's end said 'not out'. I happened to be on television with Bill Lawry at the time and said instantly that Waugh wasn't out, in fact there was no way he could be out under the wording of the Law. For him to be out he would have needed to have broken his wicket whilst making a stroke (which was certainly not the case), or in setting off for a run immediately after the completion of his stroke (which, equally, was certainly not the case).

The door to the South African dressing-room at the Adelaide Oval was never the same again after the fielding side had stormed back into the pavilion at the conclusion of the game. Hansie had walked off the field with a stump in hand at the close of play and that stump was responsible for whatever repairs needed to be made to the door. The Australian Cricket Board accepted his written apology for the damage done. No one seems to know if he apologised as well, as captain, for being ignorant of the Law of the game concerning Hit Wicket, which stated quite clearly that Waugh couldn't be out and that the umpires had made the correct decision, the only one possible.

That Adelaide match, 30 January to 3 February, 1998, concluded the South African tour of Australia, with the Limited-overs Internationals having already been played between the start of December and 27 January.

Cronje then captained his country at home in two Tests against Sri Lanka before he led them in England in 1998 in a tough, competitive series. With the teams level at 1–1, England won the final game at Headingley by 23 runs, but I still hadn't managed a meeting with the South African skipper. Circumstances more than anything else, I guess, and a considerable change in work schedules, meant it was pushed on to the back burner.

In 1999 Australia won the World Cup, having tied with South Africa in the semi-final at Edgbaston and then they defeated Pakistan at Lord's in the final. New Zealand beat England 2–1 in the Test series, after England had won the First Test of the series by seven wickets.

The Australian team had a busy time between then and 7 April, 2000; they beat India 3–0 in a Test series in Australia and won the VB Limited-overs series by defeating Pakistan in the best-of-three finals. Then Steve Waugh's team dashed across the Tasman and won the three-match Test series by 62 runs (Auckland), by six wickets (Wellington) and six wickets (Hamilton). That Hamilton match ended on 3 April, 2000, so for them it was straight on to an aeroplane from Sydney to Johannesburg for the three-match Limited-overs series against South Africa. Their first match was to be played on 12 April at Kingsmead, Durban and, with all the successful cricket they had played, they should have been confident and in top form.

So too, for that matter, Hansie Cronje and his South African team. They had just played two exciting series in India and Sharjah, India from 9 March to 19 March and Sharjah 22 March to 31 March, 2000. India had won the first series 3–2 and Pakistan had beaten South Africa in the Grand Final in Sharjah by 16 runs, with Cronje top-scoring for his team.

That was the chronology of the playing side of things leading into Hansie and Steve Waugh pitting their wits against one another at Kingsmead.

There was though an extraordinary unknown factor about to make an appearance.

In India, a Delhi-based crime branch detective, Ishwar Singh Redhu, was listening to some taped conversations concerning possible extortion in the Indian business world, and Cronje's name was mentioned. It caught Redhu's attention, as did other conversations relating to cricket matches between India and South Africa. Then a voice, assumed to be that of Cronje, was heard discussing matches and money. Detective Redhu immediately filed a report with his Joint-Commissioner of Police, K.K. Paul.

Mr Paul then listened to telephone conversations between a variety of people, one of whom, in fact, turned out to be Cronje. Like me, Mr Paul had never met Cronje and although the whole purpose of the phone taps was the business extortion racket, Mr Paul was left wondering how the person named Cronje was talking on this particular mobile to other people in such an odd way about certain matters connected with cricket. It just happened that Hansie had been given a mobile phone by an Indian friend for his personal use during the tour of India. As far as Mr Paul was concerned at that stage the phone was simply one being monitored by police, including Detective Redhu, investigating those extortion threats in the corporate world. Cricket, in fact, was, at first, the least of their interests in connection with the telephone, but it soon became clear that some of the conversations automatically monitored had a far more compromising aspect to them. Mr Paul seems to have been an outstanding investigator, calm and purposeful, and on 7 April he and his team of detectives charged Cronje and three of his team-mates with being involved in match-fixing of cricket.

Cronje said of the charges that they were completely without foundation and that he was stunned by what had been said. He added that he had never approached any of his players to ask them if they wanted to fix a game.

A strong vote of confidence was given to Cronje by Dr Ali Bacher, South Africa's United Cricket Board managing director, who described the allegations as rubbish. He added that Cronje was known for his unquestionable integrity and honesty.

At the same time K.K. Paul was receiving robust telephone calls from South Africa, most of them insulting, for having had the temerity to question the honour of the South African captain, the team, and South Africa in general. This was happening between 7 April and 9 April and the only thing I had seen to that stage was the bare bones of the Internet story. We were in Europe where we were watching on television the US Golf Masters at Augusta. There was a further 24 hours of intensive ridiculing of K.K. Paul and his men to put pressure on them, until Mr Paul released details of a tape recording of Cronje speaking in Afrikaans about match-fixing to a punter or bookmaker in South Africa.

Then drama unfolded. On 11 April, Cronje telephoned Ali Bacher at 3 a.m. to inform him he had not been entirely honest about his comments two days earlier. Then he had said the charges were completely without substance and that he would never do anything to let his country down. He had told Bacher he was stunned by the police charges. Now, in his new early morning call to Dr Bacher, he admitted to accepting thousands of dollars from a London-based bookmaker for 'forecasting' results, not match-fixing. He was sacked as South African captain and the position was taken over by Shaun Pollock. Bacher said: 'We are shattered. The United Cricket Board and the government have been deceived.'

One who backed Cronje in his denials was a South African who heard the tapes and jubilantly announced the person supposed to be Cronje had an Indian accent. What he and others didn't know was that, to ensure their safety, the original tapes had very cleverly been sealed and placed under the jurisdiction of the Delhi High Court.

Ali Bacher was right. Cruelly deceived. Two days later I published in the *News of the World* my own views on what had happened and how I felt. In a word, gutted! This is what I wrote at the time.

This is the greatest crisis in the history of cricket.

Some say since Bodyline, but Bodyline was of no account when compared to the stench hovering over the game of cricket at the moment with allegations of match-fixing, bribery, illegal payments and cheating.

Bodyline in 1932–33 was perfectly within the Laws of Cricket of the time, even though it was quickly seen and acknowledged to be outside the spirit of it. It was a brief incident between two of the cricket-playing countries of the world, England and Australia, and it involved bowling at the batsman's body and was designed to curb one batsman, Bradman.

To suggest Bodyline is in a pit alongside those who are besmirching the game at the moment is to allow imagination far too loose a rein.

For the past six years, starting in Pakistan and then touched on in India and extended to Australia, with the mysterious grey-suited, shadowy and now invisible gambler 'John,' the game has been under siege.

The Pakistan report into match-fixing and bribery was concluded by Justice Malik Mohammad Qayyum some time ago, but has never been presented to the ICC. During the course of that investigation the Australian Cricket Board, in one of the more crass pieces of administration, covered up payments from 'John' for pitch, weather and team reports by Shane Warne and Mark Waugh.

The defence, if that isn't a contradiction in terms, was that the two players were naïve, stupid, dumb and then dumber. Much worse though was that they had laid themselves open to blackmail with a real possibility of blandishments then orders to fix matches under threat of exposure.

It is looking as though that same 'defence' might be thought a possibility for Hansie Cronje as he weaves his way through the worst week of his life.

I feel extremely limited sorrow at the moment for Cronje, as I did at the time for Warne and Waugh. I will feel no sympathy at all for those who come to be listed as match-fixers of varying degrees and takers of bribes, if they are found guilty by Judge Qayyum and various other inquiries.

The sorrow I do feel is for the game and people who love it and are having that feeling sorely tested by those to whom cricket means only a betting proposition.

From the age of ten to the day I retired in 1964 I spent most of *my* waking hours trying to play good cricket so that I and my team would *win* every game or, at worst, not be beaten.

For me it defies belief that people now could be spending most of *their* waking hours trying to find some way to *lose* a game.

Eighty-one years ago the greatest baseball scandal ever to hit America happened when the Chicago White Sox 'threw' five of eight matches against the Cincinnati Reds.

One of the White Sox players was 'Shoeless' Joe Jackson, a wonderful outfielder, and the most poignant sports photograph I have ever seen is of Jackson emerging from a judicial building and a ten-year-old fan, tears streaming down his face, calling to him, 'Say it ain't so Joe; please say it ain't so.'

Sheer greed is one reason for destroying the faith of youngsters and older sports lovers in this way but, as well, you need to live in some strange kind of mental environment.

It must be a grim life where you glance in the mirror each morning and be quite uncaring that, despite careful polishing, the reflection still looks grubby.

A few days after Cronje's phone call to Ali Bacher, there was disquiet expressed over the Test between South Africa and England which had been played at Centurion Park in mid-January. It was the match where Cronje took the unexpected step of forfeiting an innings and England won by two wickets in a finish of high excitement.

An inquiry was launched into the Cronje affair and it began with a firm warning from the Commissioner Mr Justice King that witnesses who committed perjury would face prosecution. There followed a sequence of events which culminated in the King Commission ending suddenly and, unfortunately, inconclusively.

- It was quickly revealed at the beginning of the inquiry that South Africa's team came close to accepting a bribe of $250,000 to throw a one-off International in India in 1996. Cronje's suggestion was that the team had laughed it off but others said it was discussed in the team meetings before being declined. South African bowler Pat Symcox gave evidence before Mr Justice King that the offer had been made.
- Herschelle Gibbs said Cronje had offered him a bribe to throw a match. Gibbs told the King Commission he had agreed to Cronje's offer of $15,000 to score fewer than 20 runs in a one-day match in India earlier in the year.
- Cronje was offered immunity from prosecution, if he made a full disclosure of his role in match-fixing.
  The South African government suggested the deal after further damning allegations were made against Cronje during three days of evidence.
- Cronje admitted taking large sums of money for giving information to bookmakers. But he told the King Commission South Africa had never 'thrown' or 'fixed' a match, under his captaincy.
- Cronje was visibly affected when he was led away in tears after completing his evidence.
- This was at the end of three days of cross-examination by a panel of lawyers, during which he confessed to receiving around $140,000 from bookmakers.
- He said: 'I hope I can put the money to good use to try to redress the wrongs I have done to my game and my country.'
- Cronje earlier admitted in evidence hiding money at his home and trying to convince people that other cash had been earned legitimately from benefits and bonuses.
- Cronje, in the *Cape Times* newspaper, admitted full responsibility for his actions and apologised to the nation.
  'There is no excuse and I have let the United Cricket Board, the team, the fans and the game down,' he said.

- Former Commissioner of the Metropolitan Police, Sir Paul Condon, was appointed the International Cricket Council's new anti-corruption investigator.

  In August Herschelle Gibbs and Henry Williams were banned from international cricket for the rest of the year for their involvement with Cronje.

  The punishment, handed out by the United Cricket Board of South Africa, followed admissions made by the two players to the King Commission – but did not apply to domestic cricket.

- Nelson Mandela issued a statement chastising Cronje for his role in South Africa's match-fixing scandal.

- Cronje was banned from cricket for life by the United Cricket Board of South Africa (UCBSA) as a result of his admission that he received money from bookmakers.

- Cronje's lawyer Les Sackstein responded immediately by saying that legal steps were being considered to challenge the ban as unlawful restraint of trade.

  Sackstein pointed out that the ban prevented Cronje earning a living in the media or even coaching under-privileged children.

- The UCB softened their stance on the ban, admitting that Cronje might be allowed back into the sport at a future time.

  UCB president Percy Sonn said: 'We acknowledge that, with effort, people are able to rehabilitate themselves over time and there may be an opportunity for the UCB to take cognisance of this possibility in the future.'

- Cronje's lawyers lodged a court application to overturn the life ban.

  'We've always held the view that what they [the UCB] did was unlawful,' Sackstein said.

- After a three-month campaign by Cronje's lawyers to declare it unlawful, the King Commission came to an abrupt halt, with Mr Justice King reserving judgment on whether Cronje told the truth.

  'At the moment that is something I have to decide upon,' he

said. 'It is something that is exercising my mind. I have been informed by [chief prosecutor] Shamila Batohi, who has led the evidence at the Commission, that there is no evidence implicating any other member of the team, former member of the team or administrator. These persons must be regarded as having been cleared.'

- The UCB stance softened further, with Cronje told he might coach in private, away from the official board activities.

In July, as preparation for Cronje's appeal gathered pace, Cronje revealed that he hoped to coach the national side in the future.

'I think one day when it comes along I would certainly like to have that, because I tried my entire career to make South Africa the number one cricket playing country in the world,' he said on BBC Radio Five Live.

- Cronje opened his campaign to have the life ban overturned in the Pretoria High Court. He submitted an affidavit accusing the UCB of restraint of trade interfering with his personal life and with his attempts to earn a living.

- On the second day of the hearing, United Cricket Board senior counsel Wim Trengove revealed that Cronje – previously banned from all cricket-related activities – was 'free to practise as a journalist by attending a match as a spectator and reporting for the print medium'.

- The court rejected Cronje's appeal, but said he could take part in certain coaching and media activities.

It had been a long, drawn-out saga, ending with complete justification for the work of K.K. Paul and his Delhi-based detectives, as well as the Indian Central Bureau of Investigation.

Mr Paul had calmly endured insults and abuse, some of which continued even after Cronje's early morning phone call to Ali Bacher, and even through the sitting of the King Commission. It is a pity Mr Paul has been hampered in his efforts to trace the money trail through the banks in the Cayman Islands and else-where but these matters seem to be ongoing, even after Cronje's death in the plane crash in June 2002.

It was a pity the King Commission ended when it did because the word was that Justice King was pressing to have permission to go back to 1992 when South Africa came back into international cricket. That would have been one way to do it; the other would be to draw a line under the whole business, which in fact was what happened.

One point made by Mr Paul when he was talking about betting at cricket was, although there was match-fixing, spread betting rather than traditional style betting is the easier medium for wagering.

The increase in the number of one-day matches at international level, and the introduction of spread betting, changed the types of wagering and the number of bets made in the 1990s. The number of overs a bowler might bowl out of the ten he is permitted, the number of runs a batsman will make, and even the position in the batting order he will have, are just a small part of the type of bets a bookmaker will take. From which ball will a boundary be hit, which batsman will hit the first six, and which bowler will take the first wicket, are matters high on the list of bookmakers and potential punters. Bear in mind that although bookmakers are the ones criticised there would be no betting on cricket if there were no punters. Also that it is to the advantage of both the bookmaker and punter if one has information the other does not possess. It is to the advantage of one of them, for example, to know who the opening bowlers will be.

Betting can be straightforward, say, in backing a racehorse. You can put money on the horse to win or place, or you can take exotic bets like trifectas or yankees. It is straightforward and is a battle between the bookmaker and punter.

In cricket a traditional bet would be which team would win the game or who will be the top run-getter or wicket-taker.

Spread betting in cricket though does widen the scope for playing around because there are so many more markets available. A spread bet could be:

The bookmaker says a player will score 50–55

The punter *buys* at a £5 stake (or whatever stake he wants)

With the bookmaker saying the player will score 50–55, the punter wins or loses his stake multiplied by the difference between prediction and result

Player scores 70 runs. Punter wins £75 (70–55 = 15 × 5 = £75)

Player scores 48 runs. Punter loses £35 (55–48 = 7 × 5 = £35)

It is a favourite way of gambling in many parts of the world.

4

SAY WHAT YOU THINK

Arthur Mailey and Don Bradman

Cricket has always been a game of character and characters and, of the latter, Arthur Mailey was right out of the top drawer. To that you can add he was a fine cricketer, a good writer, an artist who drew caricatures and was one of the more modest and genuine people you would ever meet.

When I first read *10 for 66 and All That* I thought it one of the best books I had read on the game. It was published in the year I captained Australia for the first time, 1958, and it provided a clue to how Arthur and I came to be luncheon partners at Jack Lee's Jersey Road, Woollahra, home in the early 1960s.

Arthur told the story of practising bowling or sometimes going to the National Art Gallery in the Domain to browse over the great pictures. His favourites were 'Rorke's Drift' and 'The Scoffers' by Frank Brangwyn, one of 'Arundel Castle', drenched in burning sunset, and 'Visit of the Queen of Sheba to King Solomon'. It was also on one of his trips to the Domain, when he was passing Waterloo Park, that he was allowed by some youths to join in a game of cricket and one of them had the ability to bowl the 'bosie' or 'wrong'un'. Arthur bowled the leg-break but this was a revelation, a ball introduced to Test cricket by Bernard Bosanquet around the turn of the century.

He told me that story when we lunched at Jack Lee's home and the other two guests were Russell Drysdale and Stan Rapotec.

Arthur revered both of them for their painting skills, Drysdale as one of Australia's greatest and Stan because he had twice won the Blake Prize for religious painting.

Stan was also a barracker! I knew his voice because I was a player and I'd heard all the different noises from 'The Hill' at the Sydney Cricket Ground, and had been on the receiving end of many of them. He wasn't of the boring 'ave a go yer mug' group but, in a short sentence, he could paint the picture of an inept batsman or a hapless bowler. Stan Rapotec loved cricket with a desperation that makes the game what it is for a lot of people, he appreciated all the nuances of the Sheffield Shield and Test matches and it was part of his life, as indeed was the case with Drysdale.

Cricket was very much part of Arthur Mailey's life as a child, a teenager and a young man. He was a prodigious spinner of the cricket ball. He was also a bowler whose length was variable and, as will always be the case with bowlers of that type, they can be expensive. He never veered from his aim to turn the ball more than any other slow bowler in the world. Life would never have been the same had he concentrated on length and direction rather than an extraordinary amount of spin. 'Take no notice, cobber. They're crazy. Millions can bowl a good length but few can really spin the ball. Keep the spin and practise, practise, practise.'

Those lunches at Jersey Road in the early 'sixties were memorable for me, to be in the company of great artists, a man of stature in the film world, Jack Lee, and a splendid cricketer in Mailey. I listened to all of them.

The story of the dismissal of his hero Victor Trumper in the match Redfern against Paddington, and his subsequent 'I felt like a boy who had killed a dove,' has gone down in cricket history and it reads just as beautifully in 2005 as it sounded in 1958.

There were poignant stories of his mother who worked at Petty's Hotel, so too the delightful recounting of the day he was sent by the Sydney Water Board, for whom he was working, to repair a water meter at Farmers' store in Sydney. Having made the repair, he exchanged overalls for suit, walked from there to the Australian cricket team reception in the directors' lunch room, where he received an abject apology from the chairman for the late start, 'because some damned fool from the Water Board cut the water off'.

Arthur, who bowled as though he wanted to spin the leather off the ball, and Bradman who taught himself to bat by throwing a golf ball against the brick base of a water tank and hitting the rebound, were examples of the fact that in Australia anyone can play cricket for his country providing he has the skill and that money and influence are unimportant matters when compared with that skill.

In 1956 I played in a Test trial at the Sydney Cricket Ground. The beneficiaries in this testimonial match were Arthur Mailey and Johnny Taylor. There was no ready explanation as to why they had to wait so long for financial acknowledgment from the aptly-named Board of Control, though the NSWCA did sack Arthur in 1929 after the first match of the season. Arthur's crime was that he had forgotten to obtain permission in writing for the coming season where he would be continuing his career as a cartoonist and journalist. He had been happily pursuing those professions for several years, doing no harm to anyone, but that was of no account to the humourless ones down at the Cricket Association. He played in the one match against Queensland before the pen-pushers realised they hadn't had the letter from him so they gave him the shove and legspinner Hughie Chilvers made his debut for NSW on Boxing Day 1929.

I have always been interested in reading cricket books. A legacy I guess of being the son of a schoolteacher and growing up at a time when books and the wireless were the only sources of information. An inquiring mind was a necessity. Occasionally one can find a surprise and Mailey provided it for me. Jack Fingleton's *Brightly Fades the Don* remains one of the best cricket books of the immediate post-war period, the story of how the Australian team in 1948, captained by Bradman, went through the tour unbeaten.

'Fingo' and 'Tiger' O'Reilly made it clear on many occasions they never wished to be among Bradman's close friends. Jack was always of the opinion that he should have toured England with Bill Woodfull's team in 1934. The place went to Bill Brown and, although Bradman wasn't a selector, the 'Fingo' finger was dogmatically pointed at him. It always seemed to me to be a very odd call. In that summer of 1933–34, with the team to be chosen for England the final evening of the match, NSW v Victoria at the SCG, Fingleton made 655 runs at 60 an innings, Brown 878 at 68 and Bradman 1,192 at 132.

In what was the Test touring team trial in the last game mentioned above, Brown made 205 and Fingleton 145. Everyone is unlucky at some stage of their lives but I reckon Brown would have been decidedly unfortunate to miss selection for that tour. *Wisden*, in the summing up of the tour, singled out Bradman, Ponsford, McCabe and Brown as the four batting stars, Brown being rated as possessing a *classic* style. Looking at the scores and batting orders throughout the tour, it is quite clear the captain, Bill Woodfull, had determined he would be going in first with Bill Ponsford, Brown was the third opener and McCabe would occasionally be used in that position if needed.

Brightly Fades the Don, from its historical view and skilful writing, was particularly interesting to me, because one chapter, Chapter 17, was titled, *What the Critics Think*.

Those asked to put their views of Bradman in writing, and agreeing to do so, were: Sir Pelham Warner, R.C. Robertson-Glasgow, Reggie Spooner, Major 'Beau' Vincent, Denzil Batchelor, Jim Kilburn, Charles Bray, Ray Robinson, Brian Sellers, John Arlott, Arthur Mailey, the Right Hon. R.G. Menzies.

It provided a cross-section of personalities. The most interesting omission was Bill O'Reilly and I have always wondered why 'Tiger' wasn't asked to contribute, or declined to contribute, or had no interest in contributing to his great friend's book.

It was, though, Arthur Mailey's contribution which caught my eye.

The *Sydney Morning Herald* in early 2001, during an exchange of letters, quoted the first three paragraphs of the Mailey summing-up of Bradman but, surprisingly, not the remainder. The quotes were correctly noted as being from *Brightly Fades the Don*.

The full Mailey quote is: Arthur Mailey: (Sydney *Sunday Telegraph* and prince of slow bowlers):

> Don Bradman will be remembered as one of the most remarkable sportsmen who ever graced the sporting stage of any country.
>
> Bradman is an enigma, a paradox; an idol of millions of people, yet, with a few, the most unpopular cricketer I have ever met.
>
> People close to Bradman either like or dislike him; there is no half way. To those who dislike him there is no compromise, no forgiveness, little tolerance. There are at least two major reasons: jealousy and this great cricketer's independence.
>
> I have watched Bradman's career since he left Bowral, since he wore black braces at the Sydney Cricket Ground (he still swears he was never guilty of such sacrilege), have seen every innings he has played in Tests against any country, have seen him during periods of rich success and in his moments of embarrassment and frustration; have seen him pleased and annoyed; have seen him grin and sob almost in the one moment, but never have I seen him deviate very far from that line which was intended to lead him to power and success.
>
> Unlike many people who attain power, Bradman has never, to my knowledge, resorted to political intrigue or compromise. His personal success on the cricket field has provided him with a passport which he never hesitates to use.
>
> His intuition, tenacity, and calculating mind have given him an individualism which demands attention and, in most cases support.
>
> Bradman has a very acute brain. But there are some aspects of his mental outlook which lack the benefit of finer thinking. He is dogmatic

on subjects or opinions which even an expert or a master would treat with great care and discretion.

That he can express a more sensible opinion than most cricketers on any set of subjects there is no doubt, and in this particular connection I would mention speechmaking. Bradman has surprised many listeners with his ability to make an after-dinner speech. His complete coverage of interesting points and somewhat unorthodox points of view have given him a reputation that a more efficient orator would be proud of.

During his career Bradman has fallen foul of many factions directly or indirectly connected with the game. The Board of Control fined him £50 for breaking the player-writer rule. Other players were disqualified for a similar breach, but Bradman was considered greater than the game, and certainly greater than the administration.

And as a team-mate, I have always found Bradman dependable, a good sportsman. As an interviewer I have found him reliable, fearless and fair, but most unsatisfactory; unsatisfactory because he appears to be suspicious of the Press generally. Nobody handles his own publicity as well as Bradman himself. While he gives the impression of avoiding the spotlight, he is sensibly conscious and perhaps appreciative of its power.

When Bradman suggests an alteration to the laws of cricket he is listened to with the greatest respect.

Bradman is a law within himself. This has been proved over and over again, and it is his amazing success as a cricketer, plus his perfect timing and tremendous respect and faith in his own judgment, that have demanded attention where others have been ignored – in some cases ridiculed.

When I asked him if it were true that he had been offered a knighthood, he replied, 'I know nothing about it.'

'Would you accept if it were offered?' I persisted.

'I cannot answer a question which to my knowledge has no foundation,' said Don. The dialogue was similar when I asked if he intended to stand for Parliament.

A difference with the New South Wales Cricket Association probably caused Bradman to leave the state. There was a mild mutiny among certain players when he first led the Australian Eleven. Then he crossed pens several times with his old enemy, the Press.

In all these skirmishes he came out best, but there are still a number of his adversaries licking their wounds and waiting to have another 'crack' at the 'one-man' army.

Jealousy, according to the dictionary, is 'apprehension of being supplanted in favour of another', and here we put a finger on the sore spot of Bradman's unpopularity with certain players.

The ambitious Master Bradman climbed right over the heads of his contemporaries, some of whom felt that priority entitled them to the plums of captaincy.

Many of these men had accepted the captaincy of Australia or their states in similar circumstances, but consoled themselves with the thought that, in their cases, it was a reward for efficiency.

Bradman was brought up the hard way, the lonely way. That's why he practised as a boy by hitting a ball up against a brick wall, and when he felt the cold draught of antagonism within the ranks he kept his counsel, remained unperturbed, and knew his greatest weapon was centuries and more centuries.

Apart from that, his tremendous success on the field and his value as a box-office attraction made him a valuable asset to those who regard big gates as a proof of efficient administration. Bradman never made the mistake, common to many, of thinking that personal popularity is more potent than success.

Bradman's humour is not particularly subtle, although there is a cynicism about it which makes it more acceptable than the red-nose stage type of wit. Don is more alert than most people in repartee.

I believe he is quite ready to 'swap' wisecracks with Bernard Shaw or any other creator of smart sentences, not because he believes he can out-Shaw Shaw, but simply because he refuses to be silenced by greater personalities.

That is one of the best short pieces of writing I have ever come across concerning Bradman and other people.

*　　*　　*

Bradman himself was never one to rush hastily into print. He wrote an article for *Wisden* in 1939 after the conclusion of the 1938 tour of England and his contribution then concerned the lbw Law, as well as other matters. In regard to the lbw Law he suggested that the lot of the bowler be improved by changing the Law existing at that time *to allow a bowler to gain a decision when a ball pitched in a line between wicket and wicket, or on the offside of the pitch and would have hit the stumps.* He believed the Law existing at the time, under which he had played for ten years, was too much in favour of the batsmen. Sensibly the Law was changed for the better.

He also mentioned the idea which had been suggested that summer that the method of tossing should be changed. The thought then was the same one that has been broached in recent times that the toss should be alternated during the series. Bradman said, 'To enable one captain to know in advance which team would have the choice of batting would pave the way to so many undesirable possibilities that I do not think it an idea worthwhile discussing.'

In 1986 he wrote a brilliant article about the two existing versions of cricket, the Test matches and Limited-overs Internationals. By 1986, and because of World Series Cricket, the Limited-overs Internationals were sometimes played in the daylight hours; sometimes they were day-night matches.

Bear in mind this was only nine years after the start of World Series Cricket, only seven years after the conclusion of what was one of the most historic and tumultuous times in the game. It is an article entitled 'Whither Cricket Now?' and sets out to suggest what might happen in the game up to the turn of the century. As we are now well past that moment, it doesn't do any harm to consider his thoughts because, although the longer version of the game was part of World Series Cricket, day-night limited-overs matches more than played their part.

There were people in 1987, after *Wisden* was published, who said to me how disappointed they were that Sir Donald had even considered writing anything by way of approval concerning one-day or day-night matches, but he was shrewd enough to realise and to put forward the idea that there was much merit in the one-day game. The disappointment I mention above is perhaps the reason so few people comment on Bradman's remarks, whereas there is no doubt in my mind that, had he been critical, his remarks would have been widely quoted over a long period of time. Miserable and selective thinking.

Don wrote that there was a stirring of emotions at a limited-overs game between those of a new and largely young audience, who yell and scream their support, and those dyed-in-the-wool lovers of Test cricket who yearn for more peaceful, bygone days. He pointed out that, as with so many things, reconciliation between the factions is well-nigh impossible. And he added that, despite a deep feeling for the traditional form of cricket, his conviction was that we must accept we live in a new era. He correctly noted the Achilles' heel of the limited-overs game, that premium is placed on defensive bowling and negative and defensive field-placings, so one can be bored by countless singles being taken with no slips and five men on the boundary.

He pointed out though that the limited-overs contest has done something else: it has got rid of the unutterable bore who believes occupancy of the crease and his own personal aggrandisement is all that matter. He commented on the lift in the standard of fielding and that running between the wickets had taken on a new dimension. Risks must be taken to keep up a good run-rate.

The latter two aspects have increased dramatically in the near 20-year period since Bradman wrote that article. Fielding has continued to improve in exciting fashion, runs being saved with the slide, pick-up and throw in the one action, running between the wickets has become more challenging with fielders moving faster and with brilliant agility.

As was most times the case with Bradman, he was ahead of the game. In that 1986 article, before anyone else was thinking about it, he suggested there would be no loss of face or pride if television were to be used to adjudicate in certain decisions. These covered run-outs, stumpings and disputed catches. It wouldn't work, he added, with lbw appeals. That first section has become part of the game and lbws are still not in the frame. Technology has advanced in cricket but, fortunately, the cricket administrators are thinking very carefully about every aspect.

Just on 20 years after that article, there is another side to all this. From the time Mark Taylor, then Steve Waugh and now Ricky Ponting captained Australia, there was a different approach to the game in the way in which the batsmen and the team approached their task. In the limited-overs matches, the Australians found the harder they went at the opposition the bigger advantage they seemed to have as the match progressed. They then deliberately translated this to Test cricket and, starting with the opening batsmen, they tried to carry the attack to the opposition right from the opening delivery.

Although other countries have moved forward in this regard, it has been the Australians who have done it best and it has been remarkable to see how they have lifted the excitement of the Test match game to encompass scoring at around four an over and sometimes making 350 in the day. Very occasionally they have missed out but generally, with the bat, their attack and then superb counter-attack, has worked. It has also made it a brilliant game to watch. Some months ago they were talking about making 400 in a limited-overs innings.

One of the best Law changes in my time in the game has been the one where the lbw Law was again changed to read in effect that the requirements to gain a decision were *that the ball either pitched or would have pitched in a straight line between wicket and wicket, or, the ball pitched outside a batsman's off-stump and in the opinion of the*

A combination of sightseeing and research. The village of Benaud in France, from which the first Benaud journeyed to Australia on the *Ville de Bordeaux* in 1838. Daphne and I spent a lot of time scanning the archives in Clermont-Ferrand and Vic-le-Comte in the Auvergne. We found some fascinating Benaud history around Revolution time, some good . . . some better left in the tightly-bound files.

John Pendlington, who was the first person known to have experimented with a line-by-line system of cricket scoring, rather than the orthodox innings-to-one-page method. W.G. Grace was said to be much amused by it at Scarborough in 1893.

At the time this notice was captioned 'The Death of Cricket'. Instead, it turned out to be 'The Birth of the Ashes'. Billy Murdoch was captain of the 1882 Australian team to tour England. Fred Spofforth's exhortation, 'This thing can be done', was the rallying cry in the dressing-room.

Photographs were scarce and often casually organised at times in 1882; these are some of the players victorious at The Oval. The full Australian team was W.L. Murdoch (captain), A.C. Bannerman, G.J. Bonnor, S.P. Jones, H.H. Massie, F.R. Spofforth (New South Wales), G. Giffen (South Australia), J.M. Blackham, H.F. Boyle, T.P. Horan, P.S. McDonnell and G.E. Palmer (Victoria), with C.W. Beal as manager.

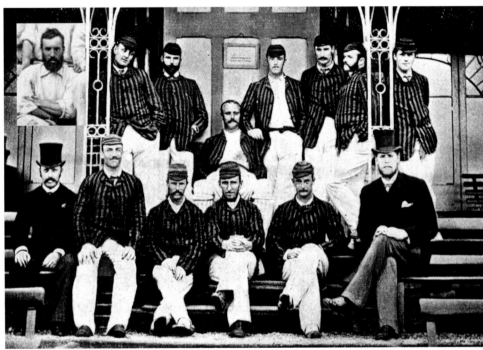

Four of a kind, but each completely different. Clarrie Grimmett (*above left*), born in New Zealand, played for Australia on 37 occasions. His round-arm legspin was too much for batsmen of all countries. Arthur Mailey (*above right*) wanted to spin the leather off the ball and was one of the great characters of cricket, as well as being a delightful person. Bernard Bosanquet (*below left*) bowled leg-breaks and then developed the 'bosie' at the turn of the 19th century. William Joseph ('Tiger') O'Reilly (*below right*) disliked batsmen and bowled slow medium-pace legspin and 'bosies' with all the aggression, demeanour and enjoyment of a fast bowler.

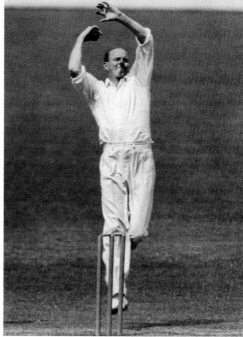

Bodyline. Perfectly legal under the existing Laws, but quickly noted later as being not quite in the spirit of the game. Two interesting shots of Douglas Jardine – (*above right*) as Australians tended to see him, rather stern-looking, possibly aloof, and (*above left*) on a tiger shoot, perhaps getting himself into the right mood for picking off Australian cricketers in what was to be the most incident-packed cricket tour of all time. The batsman in the photograph below, minus bat, is Bill Woodfull, the Australian captain, who offered a calm riposte to Pelham Warner when the England manager offered his sympathy about two Australian players being hit.

Right: There have been many fast bowlers with classic actions; Harold Larwood was one of them. The bowling attack Douglas Jardine had at his disposal in 1932–33 was quite outstanding – Larwood, Bill Voce, 'Gubby' Allen, Bill Bowes, Wally Hammond, Hedley Verity and Tom Mitchell, the legspinner from Derbyshire.

Below: Bradman missed the first Test through illness; then, in the first innings of the second Test, was out first ball, dragging a ball from Bowes on to his stumps. Bradman made an unbeaten second-innings century, 103* out of 191, Australia won the match and Bowes didn't play again in the series.

Three of Australia's greatest cricketers. *Below:* Keith Miller remains Australia's finest allrounder and is pictured here in the opening match at Arundel on his last tour of England in 1956. In the course of that tour he produced a performance at Lord's that has the game always recalled as 'Miller's Match'. When he passed away in October 2004 there were, in England and Australia, more glasses raised in tribute than there were solemn condolences.

Left: Also in a tour opener, Don Bradman (*right*) and Stan McCabe in 1934 at Worcester. Each had toured England for the first time in 1930, McCabe a surprise selection because he had never made a first-class century. Bravo selectors!

They were the days! Spectators sitting on the grass and allowed to pat their heroes on the back as they went out to field, or came back in to the pavilion. No such chance these days with the fear of players being deliberately injured: sadder times. *Above left:* Bradman is surrounded by the crowd at Headingley in 1930 after playing his extraordinary innings of 334. He made his last tour of England in 1948 (*above right*). *Below:* Australia's two greatest cricketers, Keith Miller (*left*) and Sir Don Bradman, whose portraits hang in the Long Room at Lord's.

One of the main reasons I have a love of the written word is that my father was a schoolteacher, a very good one too judging by the messages that still are received by my mother. He is at the extreme left of the picture above, taken at Jugiong School in the south-west of NSW way back in 1936. Tiny school, not many pupils, just 38 of them. The small fair haired lad, slightly to the front of the teacher, is your now grey-haired correspondent.

The picture below is of some of the Jugiong School pupils in the 21st century. Still not many of them, but in 2004 they wrote to see if, as an ex-student, I could help with some fundraising they were attempting. Not easy, as I don't have memorabilia of any kind, but we did find something from the first official Australian tour of India and Pakistan (1959–60). The money raised helped towards a swimming-pool and cricket practice nets.

umpire he made no genuine attempt to play the ball with his bat. I had been trying for this change since 1956 at Lord's when I bowled 28–14–27–1 in England's second innings. I had been contending that there must be some way of stopping batsmen using their pads instead of their bat. Colin Cowdrey was the person at the other end and England were on a mission to save the match. It was Miller's Match because of the ten wickets he took without Lindwall, Davidson and, other than for four overs, Crawford taking part. And Ian Johnson gave me a job to do at the other end by keeping Cowdrey tied down, with Peter Burge fielding a few yards from the bat. Colin made that easier by using his pads and, under the existing Law, he was completely protected until he mis-read a topspinner, padded up and was given out. The next day the English media complained that I had taken advantage of Colin being such a nice chap, which he certainly was, to put a man in so close at short-leg despite Peter May having reminded Johnson that the fielder could be hurt. The following year Cowdrey and Peter May at Edgbaston saved a match for England by playing Ramadhin and Valentine literally hour after hour with their pads.

Two years before that Lord's match Bradman, in a short article in *Wisden* 1954, immediately after my first tour of England under Lindsay Hassett, had called for a change to the lbw Law. He was talking about defensive cricket and the possibility of changing that by legislation. The bugbear was leg-theory bowling and he asked: '*Is defensive leg-theory bowling good for cricket? It restricts strokeplay and is the main reason for the game being deprived of much of its attractiveness.*' Bradman's solution was to suggest an extensive trial for a change in the Law whereby a batsman would be given out if he prevented the ball from striking the stumps without the use of the bat, irrespective of where it pitched, as long as the ball was not pitched outside the leg stump. Bradman added that such a move might induce the inswing and offspin bowlers to move their attack to the off stump and it might encourage the legspinner who would have a much better chance of success with the googly. Now which legspinner worth his salt wouldn't be interested in that? Bear in mind this was two years before the Cowdrey incident at Lord's and, to give you an idea of how slowly the lawmakers grind away, it wasn't until 1969 that it was introduced as an experimental rule to be in force for the English summer of 1970.

This was the new wording, only experimental mind you, but at least Bradman had his way, even if it took an eternity to have the lawmakers see reason.

LBW

39. The striker is out 'Leg before wicket' – If with any part of his person except his hand, which is in a straight line between wicket and wicket, even though the point of impact be above the level of the bails, he intercept a ball which has not first touched his bat or hand, and which, in the opinion of the umpire, shall have, or would have, pitched on a straight line from the bowler's wicket to the striker's wicket, or shall have pitched on the offside of the striker's wicket, provided always that the ball would have hit the wicket.

Note:

1. The word 'hand' used in this Law should be interpreted as the hand holding the bat.

    The following experimental rule will be in force in 1970:

    A batsman will be out lbw if, with any part of his body except his hand, he intercepts a ball which has not first touched his bat or hand and which, in the opinion of the umpire, would have hit his wicket, provided that either:

    (a) *the ball pitched or would have pitched in a straight line between wicket and wicket, or*

    (b) *the ball pitched outside a batsman's off stump and in the opinion of the umpire he made no genuine attempt to play the ball with his bat.*

When it became a Law of the game it proved to be one of the best ever introduced, though all these things are relative on the basis of how many good changes there have been.

Think for a moment of what a match might have been like in the 21st century had that not been done? Just fancy batsmen pushing their pads at the ball and not being able to be given out by the umpire? The problem, or really the good thing, is that the umpire still has to be absolutely certain the batsman is out. It always astonishes me when people talk about benefit of the doubt. There is no such thing as benefit of the doubt. The batsman is never given out unless the umpire is absolutely certain he is out.

5

RAISED FINGERS

N OT much changes in this game. Controversy has always existed in various areas, illegal bowling actions have allegedly been part of the game since over-arm bowling came into vogue. For the past few years the ICC, having opted to take over the whole question of bowling actions and the throwing Law, have found life to be increasingly more difficult.

Their most recent work has been done with bio-mechanists and, at a meeting in late 2004, they were attempting to make some progress and to make the whole thing easily understood by those sitting in their living-rooms, watching the cricket in a bar at the 'local', standing in the centre of the ground in a white coat, coaching the under-12s in the park on a Saturday morning, or sitting in the room of the match referee at a Test match.

A great deal has been written and said about the outcome of that meeting, far too much to be set out in full detail, but I have particularly noted concise and pertinent comments by Tim May, Jack Bannister, Allan Border and Michael Atherton.

Former Australian offspinner Tim May was a good cricketer. He has been very important in the cricket world as a leading figure in the Australian Cricketers' Association, the body which represents all the first-class cricketers in Australia. It was a sensible move to have him on the ICC's cricket committee which investigated technology which could possibly have some bearing on whether or not a bowler was infringing the Law of the game concerning bowling actions. Throwing is not quite as old as the game itself but, right from the start of cricket in the Kent and Sussex areas of England, there was always some controversy about bowlers. Even when they were bowling under-arm. In the 21st century, with bio-chemists taking a hand in the game, life has suddenly become more difficult for everyone. Most comments concerning the committee meeting were to the effect that its conclusions would provide a licence for bowlers to throw. The ICC committee studied everything put forward by those bio-chemists at that meeting in 2004 and this is a report of what May said in a summing-up on his return to Australia when he claimed the game had no choice but to change the throwing Law.

> 'The use of high-speed cameras capable of dissecting a bowler's action has enabled sports scientists to prove almost every bowler in world cricket straightens his arm to some degree in the delivery process.
>
> 'Armed with that knowledge, it is only a matter of time before the entire issue of the legality of bowling actions ends up in court,' May said.
>
> 'It is understood several Test-playing nations have prepared an initial legal brief in case any of their players are reported and subsequently suspended for throwing.
>
> 'Under that scenario, lawyers would immediately begin court action claiming the ICC were in possession of scientific information which showed that all bowlers in world cricket operated outside the throwing Law as it currently stands.
>
> 'Not only would the banned bowler plead restraint of trade, but would argue that all his contemporaries were operating outside cricket's laws with the full knowledge of the ICC.
>
> 'Faced with the prospect of the majority of bowlers being sidelined, the ICC initiated the review of procedures for dealing with illegal actions and members of the committee believe the new recommendations safeguard the game's future.
>
> 'At the end of the day, this is a pretty practical solution to a very difficult area,' May said.

'In addition to the high-speed filming and detailed plotting of elbow, wrist and shoulder extensions, images of the bowler operating in the laboratory environment will be matched against footage shot under match conditions. That will ensure bowlers do not simply go through the motions when they know they are being scrutinised.

'If they don't satisfy the testers that they are bowling as they would in a match, they will be deemed to have breached the testing protocols and suffer the penalties,' May said. 'This is not a licence to throw, this is a licence properly to police the law using the technology.'

Asked whether he – having played 24 Tests for Australia in which he took 75 wickets bowling offspin – would take umbrage at suggestions his action was illegal, May was unequivocal.

'If you said that to me two months ago without me seeing the [scientific] footage, I would have been naturally offended,' May said.

'But you could not have walked out of that room [in Dubai] with any other opinion. The fact is every bowler's arm is going to bend a bit. It's virtually impossible to get your arm dead straight.'

I enjoyed Tim May's thoughts but the disturbing aspect of all this was that suddenly the game of cricket was about to be a legal minefield and a haven for bio-chemists and possibly the bending of steel bars . . . if not Laws! Jack Bannister, who is one of the most knowledgeable cricket commentators I have known, wrote an article for the *Birmingham Post* in the United Kingdom and, first of all, posed a question. '*When does a high tensile bar suddenly veer off its 180-degree straight and narrow?*' The answer was nothing to do with an old-time circus strong-man act. It was though, all to do with sporting bio-mechanists putting it through the same high technological tests which they insist proves that no modern bowler releases the ball with a completely straight arm.

The International Cricket Council will decide that a tolerance of up to 15 degrees of flexing of the bowling arm is acceptable. This will allow slow bowlers to bowl the 'doosra' which had been considered a throw by some match referees and umpires and had been reported accordingly. The 'doosra' was said to have a flex of around 12 degrees, some 'doosra' bowlers were said to have a flex of 14 degrees.

Bannister noted that the situation had come about because the bio-mechanists had put under a magnifying glass the actions of all modern bowlers in a camera which operates at 250 frames a second, compared with 25 frames per second by television cameras. By doing this they are said to have satisfied themselves that bowlers all use a complex chain of movements such as hyperextension and adduction of their bowling arm to give the illusion of it being bent.

Then they say that the detection of a bent elbow by the human eye only happens at around 15 degrees.

Jack added that additionally the bio-mechanists seem to be saying: the angle of a straight steel bar when forced through the same mechanical motions as the bowling arm can vary from 178 degrees to 182 degrees. He made the very valid point that if the rod of steel appears to move four degrees, how could an alleged hyperflexion of twice that amount by bowlers such as Glenn McGrath and Shaun Pollock be taken seriously?

What the bio-mechanists are saying is that there is no such thing as a perfect bowling action, nor is there such a thing as a straight steel bar when subjected to the same technology. This is certainly disputed by Sir Garfield Sobers for example who claims, correctly, to have had a full sweep of the arm when bowling. And I, for one, could never believe that Jeff Thomson had the slightest kink in his arm. Bannister concludes, correctly in my experience, that anyone who has played the game can immediately spot a dodgy action.

Allan Border was short and to the point when he said that he was from the old school, that if a bowler had his arm bent and then straightened it, it is a throw.

Michael Atherton offered the view that the change in Law 24.3 came about because the original wording was never intended to be placed under the scrutiny of cameras filming at 250 frames per second. He added that such examination has rendered the Law obsolete and in this increasingly litigious society the ICC had no alternative but to protect themselves from possible legal action.

The last word was with Bannister; that the slightly bending and curving steel bar seems to present an unanswerable counter-argument against what the bio-mechanists and the ICC are suggesting.

James Phillips, the Australian umpire who, over a hundred years ago, used to spend his summers alternately in England and Australia, had firm ideas on throwing. He was one who held the opinion that to bowl a fair ball it was immaterial whether the arm was straight or at an angle as long as there was no perceptible movement in the elbow-joint at the precise moment the ball leaves the hand of the bowler.

In his capacity as an umpire he found there was great difficulty in detecting the elbow movement at the bowling end whereas, when standing at square-leg, this difficulty was overcome and every movement of the bowler's arm was noticeable.

It was Phillips who had the Law changed so that the umpire at square-leg, as well as the umpire at the bowling end, could no-ball a bowler for throwing.

Sixty years later we had the Imperial Cricket Conference version at the 1960 meeting at Lord's: a ball shall be deemed to have been thrown if, in the opinion of either umpire, the bowling arm having been bent at the elbow, whether the wrist is backward of the elbow or not, is suddenly straightened immediately prior to the instant of delivery.

Not much is new in cricket, nor in throwing.

Despite the bio-chemists and other advances made in technology, there will always be umpires in the game of cricket. Some decision-making has been taken away from them in recent years but, unless robots completely take over our lives, the men in white will continue to exist, even if sometimes for the Limited-overs Internationals they are the men in black, pale blue or pink, anything that will ensure the white ball is not lost in white jackets.

Early in 2005, the ICC Executives' Committee issued a public statement concerning changes involved in dealing with illegal bowling actions. The statement underlined that Tim May's thoughts had been accurate. The rationales for the changes were listed as below:

1. An acceptance that the focus of the Law concerning illegal actions is that it seeks to deal with the extension of the arm that is visible to the naked eye.

Research conducted by the ICC and several leading bio-mechanists around the world using high-speed cameras has established that most bowlers are likely to straighten their bowling arm to some degree during the bowling action. This is likely to be a degree undetectable to the naked eye.

It was agreed that the Law was not seeking to eliminate this imperceptible straightening of the arm.

This view was confirmed by the game's lawmaker, the Marylebone Cricket Club, which advised that it was unaware that bowlers were likely to straighten their arm to a level imperceptible to the naked eye when it drafted the laws and that its intention was to prevent straightening which is visible to the naked eye.

2. All bowlers will be permitted to straighten their arms up to 15 degrees which has been established as the point at which any straightening will become visible to the naked eye.

This limit replaces the variable limits put in place two years ago which have been superseded by the latest research into this issue.

Umpires and match referees will continue to lodge a report based on what they see on the field with the naked eye. Following a report, when the player is undergoing the analysis of his action, 15 degrees of straightening will be the threshold beyond which an action will be deemed to be illegal.

3. **The introduction of a shorter, independent review process under the central control of the ICC with immediate suspensions for bowlers found to have illegal actions.**

The first bio-mechanical analysis of a reported bowler's action must now be completed within 21 days, down from six weeks, and this process will now come under the control of the ICC rather than remain with the player's home board.

4. **The overhaul and standardisation of the bio-mechanical testing of bowlers to ensure that all tests are: a) conducted using the same equipment and standards; b) reproduced in, as far as possible, match conditions; and c) consistent in the way that bowlers are tested.**

Strengthening of the initiatives to deal with the issue at the international and regional Under-19 level.

For the ICC U-19 World Cup 2004, the ICC established an independent expert panel to observe the players in the tournament and identify any bowlers with potentially illegal actions. Any report was then provided to the home board of the player concerned to be addressed. It was agreed that this type of procedure would now be adopted by regional associations and member boards for regional and domestic age-group events respectively.

Bradman's thoughts on technology advances were well expressed in his 1986 *Wisden* article where he was suggesting television replays could be used to adjudicate on boundaries, run-outs and stumpings. Bradman was always ahead of his time with suggestions on the Laws of the game, but he was careful not to suggest too much interference with it. He was also always a great respecter of umpires and the manner in which their decisions should be observed by players.

Jack Fingleton in his various writings always pointed out that he never once saw Bradman in any way suggest that an umpire might have made a mistake. Bradman himself rated Frank Chester as the greatest umpire he saw in cricket. I only ever saw Chester in one series, the 1953 tour of England, where Lindsay Hassett was the Australian captain and Chester was coming towards the end of his career, though he did stand in the following two English summers when the touring teams were Pakistan and South Africa. He had retired by the time I toured again under Ian Johnson in 1956. The Test in which he stood in 1953 was the controversial one at Headingley where, at different times in the five days, Australia looked to be in with a chance of victory. This was particularly so during England's second innings when, at 182/6, they were in effect only 83 runs ahead of Australia with four wickets in hand.

In the previous Test at Old Trafford, with the ball turning and lifting sharply, spinners Jim Laker and Johnny Wardle between them had taken 6/18, and Hutton had been hoping at Headingley to be able to make a closure and again put Australia under severe pressure. With only the 83-run lead that didn't look possible, but then there came some dashing hitting from Jim Laker and, when we bowled England out for 275, their lead was 176 and there were still 115 minutes remaining. Len calculated we wouldn't make that many but, such was the spite in the pitch, he reasoned we might be bowled out by Laker and Lock, or at least be given a bit of a scare. Arthur Morris and Neil Harvey quickly destroyed that theory with 65 from the first ten overs and then Trevor Bailey was called into action, if that's not a contradiction of terms, to bowl his exaggerated leg-theory with a snail's pace walk back to his mark. We fell 30 runs short of the target and Alec Bedser bowled 17 overs unchanged at the Football Stand End. If we weren't disgruntled, then we weren't enthused either by what had gone on in the match. Neither umpire Chester nor Frank Lee raised a finger, or even an eyebrow at the time-wasting tactics employed, and there were no match referees and no fines for such misdemeanours in those days.

Most umpires have had some playing experience and I always think that is a good thing. In England it wasn't mandatory but, because of the county system, it was a natural progression from playing, retiring and then taking up umpiring. Chester was a fine young cricketer for Worcestershire before he lost his right arm in the First World War. He was one of the youngest ever to be given a county cap. Before joining Worcestershire he had already made his debut for Bushey in Hertfordshire aged 12 and went on to hit three centuries in the 1913 season before joining the Royal Field Artillery. It was in action for that section of the Army that he lost his right arm. Aged 26 in 1922, he joined the first-class umpires' list and within two years was umpiring his first Test, England v South Africa at Lord's. He first stood in an Ashes Test in 1926 where he was quoted as saying Jack Hobbs's century was 'the greatest innings I ever saw, and on the worst pitch'. Hobbs and Herbert Sutcliffe shared a second-innings opening stand of 172 which gave England their opportunity to regain the Ashes, with Wilfred Rhodes bowling out Herbie Collins's side for only 125.

In 1953 I played in the first match against Worcestershire, but not in the second at Leicester where Chester stood as umpire, so my first experience of bowling with him at the non-striker's end was in the game against Oxford University. Oxford had in their side one Australian, Alan Dowding from South Australia, Charles Williams, a useful number three batsman who played for Essex against us in 1956 and later wrote a biography of Bradman, and also Colin Cowdrey was in the side, his reputation as a fine young player of the future had preceded him. A year earlier he had hit a brilliant century against the Indian touring team to save Kent from defeat. Cowdrey missed out against us in that Oxford match early on the 1953 tour, Miller bowled him in the first innings for one and I bowled him in the second for five. I did also have a big appeal against him for lbw and wasn't certain how umpire Chester could possibly have given it not out. Gilbert Langley, our 'keeper, put me straight. 'Just the faintest inside edge,' he said. 'Brilliant decision.' Later that tour we had a problem or two in that Headingley Test, one with a very strange run-out decision, but I'm quite prepared to accept Bradman's opinion that Chester was the best he ever saw.

The best I saw was another Englishman, Syd Buller, who umpired his first Test in 1956 at Trent Bridge in what was a drawn game between England and Australia. He had umpired in another seven home Tests by the time I watched him officiate again and that was in the Lord's Test in 1960 when England hosted South Africa. I was still playing and captaining Australia at the time and had just successfully captained the first ever official Australian team to tour India (five Tests) and Pakistan (three Tests). The next team scheduled to visit Australia was the West Indies and, at that time, we had no idea of what lay in store for us, with a Tied Test and an astonishing series with record attendances and a tickertape farewell for Frank Worrell's team in Melbourne at the conclusion of the series. In early February 1960, George Greenfield, my literary agent with John Farquharson in London, wrote to say that the BBC had been in touch to ask if I would consider covering the five-Test South African tour for radio. They were aware I had done that specially-organised BBC course in 1956, where I was trying to learn about television because that was the year TV began in Australia, and they also assumed that, if fit, I would probably captain the Australian team to England in 1961.

In 1960 I also did some work in the London office of John Fairfax Pty Ltd, who published *The Sun* newspaper. It was a good time to be there, sub-editing and also writing my own stories back to Australia. It was the time of the Rome Olympics when Herb Elliott won the 1,500 metres, one of the finest sports performances I have seen from an Australian in any area.

It was a splendid year for Australia in other sports as well: Kel Nagle won the Open Championship at St Andrews by one shot from Arnold Palmer; Neale Fraser defeated Rod Laver in the Wimbledon singles final in four sets; and, although nothing to do with Australia, St Paddy won the Derby. Watching those three sports on television gave me an opportunity to listen to those incomparable television commentators: Henry Longhurst on golf, Dan Maskell, tennis, and Peter O'Sullevan, horseracing. They were even better than when I had heard them four years earlier!

Rothmans sponsored some televised one-day games which Frank Bough hosted on Sundays on the BBC and these were very well received. I played in some and took part in as many TV interviews as possible, enjoying the chance to become more familiar with the medium. When given the opportunity, I was delighted to be interviewed by Brian Johnston or Peter West on BBC Television.

I also thoroughly enjoyed my time with the *News of the World* as a feature writer on cricket, working with the regular cricket writer, seeking and filing my own stories and liaising with the sports editor, Frank Butler. Frank was my first of only a handful of sports editors there and I have been with the paper now for 45 years as a freelancer, longer I suspect than any full-time employee.

Visiting England in 1960 was also a great opportunity for me to have a look at what they had to offer in their cricket resurgence, with an eye to the 1961 Australian tour. As it turned out, there were many other things happening, including the throwing controversy, and it was an educational five months . . . working for the BBC, *News of the World* and *The Sun* in Sydney.

As I arrived in England in 1960 I was saddened to hear Alex Skelding had passed away. He was a delightful chap and a very unorthodox umpire who had been a useful cricketer with Leicestershire. He was, to my eyes, an unusual figure when I first came across him, because he was the only umpire I had seen in England who wore white boots or shoes. These were worn in Australia by umpires, but in England it was brown brogues, or occasionally, in dry conditions, brown or navy suede. Umpires often wore brown felt hats as well.

Alex stood in some of our matches in 1953 and 1956, but the only time I played in a game when he was officiating was when we met Essex at Southend, in 1953, and he was very amusing as well as seeming a good umpire, and not solely because he gave Doug Insole out lbw to my topspinner. There was never a dull moment from a man who was highly respected by every cricketer who knew him and it was a treat to hear, 'And that, gentlemen, concludes the entertainment for the morning . . .'

In late 1960 Sir Donald Bradman, who was to take over as chairman of the Australian board, was working hard in Australia to come up with some form of agreement on the question of doubtful bowling actions, though he was careful to emphasise the difficulties in arriving at a definition. I was in England and, having summed up the mood and the general situation, started writing a series of articles back to Australia to the effect that this, in my opinion, was for Australia the most important ICC meeting of all time.

I stressed that, instead of using the board's representative in England, or it being a holiday trip for a couple of very ordinary administrators, the Australian board must send Bradman and, as their second representative, chairman Bill Dowling. The habit was that the board's representative in England would attend ICC meetings and the various social engagements and then report back to the board in writing about what had eventuated. This was going to be completely useless in 1960 because I could see there were tough discussions ahead. I hammered the point that it was essential Bradman appear as one of Australia's representatives and, as chairman, Dowling should accompany him. Bradman and Dowling duly arrived for the conference which began on 14 July.

In England, MCC had already stated they would be providing full support for any umpires who might feel the need to 'call' bowlers with suspect actions. The problem was, would the definition stand up when they finally came up with a new wording? In the 1959 season in England there had been several bowlers no-balled for throwing, including Tony Lock, who had worked on remodelling his suspect bowling action after being shown some movie films taken by Harry Cave in New Zealand at the conclusion of the tour to Australia and New Zealand in 1958–59. The same kind of thing was being done in Australia, where the word 'jerk' had been removed from the throwing definition.

Before Bradman and Dowling arrived in England there had been some no-balling of South African Geoff Griffin. The first time this happened he was merely called for dragging, by Paul Gibb standing in the match Derbyshire against the touring side. Griffin had already been called for throwing in South Africa in February and March 1959, when he was playing for Natal.

One of England's best umpires, Syd Buller, had officiated in South Africa's opening game against Worcestershire when Griffin didn't play. When the South Africans journeyed to Lord's in late May to play MCC, two other good umpires, Frank Lee and John Langridge, stood. Lee called Griffin once and then Langridge called him twice for throwing, and once he was called simultaneously for both throwing and dragging. At a meeting at the end of the match, the umpires said his basic action was okay but that he threw the ball on the occasions he was called. When Griffin was called eight times for throwing against Nottinghamshire, the team management said he would be sent to Alf Gover's cricket school for remedial treatment.

By the time Bradman and Dowling returned to Australia from the London conference, there had been much correspondence between the two boards, as well as other cricket boards around the world, and considerable progress had been made. It had been made, however, in a slightly odd fashion, with the compromise between England and Australia being that during the first five weeks of the 1961 Ashes tour, when I was likely to be captain, umpires would not call, on the field of play, any bowler thought to be throwing, but would complete a confidential report and submit it to Lord's and to the Australian team. This bears a remarkable resemblance to what has happened in recent times, with the International Cricket Council instituting a system whereby a bowler in a Test won't be called for throwing but will be the subject of reports to the ICC through the match referee.

The catalyst for the latter was the 'calling' of Muttiah Muralitharan, the Sri Lankan bowler, in the Melbourne Boxing Day Test of 1995 and the suggestions that there were several bowlers in cricket around the world who had, or have, suspect bowling actions.

In addition to the decisions on throwing in 1960, the ICC brought the following four major issues under scrutiny, which shows that nothing in this game of cricket really changes:

1. *Time-wasting was criticised.* At last cricket administrators decided this aspect of play and captaincy was to the detriment of the game.
2. *Drag was under notice.* Umpires were trying to work off the front foot and one of the officials concerned in the Griffin throwing incidents, Syd Buller, an outstanding umpire, was to be a key man in that aspect of the game when we toured England in 1961.
3. *Pitches should not be damaged by bowlers in their follow through* was another recommendation. Correct. We had already seen to our detriment in Australia, in 1958, what damage could be done, and we were about to see it very much to our advantage in 1961.
4. *Batsmen using their pads instead of their bat* came under fire, as should have been the case many years earlier. There was thought given to bringing in a Law that a batsman could be out lbw not playing a stroke, even if the ball pitched outside off stump. Administrators have always moved slowly.

That ICC meeting was during the South African tour of England, but the unusual announcement concerning the way throwing would be policed was not made until 3 November, 1960. It was unusual, not so much because it amended the *Laws of Cricket*, which was always an ongoing proposition, but because it amended them in such a way that umpires in England, during the first five weeks of the Australian tour in 1961, would not call a bowler in Australian matches even if they thought he was throwing. When is a throw not a throw? We were about to find out!

The official announcement in late 1960 was that MCC and the English counties had agreed with the Australian Board of Control for International Cricket to the following application of Law 26 during the Australian Tour to the United Kingdom in 1961:

> English umpires will be instructed not to call on the field for a suspect delivery (throwing) any Australian bowler on the 1961 tour prior to 7 June, 1961. Up to that date every umpire who officiates in an Australian match and who is not entirely satisfied of the absolute fairness of a delivery of any Australian bowler will, as soon as possible after the conclusion of each match, complete a confidential report on a form to be provided and send it to the president of MCC – a duplicate copy to be sent through the secretary of MCC to the manager of the Australian team. From 7 June, 1961, the umpires will be instructed to implement Law 26 on the field in the normal way, according to their own judgment; and the Australian bowlers will become 'liable' to be called for any infringement. At no stage of the tour will a bowler be, as it were, 'declared illegal' and he will be free to play as and when chosen at Australia's discretion.
>
> In view of the new definition of a throw and the agreement referred to above, the MCC and the English counties will consider whether or not to adopt the same procedure in all first-class matches prior to 7 June, 1961.

At an advisory county cricket committee meeting on 16 November, 1960, it was agreed that the same truce period should apply to English bowlers in matches against the Australians. At the same time the counties stated that they did not intend to have anything to do with it for championship matches. They were quite happy with the position as it stood, which was that umpires would call bowlers with suspect actions.

In 1960 it was recalled that at the 1959 Conference in England, the important and difficult problem of doubtful bowling actions was discussed and the following decision was reached and recorded:—

It was unanimously agreed that throwing and jerking should be eliminated from the game and that each country would do everything possible to achieve this end.

The 1960 Conference then resolved to reaffirm this declaration but went further and unanimously recommended that the following experimental definition be adopted:—

A ball shall be deemed to have been thrown if, in the opinion of either umpire, the bowling arm having been bent at the elbow, whether the wrist is backward of the elbow or not, is suddenly straightened immediately prior to the instant of delivery.

The bowler shall nevertheless be at liberty to use the wrist freely in the delivery action.

It is considered that the pregoing definition will result in a more uniform interpretation of what constitutes a throw and should assist greatly in achieving the object all have in mind. The question of throwing is, however, a complicated and difficult problem, especially for the umpires who are solely responsible for interpreting the Laws. The whole problem has been complicated by modern methods of publicity resulting in a danger of prejudgment.

The Conference, therefore, having reached a unanimous conclusion in a most amicable spirit, hope that all those who may be concerned with the future welfare of cricket will do all in their power to assist those whose, admittedly difficult, task is to adjudicate on this problem.

Sir Donald Bradman on his return to Australia from the Imperial Cricket Conference said that, if allowed to get out of hand, the throwing controversy could lead to the greatest catastrophe in cricket history. 'It is the most complex question I have known in cricket, because it is not a matter of fact, but of opinion and interpretation,' he said. 'It is so involved that two men of equal goodwill and sincerity could take opposite views. It is quite impossible to go on playing with different definitions of throwing. This was the great hurdle of the 1960 Conference and it unanimously and amicably agreed on a uniform definition. It was a major achievement, but it still has to run the gauntlet of time. We must find some answer which places due regard on the integrity, good faith and judgment of all countries, their umpires, players and administrators. I have good reason to think that certain proposals under examination might lead us into calmer waters. I plead that a calm, patient attitude be exercised while we pursue and resolve the problem.'

While the Imperial Conference was deliberating on the issue of throwing, it was seriously suggested in some quarters in England and Australia that for the good of cricket it might be expedient to postpone the Australian tour of 1961. It was that close to severing cricket and political relationships between the two countries.

It underlines that there has never been a more controversial aspect of the game of cricket than umpiring. The men in the white coats of modern times were preceded by beautifully-dressed men in civilian garb, each carrying a bat and standing away from the stumps at either end of the pitch. With technology being used more and more these days, the ICC have had the task of bringing umpiring into the 21st century. Part of the challenge has been that umpires independent of the teams taking part in the international match will be in the centre of the ground. Also that their skills will need to be monitored so there can be regular assessment of their performances.

Nothing is easy for an umpire these days. On free-to-air television, and Pay TV as well, the technology is most times of benefit to the umpire, showing that he has it right. Sometimes, but remarkably rarely, it may show he has made an error, in the same way as a player, captain, selector, media worker or administrator has made an error either on or off the field.

Channel Four in the United Kingdom lists its technology in this way:

Snickometer

A difficult decision for an umpire. Did the ball come off the bat? The pad? Neither? Both? Often it's very hard to detect by sight alone. The sound can often provide more than a clue. Using microphones in the stumps, the Snickometer can study tell-tale noises and can illustrate them on screen. An edge is shown by a long thin line extending almost from top to bottom of the Snickometer box. Ball hitting pad is a much more 'chunky' picture.

The Analyst

Simon Hughes sits in the videotape truck and he produces fascinating insights into the complexities of cricket. He's changed the way people watch cricket and now other sports productions are copying him. He is part of a brilliant production concept and he does it very well.

The Red Zone

During the summer of 2001 people started asking whether the cricket authorities should manufacture a real Red Zone on the pitch to help umpires with lbw decisions. From 2002 onwards it has been an electronic device conceived and produced by Sunset + Vine in the United Kingdom showing if the ball landed in line with the stumps, also viewers can see the stumps superimposed over the batsman.

Hawkeye

Six cameras around the ground track the path of the ball as it is bowled. The data goes into a computer and emerges with a prediction of where it would have finished. It has turned out to be a valuable coaching tool for umpires and players.

During the Australia v New Zealand series in Australia in 2004–05, there were some controversial appeals and decisions to do with lbw and caught at the wicket. They produced interesting discussion points and Steve Bucknor, who has been one of the finest umpires of the modern era, set out his position in regard to lbw and the third umpire and, at the same time, called for more discussion.

At present, the third umpire in Tests can only be called on to adjudicate on run-outs, stumpings, whether catches carry to fieldsmen and bump balls. The catching provision is the most controversial and has been dropped from Australian domestic cricket.

Bucknor said: 'I believe the third umpire should be used as much as possible. This game is being played now for so much money, the players don't make it easy for you out there because they're appealing for things they know are not out, so we need to ask what is good for the game and what we should be doing.'

Mark Taylor's view was: 'They should never have brought it in for catching. It should definitely not be used for lbws.

'You should only use technology if the technology can be proven to be very close to 100 per cent right all the time. At the moment you can't do that with catches, you can't do that with lbws.'

He said more umpires would rely on the replays for more decisions if they were allowed to.

'If it gets to that stage umpires will always refer to the third umpire, and we'll have a game that will go for only about 60 overs a day. It will become that ridiculous,' Taylor added.

My view is that I oppose any moves that would lead to more delays for spectators. There is a lot of time wasted with the third umpire at the moment with referrals to him, and we sometimes finish up playing an hour's overtime. I'm very much against that.

We shouldn't introduce anything that will extend the time wasted in the game. I'm definitely not in favour of taking lbws away from the umpires in the centre. I think they are the only ones who can judge that.

Umpiring is very important in these modern times and viewers are brought into that aspect of the game with replays being shown while the third or TV umpire is adjudicating. I receive many communications from viewers asking about umpires and how they are assessed and the ICC are very thorough.

In keeping with its objective to ensure umpiring standards are upheld, they have in place a sophisticated system of umpire assessment to aid officials in their performance and development and that is constantly being updated. It works well.

6
OFFBEAT TELEVISION

TONY LEWIS was one of the best television presenters and commentators with whom I've ever worked. He moved chairs at the BBC when Peter West said he intended to retire from the presenter's job on cricket. Importantly Lewis and West were able to stand in front of a camera without script and talk expert cricket in reliable English. In this world of cricket, you can't put your head down and read prepared autocue words, however well written. Autocues are impossible. Trust me.

Lewis's planning was think clearly and move slowly. To me he was one of the best, most knowledgeable and unflappable presenters in the medium. We agreed that a day's commentary was like a day playing Test cricket – one must have energy, a clear mind, a solid performance, concentration and quality throughout the day, always with your brain in gear before moving your lips.

In a very good summing-up of television in the United Kingdom and Australia, Tony wrote in his book *Taking Fresh Guard*:

> Television commentary boxes provide privileged viewing, allowing the commentators to sit in line with the bowling. When I began, television coverage was from one end only, but there was a spirit of innovation rushing from Channel Nine in Australia that led the world. The BBC were smeared with the old reputation of being unadventurous or, at best, slow to change. We now live in days of Hawkeye, spin vision, speedometer, a host of slow-motion replays, split screens and modern graphics and the presentation of cricket is all the more important

because it is linked to the game's commercial attraction. Sponsors and advertisers are the wellspring of funding for professional clubs and players. The more television the better, but along the way, the beautiful game has needed protecting.

Nothing makes me switch off the television quicker than over-hype from the commentary box, or a commercial plug for the local hotel in which the commentator is staying on favourable terms. When commentators talk up some of the play to make the ordinary sound outstanding, they are dumbing down the game itself.

With the reservation of over-hype, cricket on television has developed into a high-class production. In Britain, the crucial moment came when the BBC lost the contract and the game was taken on by Channel Four. There were some very talented contributors to the BBC's coverage, not least the producer-director Alan Griffiths, who loves his cricket. Highlight packages were sensitively edited and the whole unit was prepared to listen to ideas or criticisms. Richie Benaud, of course, always came fresh from Channel Nine work and would discuss possible innovations in the technical coverage, but the BBC never pushed to take a lead in the televising of the game. It was tugged along by the popular experiments of others.

Pressures on cricketers and commentators these days include adapting to the change from tradition to the modern-day whizkids who control our lives. In Canberra, for example, the politicians and others have been saying for some time that Australian cricketers will soon be playing under a new flag. That apparently will happen as soon as another referendum can be set up to allow people to decide on establishing a republic or continuing traditional ties with Britain. That will be interesting. I played for Australia for 12 years, in 63 Tests, 28 of them as captain, and I played hard and with enthusiasm and a tremendous amount of pride for Australia and the Australian flag which came into existence on 16 September, 1901. I was proud to be part of it. Although the Benaud family originally came from France in the early 1800s and married into the Saville family, who came from England in 1856, I have never had any problem feeling very Australian. As a player and captain I wouldn't have tried less hard, and definitely no harder, if it had been for a multi-coloured flag or flags and some politically-correct politician who had been voted in by the people as President of Australia. I have now been part of more than 500 Tests as a player, occasionally a watcher at the ground and a commentator on television, radio or in the print media, and I still feel the same way.

Whenever I go past Belmore Park and the Richie Benaud Oval in North Parramatta just a few hundred yards from where I lived with my parents, I never fail to think of the days when the park was more like a paddock, where the pitch was concrete and missing the ball meant quite a chase to fetch it. Now the Parramatta area is a city, not just a town, the steam trains to Central Station and the toast-rack trams from Eddy Avenue to the SCG and Coogee are no more, as the transport system is run by computers which sometimes work. You might be able to score by computer these days but cricket itself has remained a contest between a bat and a ball, as was the case when I watched my first matches.

A paragraph I have always loved was written by Dr W.G. Grace in 1899, a long time ago but still pertinent to modern-day cricket. Just substitute 60 years for the 35!

> In the thirty-five years over which my memory sweeps, cricket has undergone many changes. The game we play today is scarcely like the game of my boyhood. There have been silent revolutions transforming cricket in many directions, improving it in some ways and in others robbing it of some elements of its charm.

The good Doctor wasn't just a wonderful player – he knew about the game as well and was a great observer.

When Channel Four took over from the BBC in 1999 there was no doubt about the change in coverage. From the technical point of view the coverage became more like that of Channel Nine in Australia with the producer, Sunset + Vine's Gary Franses, doing a brilliant job in the commentary box itself and Channel Nine's Rob Sheerlock outstanding as director in the van. Franses can produce, direct, create programmes and continue an enviable rapport with commentators, production staff, cricket administrators and, above all, he has a great feel for the game of cricket. Like the BBC, Channel Four went to horse-racing on occasions during the afternoon on a Saturday or holiday, but it was very rare for Channel Four to go to a News Bulletin, which in the late 1990s had become part of the BBC's standard cricket telecast.

The newsreaders were very good and Lewis and I each had a moment we would like to forget in the handover to one of them, the experienced Moira Stuart. Mine was at Lord's where I told a few million people that we would be back at the Test very shortly . . . *'first though, here's Moira Shearer in the BBC Newsroom.'* There was a long silence from everywhere, then a roar of laughter in the commentary box, a muttered expletive in my earpiece, but only a slight quirk of the lips from Moira as she said, 'Good morning,' and proceeded to read the news. She then handed back with another quirk of the lips but in a firm voice, *'To Richie Benaud at Lord's.'* I said, as a throwaway line, *'Thanks, Moira, our newsreader wearing Red Shoes.'*

That was fine, and I thought quite clever. But that evening I was taught that it doesn't pay to be too smart-arse when you have made a mistake because, having a drink with friends, I was asked what on earth I had meant by the remark about Moira and the Red Shoes. The friends had turned on the television in the middle of the newsbreak and therefore hadn't heard my initial blooper, so to them it was all a piece of nonsense. And possibly to scores of thousands of other viewers who also had tuned in when the newsbreak was in progress.

Tony Lewis, known by some as A.R., tells against himself the story of when, in the late 1990s, he and Geoff Boycott were on the roof at the Edgbaston ground doing a chat show concerning 'Best Catches' and 'Viewers' Questions and Answers'. Keith Mackenzie was directing and the instructions were that at the end of the session, Tony was to hand back to Moira Stuart at Broadcasting House. The handover had to be perfectly timed. One problem I could visualise from the commentary box was that the positioning of the monitors on the roof was such that the blazing sunshine was making it close to impossible to see what was on the screen. Tony said later that 'close to impossible' was well short of the mark, it was totally impossible. He filled exactly the twenty seconds required, threw to Moira Stuart, in his ear was given the all clear and assumed that to be correct. Never has the phrase 'assume nothing' been more pertinent because the correct cut-off switch had *not* been pressed in the van, or in London, or possibly both. That was why A.R.'s 'For fuck's sake' made it to Moira at the news desk and to a few hundred thousand living-rooms around the country, also to the office desk of Jonathan Martin, BBC's Head of Sport.

After lunch A.R. read out a prepared apology and also apologised to the head man of the BBC. He needed a bit of lightening up which was provided a few hours later when Ian Chappell sent him a message which read simply, *'Congratulations A.R. mate, one-all.'* This was a reminder to the effect that Ian had previously made a similar error, having been told he was 'off-air' when in fact the wrong switch had been pressed and he was still 'on-air'. It wasn't long before 'Chappelli' had taken a 2–1 lead in the 'assume nothing' stakes. Lewis decided on retirement, not because he thought he might keep playing catch-up with Ian, but because he decided to leave television and secure the 2010 Ryder Cup for Wales.

He did it too with a little, or a lot of, help from his friends and by working something like a 20-hour day for many months. On 28 September, 2001 the announcement was made that Wales had been successful and the Cup would be played at the Wentwood Hills course at Celtic Manor. Glasses were raised in a delightful Georgian country house called Castellau in Wales and in Coogee, NSW, where the Benauds reside. We knew how hard he had worked and what flair he had brought to the bidding process, just as he had done for many years to the BBC commentary box.

Television is a very interesting and challenging medium and the commentary box requires intense concentration. There is never a shortage of little glitches through the wires which transport the sound and pictures from the producer's van. It is astonishing though that there are so few of them in either Australia with Channel Nine or in the UK with the BBC or Channel Four. In England, BBC's Keith Mackenzie was an executive producer for many years, a man who learnt his cricket in Australia and knows many other sports as well. He produced the Grand National, used to produce the Cheltenham Gold Cup Festival until Channel Four gained the rights, handled the snooker production for a considerable time and was, and is, a highly-regarded producer in the line of those who have handled cricket for the BBC over the years. In recent times he has been producer for Formula One.

Alan Griffiths of the BBC is a cricket and Rugby man and, like some other BBC producers, can produce or direct anything and do it with flair. There are times when, sitting back in your living-rooms, you might think from the slight rise in tone in the commentator's voice that he is excited or, without you knowing it, it could be that one of those little glitches has appeared. It might be that a camera has 'gone' just at a crucial moment, or a cameraman has been defeated by an on-drive that goes past point, something to do with sound, or someone may have pressed an unusual button somewhere in the world. It might be something to do with the commentator, it could be something to do with production in the director's van at the ground and, on the rare occasion the latter might occur. I have been known to say softly into the 'lazy' mike, 'Everything all right down there . . . ?'

Just after the England v New Zealand Test at Old Trafford in 1994 we went to Headingley to cover the NatWest match between Yorkshire and Somerset. Alan Griffiths was on his own as the main producer, though John Shrewsbury was also there to lend a hand on what turned out to be a rain-marred day.

Because of the rain, the commentators' roster turned into a dog's breakfast with additions, deletions and initials everywhere and Tony Lewis, as presenter, was doing another brilliant job of providing interviews, detail and all other things necessary when nothing at all is happening on the field. Coming up to what would have been tea-time, I knew that I, in the commentary box, needed to keep an eye on things for Jack Bannister who was on air in the studio with Tony and Geoff Boycott but, for some reason, I put my brain into Plan B mode and settled down at the small table, earpiece in my ear listening to the discussion, and started on a sandwich and a cup of tea. I was able to hear the interesting chat between Tony, Jack and Geoff and see it on the monitor on the table beside me. Suddenly there was a frenzied shout from the van and in my ear because Tony had said, 'And now to Richie Benaud in the commentary box.' Plan B changed to Plan A in an instant. I moved at considerable speed and with mixed success.

I dropped the sandwich on the floor and banged my right knee hard on the side of the chair. With the pain from that, I dropped my binoculars on the chair and my earpiece, which was connecting me with the shouts from the van, became entangled in the connecting wires. When I joined it all together, I found the plug was out of, instead of in, the sound box.

Eventually, while everyone else was hysterically helpless, I was able to say in a suitably calm voice, with only a slight edge to it, 'Now that you've had time to study the scorecard at your leisure . . . !'

In my ear there came an equally calm Welsh voice, but with a definite hint of laughter about it: 'Everything all right up there . . . ?'

It was the ultimate Welsh *'touché'*.

Although Brian Johnston finished with television in the late 1960s and 1970, he and Peter West were examples to everyone with whom they worked as regards both skill and preparation. The meticulous nature of Brian's preparation was never better illustrated than in the aftermath of the splendid practical joke that had been played on him by Jonathan Agnew. Jonathan was in the radio box covering the Australian tour, where the touring team was captained by Allan Border, and Shane Warne, after the 'Gatting ball', was one of the main participants. During the Headingley Test, Jonathan, something of a new boy on the block, had 'pulled one' on Brian by pretending not to be available one morning.

It meant Brian had to do several little five-second recordings and also recorded were all the goings-on in the commentary box. It made up into a brilliant tape, was extremely funny and a very good practical joke. Brian, described on the tape as a veteran long-nosed commentator, took it in good part. Trouble was 'Aggers' wanted to tell the world about it. I thought at the time this was a highly dangerous thing to do. Brian worked on the basis of never get angry, just get even, and when he played a joke it always had about it an original touch.

The one he came up with at Edgbaston during the next Test was a ripper. Keith Mackenzie was producer/director of BBC-TV cricket and Brian had a chat with him, the upshot of which was that the whole of the television outside broadcast team, sworn to secrecy, did their bit for 'Johnners'. Edgbaston is a cosy ground for broadcasting, television and radio boxes are only a matter of yards away from one another and that added to the intrigue.

It took the form of Mackenzie hinting to Jonathan Agnew that there might at some stage be a place in the TV team for someone. He didn't know any more than that but *Grandstand* had asked if Jonathan would do a ten-minute interview on England's fast bowling resources. He would be interviewing F.S. Trueman and Jack Bannister, Fred as the great England bowler, Jack as one of the Warwickshire pace bowling stalwarts over the years and a cricket writer and commentator who had a wide knowledge of every aspect of the game. The interview had to be precisely ten minutes long and it was to be hard-hitting in content.

The only 'prop' they used was that Fred lit his pipe and blew smoke over Jonathan just before the interview began in the in-vision position upstairs. I was watching with Tony Lewis when 'Aggers' put his first question to Bannister who looked calmly back at him and said, 'I've got no idea.'

Correctly, Aggers switched to Fred, who took another puff on the pipe, blew more smoke and said, 'Don't know.'

Now we could see the first beads of sweat forming and it continued in that vein with Fred, when asked about pitches, giving an educational dissertation on fly-fishing and its benefits to fast bowlers in the strengthening of shoulder muscles. Jack recalled briefly the day Fred Gardner and Norman Horner gave the Australians a pasting at Edgbaston and then contributed the story of how Eric Hollies almost won the game against Lindsay Hassett's side in 1953.

Neither Fred nor Jack once mentioned England's fast bowling resources!

At the end of the ten minutes, as the shaken 'Aggers' handed back to the mythical *Grandstand*, his TV career possibly on hold for a day or two, a familiar voice came through his earpiece. It was Johnners who had been sitting alongside Mackenzie throughout and he murmured gently, 'I think the veteran long-nosed commentator might have had his revenge!'

The perils in being the senior commentator are those associated with the name itself, which might be an indication of being more aged and infirm than your colleagues. Occasionally, senior or junior, things go to air and you wish they had not, but it is difficult to pull them back as they are leaving your mouth. Sometimes though the position produces some interesting and amusing situations, one of which occurred at Brian Lara's home ground, Queen's Park Oval in Trinidad, during the Third Test of the 1991 Australia-West Indies series. The first day was washed out at 2.50 p.m. and on the second morning I did the usual in-vision presentation in front of a grandstand in the outer.

Throughout the Caribbean this was the equivalent of making one's way from the Channel Nine commentary box in the Bradman Stand at the SCG to a spot five metres from the front row of a packed Hill. For Channel Nine in the Caribbean no luxuries such as air-conditioned studios and commentary boxes. On my way to this open-air, in-vision position, I walked past the armed guard at the entrance to the playing area and we exchanged a civil 'good morning'. Twenty minutes later, when I returned, my very good friend, the armed guard, had been joined by what was either a dog or possibly a large wolf, an animal approximately two metres long and a metre tall, and made of an extraordinary number of muscles and teeth. It was the original steroid dog. It was a Doberman.

Common sense dictated that I stop, and there was a very good reason for this: the Doberman was standing between me and the entrance, or, as it was now, the exit.

We looked at one another for a considerable time. When he drew back his lips and smiled, and then barked, I leapt only nine inches or a foot in the air, but quickly adopted Plan B. This involved saying nothing and locking eyes with the armed guard rather than the dog. After a minute or two it worked. The guard said nothing but stood up, led the dog out on to the playing field and I made for the exit with calm assurance.

It was then I noticed several Trinidadians helpless on the asphalt, rolling around, overcome by laughter. They are nothing if not resilient in moments of comical stress however, and one of them recovered fast enough to shout, to the delight of the stand, 'Hey, man, you face Wesley Hall, what for now you take a backward step? That puppy's teeth only made of rubber . . .'

A short time later, in Barbados, I found a spectator possessing typical Caribbean humour and repartee which, when combined with a good memory, provided a devastating effect.

In 1955 I toured the West Indies and played in all five Tests. Led by Ian Johnson, Australia won the First Test by nine wickets, drew the Second and won the Third in Georgetown by eight wickets in only four days. When we played the Fourth, in Barbados, we made 668 and had them in all kinds of trouble at 147/6 on the third evening. The next day, the overnight batsmen, Denis Atkinson and Clairmonte Depeiza, batted throughout the five hours' play. The following morning, I bowled Depeiza straight away with one that ran along the ground.

Now, in 1991, I was in Barbados and just about to host the Channel Nine 'intro' to the one-day game eventually won by the Australians. The crowd were in high good humour at Kensington Oval and some, pre-match, were even celebrating their anticipated victory. Loudly! In my earpiece the voice of director Geoff Morris said, 'Fifteen seconds to on-air' and, at the same time, the ground went quiet.

Then, 'Hey, Sir Richard Benaud. You the son of that guy who couldn't get out Atkinson and Depeiza all the fourth day in 1955?'

Right match, wrong family connection.

'If you couldn't bowl them out, you do right to take up television, man,' he continued, just as I began my intro.

'Good morning and welcome to this delightful island of Barbados in the Caribbean.' I said it through my own laughter and that of hundreds of spectators in the Kensington Stand right behind me.

Above all, remember a job as a cricketer or a TV commentator might need fierce concentration but, just as important, you also must have a bit of fun, otherwise it could turn into an ulcer-making dirge!

One thing of which you can be certain about television commentary is the advice noted earlier, that silence is your greatest weapon. Timing is another. It is no use talking about something, making comment on a happening if there is nothing to do with that on the screen.

We were covering a Test match at Lord's in the 1990s when there was a commotion of sorts on top of a building on the eastern side of the ground. There was a small group of people having a barbecue on top of one of the rooftops and along just a little further was a lady who, even without the benefit of binoculars, I could see was dressed in slightly eccentric fashion. What there was of her garb seemed to be black. Closer examination showed it to be flimsy black, possibly lace. She was standing in front of some lettering but I didn't have time to pay attention to that because the bowler was running in at the Nursery End.

In between balls there were murmurs from the crowd who by now were paying as much attention to the lady on the roof as they were to the game. Keith Mackenzie, our producer/director, said into my earpiece, 'With all that noise, I'm going to have to show what's going on if nothing happens next ball.' I said, 'Okay, but I can't see anything from this angle' and then made a comment about the quick single that had been taken. Keith cut to the roof across the road and there she was, looking different now on the screen from the way she did to the very naked eye. The lady, clad in black fishnet stockings and with a thick piece of string across her frontage, was draped over a well-lettered, well-planned and painted sign advertising vodka. It proclaimed, 'Fiona Vladivar loves Richie Benaud.' I said, 'And just think, that's only her mother.'

When I went through the BBC Television course in 1956, the three commentators I've mentioned as being memorable were Henry Longhurst, Dan Maskell and Peter O'Sullevan. Peter is still with us, Henry and Dan sadly have left, but their influence lives on. I've always regarded them as the greatest and, although it is impossible, and potentially disastrous, to copy anyone, it was possible for me to learn from the manner in which they did their jobs.

Peter Alliss of the modern-day golf commentators is outstanding and is a master of the pause and build-up. He was responsible for one of the best pieces of sports television commentary I have ever heard. It was during the Dunhill Masters at Woburn in 1985 when Seve Ballesteros was playing the eighteenth, which is normally the first hole for club members. It was very late in the tournament and Seve had slightly pulled his tee shot to within a yard or two of the fence alongside the road. He had been saved from being out of bounds by the ball brushing a gorse bush but his stance was still going to be impeded by more gorse. Seve gave it everything when he arrived down there. He took his stance then he changed it, then he put on his waterproofs and took them off and all the time there was the camera behind him at ground level. Alliss, after telling the viewers what kind of shot Seve might be able to fashion from virtually nothing and reminding them that a birdie was essential, remained quiet. There was plenty going on for the viewers to see, which is what television is all about, but there are some commentators who would have been chatting away and describing what the viewers could see for themselves. When Seve finally settled into the gorse again and wriggled around several times with a very pained expression on his face as his buttocks were scratched and torn, Alliss finally used just one sentence to add to the picture and the viewers' enjoyment. 'Ah yes,' he said, 'but how will he explain all that to his wife when he gets home?'

In 1994, Channel Nine organised a special match for Allan Border at the 'Gabba. It was a tribute to a great cricketer and the personnel taking part varied from current players to those out of the game some years, and then to one or two show business personalities and footballers. It was a 16,000 all-ticket sell-out and was very successful, something which doesn't always happen with matches of that kind. They have to be done very carefully or they will quickly become run-of-the-mill. Channel Nine did it well and used a variety of experiments, with microphones on players and umpires and various other little touches, in a match which lent itself to entertainment. At the end of the game when I was racing for a taxi to the airport, with little time to spare, I was bailed up by a cricket fan who had been watching the game on television in the Queensland Cricketers' Club next door. A couple of pokes in the chest with his forefinger helped make his point. 'Been watching all that stuff you've been doing with the microphones on the players, talking to one another and being quizzed out on the field by the commentators. Bet you're cranky you weren't able to do that in your day?'

Just shows nothing is new under the sun, because back in 1963 I played in a Lord's Taverners match at Lord's with Denis Compton and others and Brian Johnston was the BBC Television presenter for the day. He did a three-way conversation with me and with Compton, in which I was describing what I would bowl, Denis was commenting, and then, for variety, we did it with communication to Johnston and the viewers, but not between ourselves. It was said at the time by those watching the television that, 'it was wonderful to watch, great to listen to and close to unbelievable the things that can be done with modern communications'. Little did they know.

7

TECHNOLOGY –
A PROBLEM?

F OR six years Michael Atherton and I had a lot of fun working for Channel Four cricket and being part of *Morning Line,* the excellent racing show which prefaces the cricket on Saturdays.

Being a television commentator is one of the more difficult assignments in the world, being a sports television commentator I believe is one of the hardest aspects of the general TV scene. One of the first things to learn is that no matter what your heart tells you, and your nearest and dearest swear to you, you are not being paid by the word, unless that phrase is an integral part of a very special clause in the contract you have with a Network. Sometimes, your nearest and dearest might turn out to be, if not your worst enemies, then at least your poorest advisers when they inform you that Joe Bloggs seems to be getting more time on air than your admirable self.

Not everyone can make the transition from player to TV commentator. That applies to all sport, tennis, athletics, football. It doesn't matter what the task might be but you can trust me when I tell you television will make your life more fraught. Michael has made the transition in splendid fashion and one of the sadnesses for me is that we won't be working together after the 2005 summer, unless, as I hope it will be, it is with Channel Nine in Australia in the next Ashes battle in 2006–07.

Michael writes outstanding copy for the *Telegraph* newspapers in the United Kingdom, something like 1,000 words on a Saturday, and although my output for the *News of the World* is considerably less than that, we each work to a tight schedule. There are always things you must look for in a 30-minute workload on television. Other time frames have been tried, but the general consensus from those who work on cricket on Channel Nine, Channel Four and the BBC is that 30 minutes is the ideal amount of time for a stretch of fierce concentration. Anything can happen and you have to be alert enough to pick it up and then have your brain in gear so that what you are saying might make a bit of sense. And always remember technology might just be about to grab you by the throat.

What happened at Lord's in 1994 with Michael, BBC TV producers and commentators, gave him a good insight into the problems captains and commentators might share. Both groups became instantly a prominent part of the history of cricket. It was, in many ways, a lesson to all those involved in any way in the incident. Every time I relive it, I'm reminded that television is instant, it is live and it is often very controversial, even dangerous.

Tony Lewis was the commentator in question at the time, though we all shared the story as events moved on. That story was the moment where the captain of England was seen, on the Saturday afternoon of the Test, to be doing something to the ball being used on the field. I had a monitor in front of me at the back of the commentary box as I was typing my story for the *News of the World*. As I looked at the screen during the over it seemed to me Atherton took something from his pocket and rubbed it on some part of the ball. It was gone in a couple of seconds. Tony Lewis, commentating, called on the 'lazy' mike to Keith Mackenzie, the producer, asking if he could see in the next break between overs a replay of what had occurred.

As it happened, it didn't need to be replayed because Michael did precisely the same thing during the changeover. Lewis, with all kinds of things going through his mind concerning the implications of doing anything with or to a match ball, had his brain in gear and said, 'It looks as though he's giving it the Aladdin's Lamp treatment.'

It was one of the best lines I've ever heard in a commentary box. It called the attention of the viewers to the fact that something was happening, or had happened. It was light, but accurate, because it involved 'rubbing' of some kind and it left everything enough up in the air that people would be intrigued by what might follow. If in fact there was ever to be anything following.

Time constraints in the newspaper world meant I was only just able to catch an edition which therefore made for limited coverage. I stated what I had seen, saying that to my eyes it seemed very odd and I pondered on what the umpires, Dickie Bird and Steve Randell, might say about it, what Peter Burge, the match referee, might think about it, and what Raymond Illingworth, chairman of selectors, and Michael Atherton might eventually do about it.

There was a hearing after the day's play and Burge issued a kind of ICC 'form letter' statement describing what Atherton had done to the ball as 'an unfamiliar action' and stating that Burge had accepted the explanation given to him and that no action would be taken. I was uneasy about this statement, not because of what I had seen on the monitor, or that Burge had said no action would be taken. But I was extremely uneasy that Michael had been instructed by England's cricket authorities to say nothing. Why on earth would they do something as ridiculous as that?

That instruction was enough to have me ask, in part, in the late editions of the *News of the World*:

> Has everyone in this cricket world gone bonkers? When the Pakistan ball-tampering allegations involving Wasim Akram and Waqar Younis were made in 1992, the ball in question mysteriously disappeared to a vault remarkably close to Thomas Lord's old ground in St John's Wood. I said in regard to that extraordinary action, and the refusal to tell the cricketing public and others about it, that cricket authorities should

know better than to think they would be able, deliberately, to deprive the cricket public of such knowledge. Exactly the same applies to this Atherton case.

By sewing tight the lips of the England captain and the match referee, and refusing to allow the cricketing public to know the facts, the cricket authorities are doing a grave disservice to the game.

Apart from being fraught with danger, it was sheer stupidity!

That Saturday evening, in the light of the information he had been given, Raymond Illingworth had said the Atherton matter was now closed. When he read the Sunday newspapers, including the *News of the World*, he decided action not silence was what the game needed. Consequently he organised a chat with his captain at Lord's and later the manager and captain issued statements.

Atherton's statement included an apology. The reason for the apology was that in his explanation he said he had put his hand into his pocket to dry his fingers, but he had not said he was drying them with dirt; therefore his response to the questioning had been incomplete.

Illingworth's statement said that, after talking with his captain, he was aware the match referee had not received all the details of what had taken place and he was fining Michael £2,000, £1,000 on each of two counts.

The first was for using dirt on the ball.

The second for giving incomplete information to the match referee.

Raymond then said that the Atherton matter *was* closed.

That may have seemed to be the case or even an ideal scenario, but assume nothing! Timing and inclement weather changed the script. We were travelling to Swansea for a NatWest quarter-final match between Glamorgan and Surrey where it rained through the night and the first day of the match was eventually abandoned. Keith Mackenzie, having managed to get through the hustle and bustle of Lord's, had to fill air-time with a cricket feature and the logical choice concerned the happenings at Lords.

Keith put together a very good programme at the Swansea ground with Tony Lewis in the chair and David Gower and your grey-haired correspondent as observers. My view was that all that mattered about Michael's future as captain of England was what had been in his mind on the Saturday of the Test when he rubbed dirt on the ball.

If, in his own mind, he knew he had done nothing wrong, if he were able to look in the mirror when shaving the next day, then there was certainly no question of any thought of resignation and he should definitely captain England at Headingley, which he did and made an excellent 99.

Michael is a stubborn character, steely as a player, which he had shown many times with his cricket and underlined later in that series against South Africa when he led England to victory in The Oval Test. It was the game where England squared the series and we had the great pleasure of watching Devon Malcolm bowl very fast and very well.

Raymond Illingworth's acute mind, equally steely touch and straight-down-the-line attitude, saved Michael's bacon during that Lord's Test. It was Raymond who *forced* the England authorities to take action rather than be satisfied with inaction, and this was Illingworth at his best and most determined. I've always had Illingworth on my short list of great captains. Not even when regaining the Ashes from Australia in 1970–71 had he shown greater leadership qualities than in this Lord's affair, in the course of which he made another real contribution to English cricket. The ECB showed no qualities other than an extraordinary lack of common sense.

The whole episode remains one of the most spine-tingling incidents I've known in the world of sports television.

*   *   *

Another incident, more interesting than spine-tingling, has appeared in the past two years of watching from the commentary box.

In 2003, at the World Cup, Adam Gilchrist walked without waiting for the umpire's decision. Basically that is only a moderate news story but, in this case, it was one which ran, and ran . . . and continues to run.

The New Zealanders toured Australia in 2004 to play two Test matches because the West Indians had reneged on an agreement with Cricket Australia to play three Tests, with Pakistan playing another three. This would make up a normal Australian programme where either five Tests or six would be played in the early part of the summer. Australia won both matches against New Zealand quite easily and the latter part of the match at the 'Gabba was remarkable only for the altercation between Gilchrist and Craig McMillan when the latter was caught behind off a very thin inside edge and waited for the umpire's decision, which was 'not out'. McMillan was out lbw next ball and, whatever words were exchanged between the pair, then continued to the edge of the boundary at the end of the game when the teams were smiling and laughing, thanking one another and saying what a great time they'd had over the few days. It turned out later that McMillan had told Gilchrist he was a player who waited for the umpire's decision and then obeyed it. He was not a walker.

I thought the New Zealand captain Stephen Fleming had it right when he said at his press conference that there are a few guys on a walking crusade, but that was unlikely to change the ways of 95 per cent of other cricketers around the world. Fleming said, 'It's still an individual decision. We all like to see the game played in the right spirit but if individuals choose to look at the umpire and have him make the decision, and it's their right to do so, it has to be respected either way.'

Australian captain, Ricky Ponting, was of the opinion that

Gilchrist's walking decisions and opinions didn't put pressure on his own team-mates or on the opposition players. Ponting said, 'Adam doesn't expect any Australian player to walk, so he can't expect it of any of the opposition players either. They've got to make up their own minds if they're going to walk or not and do what they think is best for them and their team.'

It's nothing new for walking to be a contentious subject in cricket.

Walking, or not walking, has been around as long as the game of cricket has existed. So too has been the stricture, sometimes disregarded, that no one should ever do anything on the field that could in any way be derogatory to an umpire. Of those two aspects of the modern-day argument, I strongly favour the latter. It's a question of how you were brought up by parents, mentors, captains or advisers. My upbringing was always to respect the umpires and to do exactly as they said, whether it was out or not out.

My father instilled in me that if I were batting, and there was an appeal made against me, the first thing I had to do, instantly, was look at the umpire whose job it was to make the decision. Then obey instantly whatever decision had been given. No hesitation and certainly nothing that might in any way allow the spectators to believe the umpire could have made a mistake.

Walking was very much an English thing and part of it was that umpires in England, standing in county matches, were almost always ex-players. They knew those taking part in the matches through having played with or against them in previous times and a batsman who didn't walk was soon known around the circuit in that regard.

Australians tended to remain of the view that they should obey whatever the umpire said and that generally decisions evened up over a time. The argument has often been produced by batsmen that they have been on the end of poor decisions; sometimes say three on the trot. Two of those might have been inside edges on to the pad and the umpire's finger was raised for lbw and the batsman had to go. Then next time at bat he was given out caught down the legside when in fact the ball had flicked his thigh pad and there had been no bat contact. The argument went on that if, in his next innings, he feathered a ball outside off-stump and to a half-hearted appeal was given not out, should he have walked?

In 1961 I captained the Australian team to England and walking was a public issue. Would the Australians walk was one of the many questions at the commencement of the tour which took place immediately after the Tied Test series in Australia. When Neil Harvey (vice-captain), Colin McDonald (third selector) and I had a meeting on board the ship a few days out of England, we decided there were in fact far more important things than the walking question to be put at the top of our agenda.

At the press conference on arrival I stressed the team would be endeavouring to play the most attractive cricket possible for the spectators at the ground, television viewers, radio listeners and readers of newspapers. We would try to do this by bowling our overs as quickly as possible, moving smartly between overs and not wasting any time. If we batted first in the games against the counties we would be trying to close our innings on the first evening, we hoped to be able to set challenges for the opposition and receive challenges from them. We would not be worried about losing any of those matches and we would definitely not be using the lead-up games to the Tests simply for practice, as had been done in 1956.

On walking, it would be a matter for each individual in the team to make up his own mind. I said some of the team had decided to walk; others had been brought up to wait for the umpire's decision and accept it without demur. We did stress, and it was noted in *Wisden* 1962 in the summing up of the tour, that on controversial issues we intended to leave matters entirely in the hands of the umpires. Additionally *Wisden* said, 'Encouraged by Benaud, the

Australians never queried an umpire's decision and, at times, when they knew they had touched a ball, did not wait to be given out but went their way, as did the England players. Moreover the Australians formed a high opinion of the ability of the English umpires, especially J.S. Buller.'

For my part, I had made up my mind to walk. When we played Sussex at Hove just before the First Test I was out for a duck in the first innings, caught at short backward-square off medium-pacer Ian Thomson. On the last day we had an exciting contest going, with Colin McDonald making runs and looking for victory when I went out to bat. Ronnie Bell was bowling, he was a left-arm orthodox spinner and was bowling into the rough and spinning away to slip. I tried to drive him and the ball landed in the rough and spun to Alan Oakman, who dived to his left and caught it amid shouts of joy from the fielders. Instinctively, on the shouts, I had turned and taken a pace to the pavilion when suddenly I thought, 'Hell, I didn't hit that.' I also thought instantly of the headlines had the Australian captain turned and walked back to the crease. So I kept walking, out for a pair, but not out and unable to do anything about it.

We managed an exciting draw, one wicket in hand, Norman O'Neill unable to bat, nine runs needed and Colin McDonald 116*. Half an hour later the players of the two teams were having a drink at the bar before we caught the train to Birmingham and the Sussex chaps were laughing their heads off asking why I had walked when the ball had clearly missed the bat by inches. All I could do was laugh with them, say it was a long story and would they like another beer?

The crunch question of walking really comes down to a scenario of Australia in possession of the Ashes. One match all in the last of the five matches in the series. Australia, deep in trouble, have lost nine second-innings wickets and the final over of the match is being bowled with fieldsmen crouched around the defending batsman. If England take a wicket the Ashes are theirs after 18 years. The Australian batsman plays a flurried defensive stroke, he knows there was the faintest feather touch on his glove, but no one else does and there is only a very half-hearted appeal from one close-in fieldsman when the ball is caught via the pad. The umpire takes his time. Does the batsman walk?

I know that is a difficult question but it is also a perfect scenario to use as an example in these days when technology plays such a big part in decision-making in the commentary boxes. There will be different opinions on the answer to the question posed. Whether technology can ever be geared to be completely accurate and provide extremely fast decisions is another matter, as is the question of walking.

8

BEING A SELECTOR

I N recent times it has become fashionable to choose best teams, greatest teams or most enjoyable teams, which is what I did with *My Greatest XI*. Also there have been countless players of the match, the series, the season and the year, not all the nominations free from controversy, as I have found. As other selectors have recognised over the years, it is very difficult to have more than eleven players in a cricket team.

The media, in all areas, are quite keen on choosing people to nominate important events and, in 2003, the Melbourne *Age* newspaper asked ten prominent cricket people in Australia to list their ten most important cricket moments relating to Australia from the time cricket was first played in that country.

1861 was chosen as the starting point as it was that year the catering firm of Spiers and Pond arranged for an English cricket team to go to Australia to play a series of matches. This was after they had failed to persuade Charles Dickens to make a tour and then George Parr also declined to take a cricket team because the financial terms were not what he and his Nottinghamshire players wanted.

H.H. Stephenson of Surrey eventually took a good team to play a series of matches and financially, for the players and for Spiers and Pond, the tour was a great success. Those 1861 matches are regarded in Australia as being the beginning of international matches between England and Australia, though not Test matches.

The next international exchange occurred in 1868 when a team of Australian aborigines, under the leadership of Charles Lawrence – who had gone to Australia with Stephenson's side and remained out there as coach – toured England. The side was not capable of playing English first-class counties but opposed strong club sides and, in addition to cricket, gave exhibitions of boomerang throwing and other similar attractions.

James Lillywhite organised and captained the fourth English side to Australia in the autumn of 1876. The team were beaten by Fifteen of New South Wales in their second match and then by Fifteen of Victoria. This was followed by a crushing defeat in the return v Fifteen of New South Wales, who immediately challenged the tourists to an eleven-a-side game. The match was drawn, much in favour of Lillywhite's men, but it set the stage for the first proper eleven-a-side match between 'England' and Australia, which was played when the tourists returned from a visit, in mid-tour, to New Zealand. The match is regarded as the 'First Test' and was played at the Richmond Paddock, the fourth cricket ground owned by the Melbourne Cricket Club which had come into existence in 1838. The first three grounds were where the Royal Mint now stands, Spencer Street Railway Station and an area close to Emerald Hill. The Richmond Paddock, now the Melbourne Cricket Ground, has changed to a marked degree over the years and will hold 100,000 spectators for whatever the activity in progress might be.

The ten cricket figures asked to nominate their most important ten events out of 50 listed for consideration by the Melbourne *Age* were:

Darren Berry (Victorian captain), Belinda Clark (Australian women's cricket captain), Dick French (Test match umpire), Dennis Lillee (great Australian fast bowler), Tim Lane (broadcaster and radio cricket commentator), Brett Lee (Australian fast bowler), Ashley Mallett (Australian offspinner), Steve Rixon (former Australian wicket-keeper, NSW, New Zealand and Surrey coach), Paul Sheahan (former Australian Test batsman) and Richie Benaud (former Australian Test captain and cricket commentator).

My list was:

1. Australia defeat England, The Oval 1882
2. Tied Test, Brisbane 1960
3. World Series Cricket 1977
4. First one-day International 1971
5. Bodyline 1932–33
6. The inaugural Test 1876–77
7. The Centenary Test 1976–77
8. Australia makes 404/3, Headingley 1948
9. Old Trafford Test 1961
10. Australia regains Frank Worrell Trophy, Jamaica 1995.

There were interesting choices in the other lists. Dennis Lillee had as number one the aboriginal pioneers of 1868; Belinda Clark went for Steve Waugh's 'Ton of Drama' 2003 as her top choice, Steve Rixon, Dick French and Brett Lee chose Bodyline. Tim Lane had at numbers 1 and 2 Bradman bats and bats and bats, 1930, and Bodyline 1932–33. To me a very thoughtful line of one naturally following the other.

It was one of the more interesting media promotions of the summer and produced a great deal of discussion, argument and provoking thought around the cricket community in Australia.

A summation of the choices of the ten judges was:

1. Bodyline 1932–33
2. World Series Cricket 1977
3. Tied Test 1960
4. Centenary Test 1976–77
5. Bradman duck, The Oval 1948
6. Under-arm ball, MCG 1981
7. Steve Waugh's Year of 2003
8. Australia beat England 1882
9. Inaugural Test 1876–77
10. Warne bowls Gatting, Old Trafford 1993

Three years earlier *Wisden* embarked on what seemed at the time a task which was close to impossible, the nomination of the Five Cricketers of the Century. One problem they faced was that no one saw all the Test cricket played from 1900–2000 but, like most great ideas, it eventually worked.

Wisden asked 100 people to be selectors and, in a clever additional aspect, they weighted the numerical composition of the selection committee to reflect each country's playing role in international cricket over the century. There were three women selectors and 97 men, the committee covered all aspects of cricket, and the basis of asking people to contribute was either their having played Test cricket, watched a lot of it or being known for having contributed in the media and other areas.

In the end the 100 selectors cast votes for only 49 cricketers, a remarkably small number, but not one of the 100 selectors chose all the top five players, not even in a changed order. The five were:

Don Bradman	100 votes
Garry Sobers	90
Jack Hobbs	30
Shane Warne	27
Vivian Richards	25

The most interesting aspect for me, in looking at the five, was that all of them had changed the game in some way during the time they played. A rare quality.

That the 100 selectors from all over the cricket world managed to encompass that attribute in the five choices was, to me, a remarkable achievement.

In 2004 I was one of a multitude asked to choose a personal best team of the century. There had already been teams of the century announced for England and other countries, some covering the thought of best team of the century.

I declined, on the basis that these similar combinations had already been produced, Australia's team of the century had been announced with a flourish four years earlier and had been along the lines of the Australian Hall of Fame inductees.

The Australian team of the century was:

1. Bill Ponsford
2. Arthur Morris
3. Don Bradman
4. Greg Chappell
5. Neil Harvey
6. Keith Miller
7. Ian Healy
8. Ray Lindwall
9. Shane Warne
10. Dennis Lillee
11. Bill O'Reilly
12th man: Allan Border

Eventually I agreed to do it, but it had to be in my own fashion. I said it would be called *My Greatest XI*, and I decided that, as this was to be my team, it would be one I would like to watch and be with during whatever matches they might play. The players would be first of all brilliant cricketers; they would be characters as well and good mixers with the opposition. They would be representing me on the field.

I also decided to choose the final eleven in the same way I have always chosen teams, with, on the left-hand side, the team to take the field and then two back-up players, so that in effect I was looking at thirty-three players and I would finish up with three sides capable of taking the field and being reasonably well balanced. The criteria used was two opening batsmen, three, four, five batsmen, allrounder at six, fast bowling allrounder at seven, wicket-keeper-batsman at eight, legspin bowler nine, pace bowlers ten and eleven.

I set down a rule that matches would be played on good pitches, allowing bounce for the bowlers and for the batsmen to play their strokes. Progressively through the match the pitch would allow spinners to come into the game. What you might term an ideal pitch in Australia.

I have met all of the final eleven I chose and, when I narrowed it down to 33 from 66, I had met all but one in the three teams, each of which could give a good account of itself.

TEAM

1	2	3
J.B. HOBBS	L. HUTTON	V.T. TRUMPER
S.M. GAVASKAR	A.R. MORRIS	C.G. GREENIDGE
D.G. BRADMAN	W.R. HAMMOND	G.A. HEADLEY
I.V.A. RICHARDS	G.S. CHAPPELL	R.G. POLLOCK
S.R. TENDULKAR	F.M.M. WORRELL	B.C. LARA
G. St. A. SOBERS	K.R. MILLER	I.T. BOTHAM
IMRAN KHAN	R.J. HADLEE	KAPIL DEV
A.C. GILCHRIST	R.W. MARSH	I.A. HEALY
S.K. WARNE	W.J. O'REILLY	ABDUL QADIR
D.K. LILLEE	R.R. LINDWALL	G.D. McGRATH
S.F. BARNES	F.S. TRUEMAN	H. LARWOOD

12th Man: K.R. MILLER
Manager: F.M.M. WORRELL

One of the aspects of my selection was that I would pay a great deal of attention to those players I believed had a beneficial effect on the game, those who stood out both as champions and who are remembered as being outstanding in their own eras. Also, they had an influence on cricket itself.

For a start I looked for an opening combination and I could instantly see how difficult this was going to be as I narrowed it down to six players. One of those, Trumper, was the only one of the 33 I never met.

Victor Trumper: Trumper was a legend in Australia while he was still playing; the only other person I know to have achieved that was Bradman. It seems that Victor was not only a law unto himself with the bat, but was a batsman whose strokes knew no restriction. There have always been arguments in Australia about Trumper and Bradman but never other than that pair. There is no doubt who scored most runs but, in their different eras, each had the tag 'cricketing genius' attached to him.

Gordon Greenidge: There have been other batsmen who hit the ball harder or as hard as Greenidge, Everton Weekes is one who comes to mind, so too Adam Gilchrist. Greenidge though was like his fellow Barbadian Weekes, a butcher of bowlers and one whose ambition always was to entertain and remain on top of the opposing attack.

Arthur Morris: A wonderful attacking left-hander and I agonised for a long time over a left-hand right-hand combination, but in the end I had him on the second line with Len Hutton. Arthur was my first captain and a very good one too, but after NSW had one of their best seasons, Morris with both bat and captaincy, surprisingly he was removed and Keith Miller was made skipper of the state side.

Len Hutton: Len had a wonderful technique, orthodox but not restricted in the sense that when he wanted he could be a dashing stroke-player. He was also the first professional captain of England in the proper sense, captain by appointment, and this before the difference between amateur and professional players was lifted. He not only regained the Ashes in 1953, but retained them in 1954–55 in Australia, and that after he had predicted in 1950–51 in Australia that England would bring a fast bowling attack to Australia four years later and pose problems for the Australians. At that stage he had no idea he would be captaining them. One of the most famous of England's performances was when they achieved a draw under Hutton at Lord's in 1953 with Watson and Bailey batting most of the final day. Never forget that without Hutton's chanceless 145 in the first innings, there would have been *no* final day. It was the best innings I saw him play.

The two openers I finally chose were Jack Hobbs and Sunil Gavaskar.

Jack Hobbs: Hobbs was far more than the best batsman of his generation, and possibly other generations as well, but he was a player who bridged several eras. Before the First War he was regarded as an outstanding player. He played in 14 Test series for England and no one to whom I spoke when I first came to England in 1953 was in the slightest doubt that he was the best. He played his first match for Surrey against a team captained by W.G. Grace. This was against the Gentlemen of England in 1905 when he made a sensational start to his first-class cricket career. His first Test was against Australia in 1908 at the MCG when England won by one wicket and Sydney Barnes and Arthur Fielder added an unbroken 39 for the last wicket to win the exciting game. His last Test was against Australia at The Oval in 1930, Bradman's first tour, where he watched Bradman make 232. He seems to me to have been not only a genuinely great player, when the word 'great' is often used so loosely, but a wonderful team man who would be of value in my team dressing-room. He made nine hundreds against Australia and Bradman was of the opinion that two of them, on treacherous pitches, provided some of the finest batting he ever saw. One was at the MCG in 1929 where some balls, with the wicket-keeper standing up and the batsman playing forward, went over the 'keeper's head. England had to make 332 to win, Hobbs opened with Sutcliffe and they put on 105 on the Melbourne 'sticky'. Bradman never forgot it. One of the reasons I have chosen Hobbs is that I don't believe cricket to be a game necessarily meant to be played only on covered pitches.

Sunil Gavaskar: I have always been a fan of Gavaskar who came into the Indian team seven years after I retired. I saw more of him in England than Australia, when I was covering cricket for the BBC, but his most memorable effort for me was in Melbourne in 1980–81 where, as captain, he lifted his team to victory. He had been given out lbw to Dennis Lillee when he nicked the ball on to his pad and he was so livid he tried to take Chetan Chauhan, his fellow opening batsman, off the field with him. The team manager, not knowing whether to laugh or cry, stopped Chetan at the gate and sent Sunil off, not quite with a red card but, at least, fuming to the dressing-room. Sunil, still seething the next day, closed the Indian innings and, with Kapil taking 5/28 and Dilip Doshi, who opened the bowling, 2/33, India bowled out the Australians for 83 and a famous victory.

Don Bradman: There is hardly likely to be an easier choice than the number three batsman, yet the two I narrowed it down to with Bradman were *Walter Hammond* and *George Headley*, wonderful players in their own right. Headley was known as the black Bradman and, in their time as contemporaries, no one pressed Bradman harder as a run-scorer. There is some significance in the fact that the Australians of the time tried to keep both Headley and Hammond tied down by bowling at their leg stump, but had no marked success in doing so. Headley played only 22 Tests, Hammond 85, each of them with great batting averages and ratios of centuries and fifties to the number of games played.

There will be many people who would have selected Wally Hammond in their team of all-time greats, most of them as a batsman; some would have put him up against the allrounders. Bradman was one who had a very high opinion of Hammond as an all-round cricketer. The Don remarked that he was one of those bowlers for whom the ball seemed to make pace after it hit the pitch, even though he concurred with the scientists who tell us that is impossible. Bradman said of him that generally he was too busy making runs to be bothered about bowling, but when he did he was very difficult to play. 'He was a far better bowler than he was given credit for.' Alec Bedser thought Hammond was the best allrounder he had ever seen and Bill O'Reilly listed him as the finest England batsman he bowled against, yet it was O'Reilly who occasionally caused Hammond most frustrations. Bradman was of the opinion that Hammond was the strongest offside player he had seen and I imagine Bradman therefore would have had a hand in O'Reilly bowling at Hammond's leg stump. It certainly appeared that the tactic frustrated Hammond, even though he still made a lot of runs. His 231* at the SCG in the 1936–37 series, and the 240 in 1938 at Lord's, add weight to those who claim him as a magnificent player, one of the real greats.

Bradman was something else. I first heard of him when I listened to my initial cricket broadcast in Jugiong (south-west New South Wales), in 1936–37, when 'Gubby' Allen's side toured to play for the Ashes. Mel Morris, a deep-voiced Victorian, was the first commentator I heard on our five-foot high Kreisler radio which sat in the corner of the living-room. I was six at the time and was only seven when we moved to Parramatta. I was nine when I watched my first Sheffield Shield match and Bradman was captaining South Australia at the SCG. Stan McCabe was captain of NSW. Grimmett took 6/118 and 5/111, then O'Reilly ten wickets, Pepper six and Ward four, which meant legspinners cleaned up 31 of the 40 wickets to fall. Rather a good way to influence a young cricketer to become an over-the-wrist spinner.

I saw Bradman in a Test at the SCG in 1946–47 when he and Sid Barnes each made 234 and, in the final match of the series when Australia won by five wickets, Bradman top-scored in Australia's second innings. I was standing below the old Sheridan Stand at the Randwick End and Doug Wright, bowling from the Paddington End and turning the ball viciously, had Bradman dropped by Edrich at slip. It was costly at a time where England had a real chance of victory and Bradman top-scored with 63. I first met Bradman in December 1949 as a member of the NSW side in Adelaide. Everyone who bowled against him, or played against him when he made runs, which was most of the time, said that he

112

was the best and, although statistics don't always tell the tale, they did with Bradman. Statistics roughly twice as good as any other batsman.

He was chairman of the Australian selection committee when I was surprisingly made captain after Ian Craig contracted hepatitis in 1958; he was chairman of selectors and of the Australian board when the Tied Test series was played between Australia and the West Indies. He delivered the short speech at the team dinner the night before that Tied Test, where he told the Australian players the selectors that summer would be looking in kindly fashion upon players who set out to entertain the spectators, and in less kindly fashion on those who didn't. A great cricketer and, as he showed in that short speech in 1960, he had a very good grasp of what was needed in cricket.

The six batsmen vying for the numbers four and five spots are just as high quality as the ones we have been talking about earlier. *Greg Chappell, Graeme Pollock, Frank Worrell* and *Brian Lara* all fit into the category of being match-winners, a prime ingredient in this team choice, and they all batted, or still bat in the case of Lara, with grace and wonderful skill.

When Lara made his 375 against England in St John's, Antigua, in April 1994, it was only 15 months after he had made 277 at the Sydney Cricket Ground before he was run out. I won't say it was the only way the Australian bowlers looked like dismissing him, but it was close. It was one of the best innings I've ever seen and I was unlucky not to be there to see him break Garry Sobers's record in the later Test against England. Both innings were played as part of drawn matches and I know, through having been there, that the one in Sydney was on a beautiful batting pitch. I assume the one at St John's was of similar quality. Certainly that was the case when I watched him in St John's in 2004 when, in scoring 400*, he broke Matthew Hayden's 380-run record and again established himself as the highest innings-scorer in Test matches. There is no doubt his dominance with the bat has kept West Indies going in recent times when the national team has had an extraordinary amount of trouble in winning *any* matches. Lara is an outstanding player of spin bowling, and brilliant footwork and great judgment of length make him a very difficult proposition even for the best spin bowlers in the opposition teams.

I first heard about Graeme Pollock when Frank Worrell's team played in Australia in the Tied Test series in 1960–61. He was nothing to do with those matches but three years earlier his older brother, Peter, had been the young room attendant for the Australian team in Port Elizabeth when we played the final Test of the series at St George's Park. Ian Craig's 1957–58 touring team only knew the older Pollock as Peter, a lad from the Grey College in Port Elizabeth, and some of the uncomplimentary conversation about Adcock and Heine, and the spate of bouncers they bowled in that match, had Peter vowing that one day he would be a fast bowler for South Africa and he'd give the Australians a bit of hurry-up. When we were playing the Tied Test series in Australia, South African friends who were watching the matches told us about the Pollock brothers, that Peter was a fast bowler but his younger brother Graeme, then 16, was going to be a champion left-hand batsman.

I stored it away and heard that he played a few matches for Sussex 2nd XI when I was captaining Australia in England in 1961. Then, when New Zealand toured South Africa in 1961–62, I saw Peter had made a very successful debut to Test cricket and that Graeme made 78 for Eastern Province against the touring side and also an unbeaten half-century for the South African Colts XI. The first time I saw him play was when I went to South Africa at the end of the 1962–63 Australian season as captain of Ron Roberts' Cavaliers' XI. We dismissed him cheaply in the Eastern Province first innings and then he hit the most majestic double-century against us, 209* out of 355/5. I knew I was watching a champion. When he toured Australia in 1963–64, my last summer in first-class cricket, he showed how good he was. The selectors asked me to fly to Perth at the start of this South African tour so I could play in the Combined XI and Graeme and I each made centuries. I thought I did well to make 132 in what seemed quite brisk time, 205 minutes. Graeme's 127 not out was blasted in less than two hours and I knew we were in for some tough times over the next 13 weeks.

In the third match of that Test series he hit a glorious 122 out of 186 added while he was at the crease, then made 175 in Adelaide playing one of the finest innings I've ever seen in Test cricket. The pity was that he was only able to play 23 Tests, but there's no doubt he was one of the best ever to walk on to a cricket field.

I finally chose *Viv Richards* and *Sachin Tendulkar* to occupy those four and five places.

I have seen a considerable amount of both of them and Australians, in fact, were responsible for Viv Richards becoming one of the greatest batsmen and entertainers the cricket world has seen. My first sighting of him was in 1975–76 in Australia when Greg Chappell was captain of the home side and Viv was only a year into Test cricket. The West Indian selectors had given him a tough initiation in November 1974 with a debut against Chandrasekhar in Bangalore where the brilliant spinner dismissed him twice for 4 and 3. He made 192 not out in his next innings, so suddenly a great deal of notice was taken of him in Australia because West Indies were touring there a year later. When I first saw him he was all attack and disdained any form of shackling by the bowlers but, in 1975–76, Dennis Lillee, Jeff Thomson and Gary Gilmour sorted him out and he made only 137 runs at an average of 19 in the first four Tests.

Then Clive Lloyd, in desperation, or with a touch of genius, opened the batting with him in a couple of minor matches. He was successful and, opening in the final two Tests, he made 30, 101, 50 and 98, even though Australia still won both matches and the series 5–1. This was the summer which started Lloyd thinking that pace bowling would win Test series and that winning was far preferable to losing! The Australians, having got Viv into the right frame of mind, watched with interest as West Indies toured England in 1976 and he hit 829 runs in four Tests at better than 100 an innings. He never looked back and remains one of the greatest batsmen I have ever seen.

So too Sachin Tendulkar, though they are completely different types. Tendulkar made his debut against Pakistan as the third youngest player in history and that too made interesting newspaper copy in Australia. I was covering Test matches for the BBC in England and Channel Nine in Australia at the time, and this happened just after Australia's wonderful tour of England in 1989 when they regained the Ashes and, so far, haven't relinquished them in the ensuing 16 years. I knew Sachin was to come to Australia in 1991–92 but, before that, he played against England in England in a high-scoring series and I watched one of the best innings imaginable in the Old Trafford Test where he made 119 not out and was partly responsible for the saving of the match.

When he came to Australia he made two centuries, one at the WACA in Perth and the other in Sydney. This was the better innings, although Perth too was good. The one in Sydney though was flawless. It had everyone in raptures, an innings of 148 not out which, to my mind, could not have been bettered, with an incidental note that, at 18 years and 256 days, he was the youngest player to hit a Test century in Australia. It was Shane Warne's first Test, so being privileged to see the innings and note the legspinner's debut was a highlight.

Keith Miller was the greatest allrounder I ever played with or against, but bear in mind that the period covered there embraces Miller retiring in 1956 which was only two years after Garry Sobers made his Test debut. Sobers was more my time, and then a considerable distance past, but Miller was an extraordinary cricketer. He, Arthur Morris and Ray Lindwall were my mentors, three great cricketers and outstanding people. Miller succeeded Morris as captain of NSW and was the best captain I have known and certainly the finest captain never to have captained Australia.

It was a freakish and much appreciated happening that in later years I was able to watch four extraordinary allrounders in action in the one period, *Imran Khan, Richard Hadlee, Ian Botham* and *Kapil Dev*. Fancy having them all playing in the same era. It is normally regarded a great bonus to have just one in action over a similar time.

Three of the Hadlee family played for New Zealand. Walter, the father, made his debut in England in 1937 and then captained his country for the first time in the Test against Australia straight after the end of the Second World War. His eldest son Barry didn't play for New Zealand but Dayle and Richard did and Richard brought left-handedness into the world of all-round cricketers and was a splendid player.

It was unusual that the four allrounders of that era each reached the milestone of the 2,000 runs and 200 wickets 'double' in consecutive years in the early 1980s. Ian Botham was the first in 1981–82, then Kapil Dev in 1982–83, Imran Khan in 1983–84 and Richard Hadlee in 1984–85. No wonder it was such a good time to be around the commentary box.

Botham's most extraordinary Test series was the one in 1981 against Australia where all the points one makes about cricket being 'a funny game' were underlined at the one time. The game at Headingley has always been known as Botham's Match and the circumstances were extraordinary. It was a six-Test match series and Australia won the First at Trent Bridge by four wickets, with Terry Alderman taking nine wickets on his Test debut. Botham was captain of England and had just returned from the England tour of the West Indies, where he had also been captain and West Indies had won 2–0, with one Test abandoned without a ball being bowled. This happened when the Guyanese government withdrew Robin Jackman's visitor's permit and deported him. When England

and Australia met at Lord's in the Second Test in 1981 the match was drawn but Botham collected a 'pair'. It is a moot point whether Botham then resigned as captain or received the push from Alec Bedser but, for the following Test at Headingley, Mike Brearley was reinstated as skipper. Brearley's opposite number, Kim Hughes, had won the toss and fielded in the opening two Tests with Botham leading the opposition but, in this one at Headingley, Hughes won it and batted. Australia made 401 and then bowled out England for 174 and made them follow on.

To create some form of history, England needed to win, since only one other team had ever been victorious after following on; England at the Sydney Cricket Ground in 1894–95. When Botham came in to bat in the second innings, England were 105/5 and they quickly lost two more wickets for 30. Then Botham hit a century from 87 balls and shared a partnership of 67 with Graham Dilley. Botham remained 149 not out and this all happened after the England team had booked out of their hotel on the fourth morning of the match. Bob Willis then bowled out Australia for 111, returning his best-ever figures of 8/43, and suddenly the Test series was 1–1. England won by 29 runs at Edgbaston in the Fourth Test, with Botham bowling out Australia in their second innings with 5/11 from 14 overs. Australia, needing 151, lost their last six wickets for 16 with Botham's haul 5/1 from 28 balls. Quite extraordinary. Botham then hit 118 and took five wickets in England's triumph at Old Trafford and, when he went to The Oval for the final Test, he had the chance of reaching the 2,000 runs and 200 wickets 'double' in that game. It was a pity he didn't quite manage it on the last day. He made it as regards the wickets, but was 23 short with the runs; something he redressed in the following Test against India at Wankhede Stadium in Bombay.

Kapil Dev was playing in that latter game and it was only two months later he also reached the landmark against the touring West Indian team led by Clive Lloyd. I always thought Kapil better

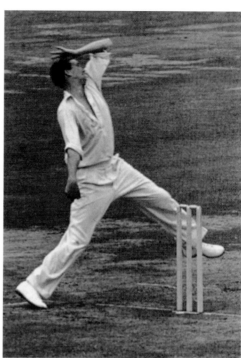

Hardly a week goes past without me being asked by a youngster if I ever actually played cricket. Despite the accompanying adults being apologetic, it is a perfectly natural question because all young people ever see of me is in a commentary box, with a microphone in my hand, but never a cricket bat or ball. All three aspects of my playing and working life are illustrated here. The photograph below was taken by Daphne in 1991 at English Harbour, Antigua. I was doing a presentation for Channel Nine Australia, as part of 42 years in the television commentary boxes of England and Australia. The above two are of me batting at Worcester in the opening match of the 1956 Australian tour and bowling against Middlesex at Lord's in 1961.

If it is true that in life you learn something new every day, it also applies to cricket. My three mentors were Keith Miller, Arthur Morris and Ray Lindwall. Here I am chatting and listening to Arthur at the Park Lane Hotel, London, early in the 1953 tour of England.

This is of the NSW cricket team that played at the Adelaide Oval in 1955, with Norman O'Neill (NSW) and Tim Colley (SA) making their debuts. Miller, always with a touch of unorthodoxy about his captaincy, pitted them against one another on the opening morning, just for a bit of fun.

right: Chatting with Len Hutton at Longparish, Hampshire, prior to the start of John Woodcock's XI v Longparish. A former England captain, a former Australian captain and one of the more perfect settings for a village match, complete with big-hitting blacksmith.

below: Memories of my first tour of England in 1953. Ray Lindwall, who was a wonderful role model for all young cricketers, bowling in the final Test at The Oval where England regained the Ashes under Len Hutton's captaincy.

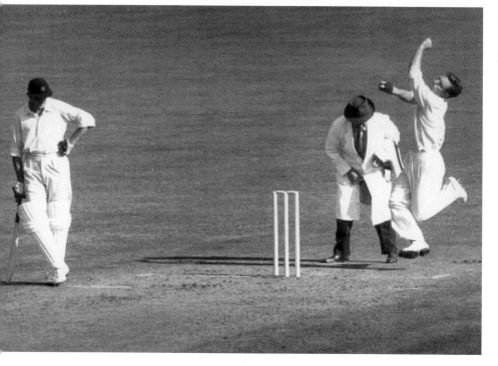

Left: Alan Davidson was one of the greatest cricketers ever to play for Australia. A fast-medium pace bowler, with great control of inswing to the right-handers and the ability to move the ball away to the slips as an alternate delivery. A powerful striker of the ball, he was also one of the finest fieldsmen world cricket has seen.

Below: Neil Harvey, one of a famous cricketing family in Melbourne, was, at 19 years of age, the youngest player in Bradman's Invincibles team, which toured England in 1948. He made a brilliant century at Headingley on his Test debut in England and remained to the end of his career one of the outstanding batsmen in world cricket. He played an extraordinary innings in Dacca (now Dhaka) in 1959 to set up a win on the matting pitch and he remained, over 16 years, one of the greatest fieldsmen ever to grace the game.

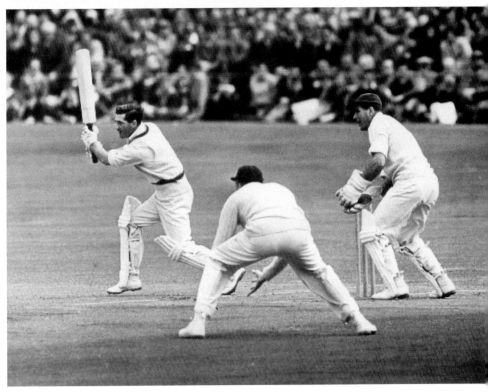

Just a practice run. Jim Laker is shown here bowling for Surrey at The Oval against Australia in May 1956. He took all ten wickets in the innings, Tony Lock, at the other end, took none. Fast forward to Old Trafford later in the season when Jim took nine in an innings and then again took ten in the second innings. Tony took the odd one!

Three outstanding English batsmen I played against, Peter May (*above left*), Ted Dexter (*above right*) and Colin Cowdrey. Peter was a wonderful onside player, Colin possessed the most beautiful cover-drive and Ted was both elegant and brutal with his strokeplay. Contrasting style and very difficult to bowl against, as cricketers and captains around the world were to find.

ɪree outstanding English fast bowlers. These were the days when England had a superb bowling ⸱tack, on hard and covered overseas pitches as well as on greener pitches in England where the ɪrface was left to the elements. Alec Bedser (*above right*) carried the England attack from June ⸰46 until the 1954–55 tour of Australia where a bout of shingles put him out of the team after ᴉe opening Test in Brisbane. He had a classic bowling action, as did Fred Trueman (*below*) who ᴉme into the team against India in 1952. Frank Tyson (*above left*) was the fastest bowler I ever ·w, fractionally shading Jeff Thomson in pace but, trust me, it was no more than a fraction.

Commentators come in different guises. When I started in England it was with Brian Johnston (*right*) and Peter West, who were outstanding and very helpful. They also served BBC, as I did, over a considerable number of years. When, in 1977, World Series Cricket began in Australia, Bill Lawry (*left*) and I were the first two commentators and, when Channel Nine started televising the official Tests in 1979, the same applied. Channel Nine in 2005 signed a new seven-year television deal with Cricket Australia.

Three very good umpires, all from England. Frank Chester (*left*) was said by Bradman to be the best of any he played under, Frank Lee (*middle*) was excellent and Syd Buller, in my view, was outstanding, the best umpire of my playing time.

suited with both bat and ball to pitches in England and India, though he certainly turned in some fine efforts in Australia at different times. He was a magnificent striker of the ball and could there be any more spectacular way to save a follow-on than what he did at Lord's in 1990? With 24 needed, and last man Hirwani at the other end, he hit Eddie Hemmings for four successive sixes. Great allrounders, all of them!

Garry Sobers, in my view, is the greatest all-round cricketer the world has seen. He was certain to be in my team as one allrounder; a brilliant batsman, splendid fielder, particularly close to the wicket, and a bowler of extraordinary skill, whether bowling with the new ball, providing orthodox left-arm spin or over-the-wrist spin. It is in the latter category I would use him in this team, though he might also be given the new ball on occasions if Bradman could extract it from the hands of Lillee, Barnes and Imran.

It was a matter of choosing one other out of Hadlee, Imran, Botham and Kapil and I selected Imran Khan. Imran was the only one I saw reach the 2,000-run and 200-wicket milestone; that was in the match between Australia and Pakistan at the MCG and he was playing as a batsman, having been injured prior to the tour with a stress fracture to his left shin. It was, even by Pakistan administrative standards, an extraordinary set of circumstances. Originally Zaheer Abbas had been named as captain by the selectors, then the president of the Pakistan board sacked the selectors and made Imran captain. Sarfraz Nawaz had also been banned from the tour because of criticism he had made of the Pakistan selectors who had not chosen him for the tour of India which preceded the Australian tour. When it was seen that Imran's X-rays would not allow him to bowl, possibly for the duration of the tour, Sarfraz was instantly un-banned but appeared in Australia at such a time that he had missed playing on the pitches which would have best suited his bowling. As it happened, Imran's batting in Melbourne saved the team from defeat. In the Pakistan second innings Lillee took two quick wickets and Lawson one, and Pakistan were 81/5 when Imran came to the crease. He added 79 with Zaheer Abbas and then 53 with Salim Malik and, in the course of making his 72 not out, became only the fifth player, and the first from Pakistan, to achieve the double.

I didn't see him make his debut for Pakistan at Edgbaston in 1971 when Zaheer Abbas hit his magnificent 274. He was run out for five by Zaheer and didn't take a wicket, nor did things immediately progress a great deal because it was six years before he was able to force his way back into the team and share the new ball. It was against Australia in Australia in 1976–77 that he really caught my eye and continued to do so for another seven years. In the Third and final Test of the short series, Pakistan achieved their first-ever Test victory over Australia in Australia and Imran took 6/102 and 6/63, bowling his team to victory in 46 overs of sustained hostility. He fits in nicely for me in this side as the pace bowling allrounder to go with Garry Sobers.

There have been many fine wicket-keepers from all countries over the years but Australia have been particularly well served in this regard in the past 30 years. In other countries Godfrey Evans and Alan Knott were very good over long periods, Jeffrey Dujon, Wasim Bari and others have impressed but, in Australia, *Rodney Marsh*, then *Ian Healy* and now *Adam Gilchrist* have been outstanding. My vote goes firmly and quickly to Gilchrist who is a fine wicket-keeper who had to move from NSW to Western Australia to have his chance of representing Australia, and then proceeded to keep wicket and bat magnificently. In 50 years of playing and watching, I have never seen anyone strike the ball *more* cleanly than Gilchrist and no one has reached 'keeping dismissals and batting targets faster in the history of the game as far as 'keepers are concerned. He has kept brilliantly to Shane Warne and Glenn McGrath, and even stumped Craig McMillan off McGrath in a limited-overs match in Wellington, New Zealand, in February,

2005. Some of his batting in the last few years has been as good as I have seen from anyone, particularly in turning his team's problems into a winning position by the most attacking batting imaginable.

Shane Warne is the best legspin bowler I have ever seen. He has also had a great influence on boosting the art and in persuading young cricketers that it is a good thing to be a slow bowler rather than one who runs from 30 yards and bowls at something like 85 mph. There is no doubt legspin bowling is an art, and a very difficult one at that. Over-the-wrist spin puts tremendous pressure on shoulders, elbows and fingers; fingers imparting fierce spin are torn and bleeding before a day is completed and there have been many bowlers over the years who have had short careers because of this.

Bill O'Reilly was all flailing arms and legs and aggression, and no lover of batsmen. He played against Don Bradman in 1925. Bradman, playing for Bowral, took an unbeaten double-century off him on the first day of the match and the following week O'Reilly, playing for Wingello, bowled him first ball. Both were country boys living no more than 20 miles from one another in the south-west of NSW. I have talked about 'Tiger' O'Reilly in other areas of this book but one thing remains clear: that when he and Clarrie Grimmett were playing for Australia, Australia's spin bowling fortunes were at their peak. The fact that he and my father both went to Teachers' College around the same time gave me some feeling of family connection and made me enthusiastic as a youngster when I was able to see St George play in the Sydney club competition. 'Tiger' made his Test match debut against South Africa in 1932 and it was there his partnership with Grimmett was forged, Grimmett having already been seven years in the Australian team. I was only a year old when 'Tiger' made his debut and my father was teaching at Warrandale, outside Koorawatha, very much in the far south-west of NSW. O'Reilly took his 144 Test wickets in just 27 Tests and knee problems forced him into retirement after the one post-war Test match in Wellington, New Zealand. He was rated by Bradman as the finest of all bowlers.

The other legspinner for whom I have great regard is *Abdul Qadir* of Pakistan who never for an instant stopped attacking the batsmen. He first came on to the Test scene in 1977–78 in the series against England and he bowled with attacking verve for 13 years right up to the time Warne made his first Test appearance.

There have been others but in my view none to match Warne who is my number nine.

There has been no shortage of fast bowlers and fast bowling combinations over the years. Australia started it off with Gregory and McDonald in the 1920–21 period, then Lindwall and Miller 1946–56, Lillee and Thomson 1974–1982. Larwood and Voce, Trueman and Statham were pre-eminent in England and, for a short time, Frank Tyson blasted all-comers. Alec Bedser, on the other hand, was for much of the time from 1946 just about on his own and was a magnificent bowler at medium-fast pace. *Harold Larwood* and Bill Voce were too much for Australia in the Bodyline tour, leading an attack quickly to be banned. Bradman's batting average in that series was merely half what was considered normal for him.

Ray Lindwall, of whom I talk in another section of the book, was a great fast bowler with a slightly round-arm action that allowed him to bowl wonderful outswingers to the right-hand opening batsmen.

Glenn McGrath is, in my opinion, one of the great pace bowlers the cricket world has seen. Not blisteringly fast, he is beautifully accurate and with a host of variations that make him a real danger to batsmen, even on the best of batting pitches.

It is always worth keeping one's own statistics, particularly on bowlers where '*low*' is best. McGrath, in the list I keep of bowlers with at least 100 Test wickets, is quite outstanding and is a model for all young bowlers. One of the aspects of his bowling which can't be quantified by a figure is his superb control of change of pace. This part of any bowler's armoury must always be subtle in the longer version of the game, though it is obvious that many varieties of slower balls can, and will, be produced in one-day matches. Many times I have seen McGrath use subtle changes of pace, particularly a slightly faster ball, to have the batsman hurry his stroke. Glenn has been playing Test cricket now for ten years and the manner in which he has come back from injury setbacks simply underlines that he is not only a great pace bowler, but a courageous one as well. I've been very fortunate to have been there on his debut against New Zealand in Perth in 1994 and to see him in action with Shane Warne. It is one of the greatest bowling periods in Australian cricket history, with Warne the world's highest wicket-taker and, at the start of the 2005 Ashes battle, McGrath needed only one wicket to reached the 500 milestone.

Fred Trueman remains for me one of the finest fast bowlers of the post-war period, a classic action, plenty of pace and no one has had a better outswinger, except perhaps *Dennis Keith Lillee*. Lillee is the first of my pace bowling attack. I saw him make his Test debut in Adelaide in 1971 and the only time he faltered was when he suffered severe stress fractures to his back and the medicos said it was unlikely he would play again. He fought his way through that injury, came back in triumph against England in 1974–75, and then played another nine years before retiring as the world's leading wicket-taker at that time.

To join him in leading the attack is *Sydney Francis Barnes*, a bowler I met but never played against but one who, from the time I have talked about cricket to older and more experienced people in Australia and England, is said by them to be the finest bowler of all time. I met him in 1953 at Stoke-on-Trent where the Australians were playing Minor Counties and Barnes bowled the first ball of the match. He had turned 80 years of age a couple of months earlier and the ball he bowled landed on a good length and the batsman played it defensively. Even then he was a tall, straight-backed man with big hands, very long, strong fingers and a firm handshake. Ability to swing the ball with great control and cut it off the pitch made him a formidable proposition. Barnes's record in Test cricket, at a time when the Australians had a splendid team, very strong in batting, and South Africa, the other nation of the time were very good, was quite astonishing.

He played only 27 matches, a mere ten of which were in England over a period of 13 years up to the start of the First World War. He took 189 wickets. When he went to Australia in 1911–12 he was up against the cream of Australian batting, including Trumper, Bardsley, Hill, Armstrong, Kelleway, Ransford and the young Macartney. Thirty-four wickets at 22 on shirt-front pitches. He must have been some bowler!

When Barnes made his debut in a three-day Test at the SCG during the 1901–02 tour, he took 5/65 and 1/74. He took 13 wickets in his next Test, which was played at the Melbourne Cricket Ground, but damaged his knee two weeks later in Adelaide and played no more cricket on the tour. The MCG was a favourite ground for Barnes and ten years after his Test debut he routed the Australians pre-lunch on the first day, taking 5/6 from 11 overs. Those present said he was as close to unplayable as could be imagined. England won by eight wickets with Jack Hobbs, included in *My Greatest XI*, making the first of his 12 Test centuries against Australia, an unbeaten 126.

It would be superfluous to have a coach with a team of this quality and character, but I do have two men I would appoint to other positions; Keith Miller as 12th man and Frank Worrell as manager. My experience with Miller as player and captain showed me that he could, if necessary, fill any position in the team and Worrell was the best I ever saw in man management. He was the first black West Indian cricketer to be allowed to captain a team away from the Caribbean and he was one of the reasons the face of cricket in Australia and perhaps in other parts of the world was changed forever because of that Tied Test series. No one but Worrell could have done it for the West Indies.

TEAM
J.B. HOBBS
S.M. GAVASKAR
D.G. BRADMAN
I.V.A. RICHARDS
S.R. TENDULKAR
G. St A. SOBERS
IMRAN KHAN
A.C. GILCHRIST
S.K. WARNE
D.K. LILLEE
S.F. BARNES
12th Man: K.R. MILLER
Manager: F.M.M. WORRELL

Choosing eleven players out of 66, eventually narrowed down to 33, simply showed me three things. First, I wouldn't want to be an official selector, though sometimes I have had the task of choosing teams for various media.

Second, no matter how you twist and turn and burn the midnight oil, you can only fit eleven players into a team. And third, that exactly one hundred per cent of the people who read the final list of names will instantly be able to come up with their better eleven and that, in those selections, all thirty-three of the names will appear!

9

'TIGER'

W HEN World Series Cricket began in 1977 it was as one of the more extraordinary undertakings I had ever known. When it finished, approximately two years later, it had provided one of the more exciting parts of my life, and Daphne's as well. Twenty years later, bowling in a Test match at the Sydney Cricket Ground, Shane Warne took his 300th wicket in Tests under the brilliant light provided, not by the sun but by light towers which had been there since the first day-night one-day fixture played at the Sydney Cricket Ground in World Series Cricket on 28 November, 1978.

If asked, in 1976, about the possibility of that being written as a script for a play, you would have been laughed out of the producer's room and people in the street would have been saying, 'This guy's only about 50 cents in the dollar.'

Warne's 300th wicket was, in a sense, the combination of the innovations of World Series Cricket and the fact that the ICC, in an enlightened moment not appreciated or agreed by all, said that where lights were available they could be used, providing there was agreement between the two countries taking part in the Test. There were, by that time, plenty of limited-overs matches which had been played at the SCG, as well as in Melbourne, Brisbane, Perth and Adelaide.

Warne's victim that day, with the game eventually finishing at 7.09 p.m., was Jacques Kallis, the outstanding young South African allrounder, and it was a ball befitting the occasion. From around the wicket, with Warne bowling from the Southern or Randwick End, the ball drifted from outside off stump to middle-and-off and then went straight on. It was beautifully flighted and it drew Kallis into what was almost a perfect defensive stroke, but, like a moth to the flame, he then allowed for the legspin, or for the angle from around the wicket. It was the topspinner on which Warne had worked so diligently and, though there seemed no gap, one fractionally bigger than the ball appeared and Kallis was gone. Like Mike Gatting, five years earlier, the brilliant South African had been beaten by a classic piece of legspin bowling.

I suppose being brought up by my legspinner father, Lou, and then being helped by Bill O'Reilly, a man who was one of the greatest ever at the art, though in a slightly unorthodox style, has had an influence in the way I regard slow bowlers. Clarrie Grimmett was in there as well because he was the first I saw at the Sydney Cricket Ground early in 1940 when my father took me to a Sheffield Shield match where Don Bradman and Stan McCabe were the two captains.

I never had a genuine interest in becoming an offspin bowler, although I needed to work hard on finding a way to counter them because two of the best played around my time. Jim Laker took 19 wickets against Australia at Old Trafford in 1956 and Hughie Tayfield, against whom I played in 1952–53 in Australia and then again in 1957–58 in South Africa, were class bowlers. They were different in style and, at the time, I had the feeling Tayfield used more flight than Jim, something I believe in retrospect was probably wide of the mark. Tayfield was always prepared to give the ball some air with plenty of variations and well-set fields. Laker, like Lance Gibbs the great West Indian offspinner, was a bowler against whom you never quite seemed able to get to the pitch of the ball, no matter how good your footwork might have been.

At any rate, that wasn't enough to have me loving offspin bowlers; my leaning was always towards the legspinner, either becoming like them or admiring them. In some way to me they always seemed more exciting than the fingerspinner.

To have been lucky enough to have dinner with Bill O'Reilly at the conclusion of the 1953 tour of England was a piece of good fortune almost beyond compare. Bill was working on the tour for John Fairfax Pty Ltd, publishers of the *Sydney Morning Herald*, and he wrote cricket feature stories. Tom Goodman, the journalist on the paper, was the cricket writer covering the straightforward, factual account of the day's play. With his encouraging words in print, he was a good friend to many young cricketers, older ones too for that matter.

Lindsay Hassett, Australia's captain on that tour, was a wonderful player of slow bowling, as evidenced by the fact that in Sydney in 1940, a fortnight after I saw my first Sheffield Shield game, I was able to watch Hassett hit 122 in each innings off a New South Wales team with O'Reilly as the main spin bowler. Now, 13 years later, I was being captained by Hassett as a wet-behind-the-ears young legspinner and O'Reilly and Goodman were in the press boxes of England watching me trying to learn as much as possible.

It wasn't easy to hold on to possession of the bowling crease unless wickets were forthcoming. I developed my own answer to all this, which was to become more and more desperate to take wickets and to try bowling six different balls an over. It wasn't working and 'Tiger' could see this from the press box, in fact he had asked Tom Goodman if he knew why this had become my rather questionable technique. Tom was able to tell him, after asking me, that it was because I was desperate to stay at the bowling crease and bowling 'tight' didn't seem the way to go for an enthusiastic 22-year-old on his first tour.

Five or six overs and then the sweater was the norm and, in later years, I understood that very well because I found, as a captain, one needed to break partnerships and go on to win matches. At any rate, Tom Goodman sensed I was having problems and asked 'Tiger' O'Reilly if he would spare one night of the Scarborough Festival to have dinner with me. By coincidence, it was a night

'Tiger' was supposed to have dinner with Hassett, something that was always a convivial and interesting affair for them. For 'Tiger' to give up such an occasion was something I appreciated very much.

The dinner was great. I can't now remember what we ate but I know I kept Bill company with a few beers. Certainly I didn't have a scotch and water because his mate Hassett, around the middle of the tour, had taught me a lesson I have never forgotten about the perils of over-tasting alcohol. It was at a party we went to on 14 June, the Saturday of the Trent Bridge Test match in Nottingham, and there was no play on Sundays in those far-off times. The party was thrown by Bert Edwards, a close friend of the Invincibles' players and connected to the Nottingham Lace company, the most famous manufacturer of that fabric. I was having an orange juice. To that stage I hadn't had a memorable match, being brilliantly caught by Godfrey Evans down the legside for three and, a few hours before this party, knocked over by a magnificent leg-cutter from Alec Bedser for a duck. Three days gone in the Test and we were certainly looking right down the barrel. Alec Bedser already had his 14 wickets for 99, Lindsay Hassett had made a magnificent century on the very awkward pitch and he was having a scotch and water at the party. In truth I didn't feel much like a party and I said to Lindsay that, because I had a Test match on Monday, I'd just have another orange juice. He looked at me with that little half smile and said, as a matter of fact, he was actually captaining the team in the same Test I was talking about and I had his permission to try a scotch and water. I had a sip, told him it was tasteless and he said to the bartender: '*Mr Benaud seems to be of the opinion that you can't pour a proper scotch, could you please bring him one he can taste?*' I was certainly able to taste the next one, and the others that followed, and I'm able to say that the following morning I'd never felt worse in my life. Nor have I since! It was a good lesson for me and for some time, having moved out of the ranks of the teeto-tallers, I stuck to beer and these days it is mostly good quality white and red wine. It was beer at Scarborough with Hassett's mate O'Reilly.

When we had finished dinner, we repaired to Bill's room and this was for the bowling advice. It remains one of the more fascinating chats I've ever had with anyone in the cricket world. It was also the most beneficial.

Bill said that my captain, Lindsay, was one of the greatest players of spin bowling the world has ever seen. Bill's view was that because of his great footwork and ability to play spin, Hassett, and other batsmen like him, had little respect for that part of the game. Knowing he had hit those two centuries in the match against O'Reilly I could understand this.

Bill's first point was that batsmen deserved nothing. They considered themselves to be the aristocrats of the game of cricket. Bowlers were merely the workers and were tolerated. Give batsmen absolutely nothing.

Okay that's where we started. Then we went on to the next step in the method that should be used against a batsman. To give him absolutely nothing involved completely discarding the style of bowling I had been using, that of bowling six different types of ball an over.

'Don't try to take a wicket every ball, strange as that may sound.

'Develop one ball as your stock ball and perfect it. Spend a year, even two years or more doing that, and don't be swayed by anyone, captains, selectors, friends, would-be friends, hangers-on, do-gooders or ear-bashers, into doing anything else.'

Now that was easy for 'Tiger' to say but I had my own questions to ask about how to do it. Was I to take it at face value and practise one ball, over after over in the nets, to the exclusion of all else? The answer was no, but the real concentration was that I had to work, say, 90 per cent of the time on perfecting the fiercely-spun leg-break that would land in the position where the batsman would least like it. 'Try it yourself,' he said. 'Go into the nets and bat and have someone standing in the next net with a piece of chalk or white shoe cleaner, something that will make a mark, and when you are bowled a ball by a legspinner, and you are forced to play it defensively, have a mark made on the pitch exactly where the ball has landed.

'After a time you will find there is a small circle or rectangle where those balls have been landing and, when you have a look at the line of the ball from the bowler's end, middle stump to middle stump, you will see where *your* ideal ball will be landing.' The basis of it, he said, was to keep it simple. 'After all, there can hardly be anything more simple than bowling in a net at a spot on the pitch you have chosen and then perfecting it over a matter of years. It will then be second nature to you to do it in a match.'

This of course fits in with what he had told me about not trying to take a wicket every ball. 'If you are bowling six different balls, like you have over the past few months, simply through frustration, it will get you out of that habit. On this tour, in one over, I've seen you bowl your normal legspinner, a slower change of pace, an overspinner, the new sliding topspinner I believe Doug Ring showed you in the middle of the season, a wrong'un and then a faster leg-break. Not even the greatest legspinner the world has ever seen could do that over after over and get away with it. Sometimes, in those ten overs you've bowled 40 good balls from which the batsmen haven't been able to score, ten of which were accurate enough and ten which have been 'gifts' and have been hit for four. No more gifts. Give him nothing.

'Never forget even for a moment that out in the centre the batsman is an enemy of yours.

'What he does to you, or what you allow him to do to you, could mean the end of your bowling career. It certainly could, if you stop making runs, mean the end of your cricket career. You might have a beer with him at the end of the day and that's good because once the day is over you can be friends with everyone. On the field, attack him, but give him nothing, absolutely nothing.

'Bear in mind too that almost every captain under whom you play will be a batsman. Batsmen know a great deal about a lot of things and often they have a good idea of how to play spin bowling. But about the technique, the correct field-placings necessary for other batsmen and the best methods and thought processes of a spin bowler, they know very little. Some of them know nothing.

'One other thing you will need to remember is that it will take you something like four years to perfect all that, even though me saying it to you has only taken half an hour. That's the most important thing I'm telling you, now we'll chat about a few other things.'

It was from O'Reilly I learned about Patience, not trying to bowl six different balls an over and of making sure you give the batsman nothing. From him too the question of Economy, with the batsman as your natural enemy; from my father, Attitude and Practice, and how to go about it.

O'Reilly was certainly not coached, though he coached himself, as did Grimmett, the latter bowling for hour after hour in a net. And with a dog trained to go and get the ball at the other end of the pitch where it had been stopped by the net and then bring the ball back to where Clarrie was waiting. No better way I can assure you of concentrating on landing the ball on a certain spot on the pitch than when you are on your own, lonely in a net.

'Tiger' had a slightly unorthodox grip of the ball when he started and the fact that he finished his career with the same grip was partly due to his own fiercely-determined nature and partly to someone he didn't recognise at the first SCG practice session he attended as a boy from the country.

Under the eagle eye of the state selectors and some famous ex-players, he had bowled three balls to Alan Kippax when a couple of those ex-players, including Arthur Mailey, wandered over and suggested he would need to change his grip of the ball which had the third finger bent back into the palm of his hand. He told them it was the grip he had always used but they pointed out that, although it might have been okay on concrete pitches in the country areas, it would be useless on turf pitches in the city.

After he had finished his spell in the net, a chap who looked as though he might have been in his mid-sixties came over to him and told him not to change. It was the great bowler C.T.B. Turner who said to Bill that when he first came to Sydney from Bathurst there had been endeavours to have him change his grip. Turner added that he had politely thanked them very much for the advice, had stuck to his own methods and that Bill should do the same.

There's no doubt in my mind that this is the way good advice should be. Short and to the point, and make sure the recipient understands what you are talking about before you go on with the next bit. That's how it was that evening at Scarborough. Bill didn't move on to his next short point before he was convinced I knew what to do about the point he had just finished.

When we came to the end of the session he made a very good observation. 'There is only one person able to do this,' he said. 'I've told you how long it will take, and I know you're a dedicated young cricketer, not averse to bowling in the nets and trying to perfect a delivery. You must first of all try to perfect the one about which we've talked. The fiercely-spun leg-break which can be used either as a defensive or an attacking ball.

'It will be up to you to work out how you practise all this, but hard work is going to be the only thing that will get you there, and the added problem you'll have is that if your spinning fingers are raw after a day of practice, then you'll need time to have them heal before you go into the matches.'

Bill was right about many things which later transpired, certainly about the spinning fingers, and Colin McCool was just as correct.

When more than 20 years later, Daphne, in one of her rare moments of mental aberration, connived to have me on *This is Your Life*, a programme which had just started in Australia on Channel Seven, Bill O'Reilly was in a way involved, even if he was out fishing when the drama all happened in a TV studio at Epping in Sydney, in front of a live audience. The producers of the programme had asked Bill if he would be able to appear. Instead, and very sensibly, he sent an old-fashioned telegram from Bright-waters in New South Wales where the flathead were biting and the tailor were in abundance. It read, simply, as he would have said it:

> Dear Richie: I was watching from the press box as you bowled every different type of ball, fast, slow, medium and spin (stop) You were very young then and tremendously dedicated (stop) Your one wish was to handle the bowling game as well as it could be handled (stop) I remember advising you to concentrate on one perfect delivery and only use the showy stuff to liven up the batsmen (stop) You'd have done it anyway yourself but I like to think I had a hand in your success (stop) Wish I could be with you tonight but took a party of friends up north fishing and can't leave them all at sea (stop) Regards Bill O'Reilly.

Bill was right about the fact that I had to work out for myself the best way to do all this. Because I believe in apportioning credit where it is due I have always, when asked, publicly said what Bill had done for me. He was inclined to gloss over it with a wave of the hand and say, 'Well, advice isn't worth anything if the person can't use it properly.'

That is true enough and it is in the proper use of the advice Bill tendered that evening that I formed my whole bowling approach from that time on. It is why, when these days I am asked for assistance on over-the-wrist spin bowling, I will send out two pages of advice on legspin bowling and how to go about it. That advice I send is a précis of what Bill O'Reilly told me in 1953. Additionally it covers what my father drilled into me as a youngster and one idea in particular from the little book written by Clarrie Grimmett, *Grimmett on Getting Wickets*. It was in that little Grimmett book where I first read about proper concentration for a spin bowler, that from the moment you turn and start your run to the crease you should only be concentrating on the spot on the pitch where you want the ball to land.

Because I have always insisted that cricket is a simple game, and everything to do with it should be kept as simple as possible, there are only the two pages.

I believe the advice is good; it is brief and is uncomplicated. It could be extended into 150 pages but that would be pointless. The youngster, or oldster for that matter, wanting to learn to be a legspinner would be wasting a couple of hours of valuable practice time.

Legspin bowling technique

For over-the-wrist spin, grip the ball so that the seam runs across the first joint of the index finger and the first joint of the third finger.

For the leg-break, and the overspinner or topspinner, the ball is spun off the third finger. The wrist is cocked, but *definitely not* stiffly cocked, which would prevent flexibility and, in delivery, would give you the feeling the ball was simply falling out of your fingers.

In delivering the ball, you look at the spot on the pitch on which you wish the ball to land, your bowling hand starts level with your face and then describes what could loosely be termed an anti-clockwise circle to the point of delivery.

The position of the bowling hand dictates in which direction the ball will spin.

At the moment of delivery the positioning of the hand is as follows:

Leg-break: in delivery, the back of the hand is facing the face. (The ball will spin out with the seam rotating in an anti-clockwise direction towards slip.)

Overspinner or topspinner: in delivery, the back of the hand is facing the sky and then the batsman. (The ball will spin out with the seam rotating in an anti-clockwise direction and towards the batsman.)

Wrong'un: in delivery, the back of the hand is first facing the sky and then the ground. (The ball will spin out with the seam rotating in an anti-clockwise direction towards fine-leg.)

You should practise the fiercely-spun leg-break 90 per cent of the time, the variations only 10 per cent. You should be side-on to the batsman and looking over your front shoulder as you deliver the ball and then your bowling hand will finish up going past your front thigh. This means, if you have done it correctly, your body will also have rotated anti-clockwise.

This 'pivot' is of great importance. If you bowl a ball that is too short, you can be almost certain it happened because your body was 'chest-on' to the batsman, rather than side-on, and you dragged the ball down into the pitch.

When you are bowling in a net, make a white shoe cleaner mark the size of a 20 cent piece, on what seems to you to be a good length; that is with the ball pitching where *you* would *not* like it to pitch if you were batting against a legspinner.

Never have your bowling arm at or past the perpendicular when you deliver the ball; it should be at least a few inches lower than the perpendicular.

Don't even think about learning the 'flipper' before you have mastered the legbreak, topspinner and wrong'un.

Keep it simple is the answer. Attend to the basics first; if you can't do that, then the more complicated things will be difficult anyway. It is possible to extend some of those points but the one thing of which you can be guaranteed is that with legspin bowling, common sense will always outweigh rhetoric and complication. Also, there are many examples which show that natural ability can be of considerable importance in bowling legspin, but hard work is essential.

The second page of advice is to do with attitude, not technique:

1. **Patience:** bowling is a tough game and you will need to work on a batsman with your stock ball, sometimes for several overs, before putting a plan into action. It may not work the first time or even the second.

   (If you take a wicket on average every ten overs in Test cricket, you will have a better strike-rate than any of O'Reilly, Grimmett, Benaud and Warne. If you take a wicket on average every eight overs, you could have the best strike-rate of any modern-day Test bowler, fast or slow.)

2. **Concentration:** anything less than 100 per cent concentration running in to bowl is unpardonable. The spot on the pitch where you want the ball to land (judged by looking from the middle stump at the bowling end to the middle stump at the batting end) should be the most important thing in your mind from the moment you turn at your bowling mark.

   (If someone offered you $10,000 if you could throw a ball and hit an object 19 yards away, in trying to win the money, would you, as you were throwing, look at someone standing nearby, or at some other object?)

3. **Economy:** this game is a war between you and the batsmen.

   (Is there some very good reason you want to allow him more than two runs an over, thus possibly giving your captain the idea you should be taken off?)

4. **Attitude:** calm, purposeful aggression and a clear mind are needed, plus a steely resolve that no batsman will get the better of you over a long period of time. Always remember as well that cricket is a game to be enjoyed and you are responsible at all times for ensuring play is conducted within the Spirit of the game, as well as within the Laws.

(In other walks of life you will want to be mentally strong and on top of the opposition. Is there some particular reason why, within the Spirit of the game, this should not be the case in your battle with the batsmen?)

5. **Practice:** all practice should be undertaken with a purpose.
   (You think hard before doing most other things, why should you allow cricket practice to be dull and boring?)

10
ILLUSIONS ABOUND

B OB COWPER caught my attention over a glass of high-class vino in St Tropez in 2004 when he was chatting about the illusions that abound in cricket. He was talking about the eleven players I had chosen to represent me in *My Greatest XI*, and the fact that I had three legspinners in the last 33 names.

His point was, there aren't many others.

I had Shane Warne, Bill O'Reilly and Abdul Qadir and although Australians tend to boast about being all pace and over-the-wrist spin, it is an illusion. 'Cowps' was starting his career in first-class and Test cricket as I was ending mine so we played against one another but not for long before I retired. He then had an excellent cricket career before he too retired from the game in order to have a job, which was the way cricket worked in those days. Nowadays no one has a job and on their immigration entry forms they write the words *Professional Cricketer*.

So, we started thinking about whether it was fact or illusion and the first thing we were able to agree on was that Australia has had more legspinners than most, although we also decided that we would need to go through the records at a later stage to see how many had represented India and Pakistan.

We also agreed that we needn't spend a great deal of time on England because they had made a very good job, if that's not a total contradiction, of getting rid of every legspinner in the land. When I first went to England in 1953, every county except Yorkshire seemed to have a legspinner, but that in itself was an illusion.

When I went to the SCG in 1940 to watch my first Sheffield Shield match, the legspinners playing were (SA) Clarrie Grimmett and Frank Ward, (NSW) Bill O'Reilly, Cec Pepper, Harold Mudge, Sid Barnes and Arthur Chipperfield. Two weeks later, the same NSW spinners played against Victoria, for whom Doug Ring and 'Chuck' Fleetwood-Smith were the over-the-wrist spinners. This was the match in which Hassett hit 122 in each innings but O'Reilly still had eight wickets in the match.

When I went to the SCG to watch the Test matches in 1946–47 there were two legspinners in the England touring party captained by Wally Hammond, Doug Wright of Kent and Peter Smith of Essex. In England in 1953 there was a very good cross-section of spin bowlers, the orthodox variety of fingerspinner being led by Jim Laker, Tony Lock, Roy Tattersall and Johnny Wardle, the latter also able to bowl over-the-wrist spin. Others of the unorthodox variety were Roly Jenkins, Jack Walsh, Gamini Goonesena, Eric Hollies, Doug Wright and John Lawrence.

Later Robin Hobbs was almost the last of them, playing for Essex and bowling his legspin between 1967 and 1971 in a small number of Tests, at a time when that type of bowling really was going out of fashion in England, and this was only half a dozen years after I had retired from the game. In fact, only Doug Wright ever reached 100 Test wickets for England, whereas there have been 14 orthodox spinners who have done so. For those who love orthodox spinners and decry over-the-wrist bowling that will be no sadness. Those who prefer the less orthodox variety raise an eyebrow because it was an Englishman who introduced the wrong'un, googly or 'bosie' to the game of cricket.

There have been plenty of spin bowlers around for more than a hundred years but the four, for me, who have broken the mould and made batsmen think seriously about what was coming down the pitch at them, have been Bernard Bosanquet, Jack Iverson, John Gleeson and Shane Warne. Neither of the first two played a great deal of Test cricket. Bosanquet, at the turn of the 20th century, played seven Tests and took 25 wickets, Iverson, fifty years later, played five Tests and took 21 wickets. Gleeson too had a relatively short time in the game, only six years. Warne has played more than 120 Tests since 1991 and took his 500th wicket in March 2004 in a Test against Sri Lanka. A wide variety of mould-breakers!

Bosanquet might have played only seven Tests but such was the unique style of his bowling that before he was dropped from the England team he had done extremely well. The astonishing thing, however, was that after he bowled England to a great victory over Australia in the First Test at Trent Bridge in 1905, taking 8/107 in the Australian second innings, he was included in the team when the next two were drawn at Lord's and Headingley but did little bowling. He was then dropped and never played again! He may have been the first of the over-the-wrist spinners to suffer from 'captain's block' as regards a type of bowler being expensive. However, he also had an extraordinary strike-rate of taking a wicket every 39 balls bowled. He had one other significant mark in cricket history, that his style of bowling was copied by the South Africans. Four of them, Reggie Schwarz, Aubrey Faulkner, Ernie Vogler and Gordon White, were over-the-wrist spinners; White was also a batsman and did less bowling than the other trio. All of them though had copied Bosanquet in some way, Schwarz more than the others apparently because he and Bosanquet were good friends. From those four South Africans, and others around the world like Arthur Mailey, Warwick Armstrong, Clarrie Grimmett, Bill O'Reilly, at considerable pace for a bowler of this type, Bruce Dooland and Colin McCool, Australia moved into the post-Second World War period in the position of having learnt quickly from what had been seen from Bosanquet 40 years earlier.

There is some argument about whether or not Bosanquet was the first to bowl the ball which spun back from the offside to a right-handed batsman, even though it looked as though it was a leg-break. Bosanquet thought it possible that a dozen years or so before he started experimenting with what would become the 'bosie' or 'bosey', there were several other bowlers who, either by accident or design, managed to get their wrists into the correct position for the new-type delivery. That he could have had such a short career, despite having bowled out Australia to regain the Ashes in Sydney in 1904, seems to me one of the more remarkable happenings in the history of the game. Perhaps it is partly because some people gave the impression they regarded the inventing of the delivery as more comical than clever and Bosanquet's retirement from Test cricket, far from being a sad affair, actually appeared in some quarters to be welcomed.

For England, after Doug Wright, 'Tich' Freeman took 66 Test wickets, Walter Robins 64, Eric Hollies 44 and Bob Barber 42. In Australia, Shane Warne is pushing towards 600 and remains the finest legspinner I have ever seen. I took 248, Clarrie Grimmett 216, Stuart MacGill has 152 and, if the selectors will give him a proper go, he will have many more. Then Bill O'Reilly 144 and Arthur Mailey finished on 99. Around the end of the Second World War there were legspinners everywhere in Australia, with Bruce Dooland, Colin McCool a little later, and George Tribe (left-hand, over-the-wrist) having to go to England if they wanted to earn proper money because there wasn't room for them in the Australian team.

Bruce Dooland's ill-luck turned out to be my good luck because he went first of all to Lancashire League cricket, as did so many Australians and West Indians in the years after the War, and then moved on to county cricket. McCool played with Somerset, Tribe with Northamptonshire and Dooland with Nottinghamshire. They were all champions, but they simply couldn't make it on a permanent basis into the Australian side in that period 1946–50. At that point Jack Iverson came on to the scene and added another dimension to the slow bowling world with his finger-flicking deliveries.

Iverson was something else. When I batted against him in 1950 at the MCG, the advice I was given was that he *must* be treated as an offspinner, even though for all the world his hand action looked as though he was bowling leg-breaks. He held the ball firmly between the thumb and first two fingers of his right hand and flicked it outwards and upwards with his second finger as he brought over his arm. Jack's grip of the ball was unique and as far as I know he was the first bowler ever to try to bowl this way. He and Bosanquet had in common the fact that they taught themselves to bowl by using a ball other than a cricket ball. Bosanquet played a game at Oxford where the participants tried to spin a ball past someone else seated at the other end of the table. It was called 'twisti-twosti', which in itself is a strange name but it was obviously popular at the university.

Iverson, who originally started as a medium-pace bowler with Geelong College in Melbourne, then became a sub-district and lower grade player in Melbourne club cricket. He was in New Guinea during the Second World War when, for a bit of fun, he flicked a table tennis ball under-arm and found he was able to spin it a considerable amount. From that small white hollow ball, he graduated to trying it out with the cricket ball, over-arm, and found it to be confusing to the batsmen against whom he was bowling in the jungle. That was the case also when he returned to Australia and his name kept appearing in newspaper articles, nothing too flamboyant and often just a paragraph or two, but the story always seemed to be that he was 'different'.

He certainly was! In that 1949–50 season when Lindsay Hassett's team were touring South Africa, in the same period as the Australian summer was under way, NSW played South Australia in Adelaide as the first part of the southern tour. Ron James, who had played with South Australia, had now taken over the NSW captaincy because Keith Miller had been called into the Australian team in South Africa after Bill Johnston had been injured in a car crash. The second NSW match was against Victoria at the MCG and Iverson came on first change. He was very carefully inspected by not only the two batsmen in the centre, Jim Burke and Clive Johnston, but by all the others in the dressing-room as well. I made 68 when it came my time to bat and was missed stumping once, by Ian McDonald off Iverson, when I dragged over the popping crease, playing at a ball which my eyes told me was a leg-break and my mind should have told me, as well as McDonald, was his normal offspinner.

By the time that Australian summer was over Jack Iverson was on his way to Test match stardom and fame. There was only one proviso. Did he have the temperament as well as the extraordinary skill to stay at the top level? In the following summer there was no question he would play Test cricket against Freddie Brown's MCC team. It was more a question of which bowler would make way for him. The selectors decided the man to go would be Colin McCool which meant, in effect, Australia would have two offspinners in the team, Ian Johnson and Jack Iverson, albeit one of them totally unorthodox.

Iverson didn't waste any time making his mark. He took 4/43, 4/37, 2/36, 6/27, 3/68 and 2/52 and, despite Reg Simpson making a very good hundred in the last Test of the series won by England, no one could honestly say they were totally comfortable against Iverson. Was Iverson totally comfortable in himself? Rumour around the traps was that he relied very much on Lindsay Hassett setting his fields and telling him exactly where to bowl. The latter instruction, almost bizarre as it may seem, could be carried out by Iverson. He could flick the ball precisely where Hassett told him to land it.

At the other end of the scale, I wasn't landing anything any- where because I had broken my right thumb in fielding the last ball of a club match and had to pull out of the Australian XI team to play MCC at the Sydney Cricket Ground, and miss several NSW matches as well. It could hardly have come at a worse time. The Australian team, as is always the case, was very difficult to break into. When Australia had played their Test series against South Africa, in 1949–50, the best eleven was Arthur Morris, Jack Moroney, Lindsay Hassett, Neil Harvey, Keith Miller, Sam Loxton, Colin McCool, Ian Johnson, Ron Saggers, Ray Lindwall and Bill Johnston. Changes by the end of 1950–51 were that Iverson had come in for McCool, Ken Archer for Moroney, and Jim Burke for Loxton, then Graeme Hole for Burke and Tallon for Saggers. Quite a bit of shuffling around!

There was though another scenario building up. The NSW batsmen had a game coming up against Victoria at the SCG. I was still on the injured list but Morris, Miller and Moroney had decided that unorthodox means were needed to counter Iverson's unorthodox bowling. They resolved to do two things, get down the pitch to him and, as well, give themselves some room for shots on the offside, on the basis that 'Jake' would not be able to handle something that threw him out of his normal rhythm. It was enthralling to watch from the grandstand. Morris hit 182, Miller 83, Ron James 59 and Moroney 43 and NSW finished with 459/7 off only 93 overs. Iverson took 3/108. Not bad figures in a total of that size but it affected Iverson that he had been hammered and certainly his rhythm had been affected. However he bounced back quickly from that setback and, in the remaining match of the summer for Victoria, he took 1/15 and 5/31 against Western Australia at the MCG.

I had enough problems with my own game between then and the end of the 1952–53 series against South Africa in Australia. I was trying to do well enough to persuade the selectors I was worth sending to England. It wasn't until Iverson didn't take his place in the Victorian side that this seemed a real possibility, but he played only one game in 1951–52 and one in 1952–53 before announcing he wasn't available for selection on that tour of England. I have never been in any doubt, had Iverson been on the 1953 tour, that Australia's bowling attack would have been good enough to retain the Ashes, but then perhaps I wouldn't have been given the selectors' vote for the tour, or it might have been Jack Hill who missed out.

Iverson never played again. Twenty-five Test wickets and 78 victims in Sheffield Shield and that was the finish for a unique bowler. The overriding feeling is that it was a sad ending for an extraordinary cricketer.

Gleeson bowled with the same bent-middle-finger style as Iverson, after starting his career as a batsman and wicket-keeper. He was one of the quiet men of sport and no one enjoyed his cricket more, whether at country town, interstate or Test level. I first saw him play, in fact played against him, when I went with Jack Chegwyn's team to the north-west of New South Wales in 1965. This was the summer when Mike Smith brought a very strong English team to Australia and at domestic level there had been many changes in the personnel of Sheffield Shield teams. I had retired from Test and state cricket at the end of 1963–64 and Neil Harvey, Alan Davidson and Ken Mackay had retired at the end of 1962–63. Bob Simpson was captain of both NSW and Australia.

This day at Gunnedah I went around behind the bowler's arm with a pair of binoculars after a time because the batsmen seemed to be having an extraordinary amount of trouble in 'reading' Gleeson. We had heard he was unusual, but surely not this unusual? It seemed easy enough from the car. When it came my turn to bat, he ran up and bowled me what was obviously an off-break pitching on middle-and-leg and I turned it behind square-leg. Or rather I would have done that, other than for the fact the 'keeper had taken it outside off stump and thrown it back to Gleeson.

That was my first sight of him on a cricket field and I always enjoyed watching him bowl. He had a genuine feel for the game and a deep love of a contest, no matter who the batsman may have been: the better the batsman, the more enjoyable the contest and the greater the prize. Having finished at first-class level, he decided to take up lawn bowls where he applied himself as assiduously as he had done several years earlier to become only the second bowler in the history of the game to bowl in that extraordinary style.

Nicknames abound in Australian cricket, any cricket for that matter, and Gleeson was known as 'Cho', an abbreviation of Cricket Hours Only because he was difficult to pin down on tour, always out somewhere trying to find out more about the culture of the country in which he might be playing. He toured India and South Africa in 1969–70, then England in 1972 and he had a relatively short time in the game. He made his Sheffield Shield debut in 1966–67 and retired in 1972–73, having played 30 matches, taken 108 wickets at 26 apiece, including six five-wicket hauls and one match where he took ten. His Test career was shorter, covering the period 1967–68 to 1972 and he took 93 wickets at a cost of 36 runs apiece.

In that match at Gunnedah he took 5/80 against a very strong team and he bowled 27 overs in a thoroughly impressive display. As Jack Chegwyn was a state selector at the time and I was a past captain, and he had bamboozled me and others out in the centre, he had a bit going for him. It didn't take long for the state and national selectors to take advantage of what to many was a completely new style of bowling, few people having retained a more than rudimentary knowledge of what Iverson had done 15 years earlier. I was still practising at the SCG nets and had a 15-minute net a couple of times a week and, on one of the afternoons, 'Cho' was practising with the NSW squad and he bowled in my net. He was always a good thinking bowler and he had developed several variations of what I had seen when I had last batted against him. Again I played down the wrong line and was bowled first ball. I shook my head and said to him I was still at Gunnedah.

With Gleeson it was definitely a case of loving the game and enjoying bowling so much that he was constantly experimenting with different deliveries, always trying to find something new. That's the way bowling should be. He could bowl leg-breaks, topspinners and wrong'uns with his thumb and middle finger behind the ball, and he could bowl orthodox offspinners as well. He was one of the characters of the game in the time he played and a wonderful example of what cricketers can do to give themselves an opportunity of playing top-class cricket in Australia.

When I went to England under Ian Johnson's captaincy in 1956, Bruce Dooland was well established in the Nottinghamshire County Cricket Club and he bowled on a pitch square that was all in favour of the batsmen. He certainly was a champion and, like Bill O'Reilly, he was prepared to pass on to eager young cricketers the benefit of some things he had learned over the years. When Dooland was in Adelaide he copied Clarrie Grimmett's 'flipper', a skidding type delivery also used to considerable effect in Australian cricket pre-war by Cecil Pepper who returned with the Services' team captained by Lindsay Hassett in 1945. Later in the time he played his cricket in England, he changed the whole of his bowling style to accommodate the flipper, shortening his run to the crease and developing the start of his bowling action with the ball slightly concealed.

When we played Nottinghamshire in 1956 very early in the tour, I was looking forward to meeting up with Dooland, though at that stage I had no idea of the offer he was about to make me. It came out of the blue, a little like the dinner with Bill O'Reilly. I had been concentrating very hard on my bowling, along the lines O'Reilly espoused, and it was working well enough, although the captain, Ian Johnson, constantly wanted me to toss the ball into the air far more than I was doing. I hadn't batted or bowled on the first day, the Saturday, at Trent Bridge, but I had watched very closely as Bruce bowled to Colin McDonald and Peter Burge on a dead flat track. On the Saturday, with no play on Sundays in those days, players from the two sides were having a few beers in the dressing-room before our team went back to the hotel. Bruce came over and congratulated me on the 160 I'd made ten days earlier against Worcestershire in the tour opener, and said he'd heard I was bowling well and that I had been working hard. We chatted about the different deliveries and I was able to confirm for him that I was much steadier now and far less prone to bowling six different-type balls every over.

'Well,' he said, 'I won't suggest you change that, but would you like to learn to bowl the flipper?' Would I ever! He said that normally he and the rest of the Notts team would be at the ground on Monday an hour before the game and, if I cared to come two hours before the scheduled start, he would be there and would arrange for the groundsman to have one net set up for that time. He would run me through the flipper and then it would be up to me, from that point on, what I did with it. He told me some people couldn't handle it at all, but added, 'We'll see how we get on.'

I caught an early taxi and was waiting for him where the net was already set up at the Radcliffe Road End and we started. His advice was that I should start practising in a net, but only bowl at the side of the net from inside. The whole thing would take a long time to learn and he felt a grip different from my normal leg-break grip would be needed until I got used to the whole feel of the project. At that point I would be able to start bowling it using my leg-break grip.

The problem was that, in effect, when bowling the leg-break, the ball came out more or less over the top of the hand, so too for the overspinner. And wrong'un. But, and it was a very big but, with the 'flipper' the ball came out from underneath the hand with a decided flipping or squeezing action. The ball never at any stage came over the top of the hand.

At the same time, with the flat side of the thumb and the index finger facing the batsman, or in this case the side of the net, the ball was squeezed out of the fingers in such a way that the tips of the fingers finished up facing the batsman, though the back of the bowling hand faced my own face, as was the case with the legspinner. It took me more than half an hour to understand completely what had to be the *feel* of the ball leaving the fingers, which Bruce said was by far the most important thing. Disguising the ball could come later, as happened with him when he made the conscious effort to change his bowling delivery so that with a shorter run to the crease, and a slight hiding of the ball, he felt secure in his action.

I thanked him very much for his time and effort and certainly his patience, because what was second nature to him was something completely new to me and it would require considerable practice. Very few spinners had ever done it successfully. He left me with the thought that I should only work on it on my own, rather than bowl it at state cricket squad practice sessions. And, most important, not to bowl it in a match until I had the confidence to run up and bowl it precisely on the spot I wanted.

I assured him I would do this and practised the ball carefully for the remainder of the tour, then did the BBC Television course while the players went for their holidays on the continent. We played the Test in Pakistan and three in India, then returned to Australia and toured New Zealand, after which I was included in Ian Craig's team to tour South Africa.

I had made up my mind that the first time I would use the flipper in a match would be in the opening game I played in Southern Africa in September 1957, either at Kitwe in a one-day match or in the game against Rhodesia as it then was, in Salisbury, now Harare. It turned out to be a good choice because in the game in Kitwe I took 9/16 and six of them were taken bowling the flipper. All the hard work in the practice nets had been worth it, though it was obviously going to be far more difficult against first-class batsmen and under tougher match conditions.

The whole tour of South Africa was a complete success as far as I was concerned as I made 817 first-class runs and took 106 wickets at 19.40 and became only the second bowler ever to take 100 wickets in a South African season, the first being the English fast bowler S.F. Barnes in 1913–14.

This South African tour had coincided with our own Australian summer and we arrived back in Sydney in February 1958. At this time I had managed, because of listening carefully to several people and working hard at putting their advice into practice, to have my game in reasonable shape. Of great importance was the fact that, alongside Alan Davidson, I was now being given a great deal more responsibility in the team. Those people noted above were:

Bill O'Reilly: I had worked hard to perfect the advice he had given me in 1953 about not trying to bowl six different balls an over but develop a fiercely-spun leg-break as my stock delivery. Fiercely-spun is a relative thing because I was more overspin than sidespin. As he had suggested, it had taken me four years to do it. And try to give the batsmen nothing.

Bruce Dooland: To practise the flipper for a year before trying it in a match. I waited just over a year and the ball helped me greatly in developing a varied repertoire over the following seven years.

Colin McCool: The splendid legspinner, feisty character and good bloke who told me '*Get those bloody fingers fixed mate or you'll have a short career in Test cricket.*'

Ivan James: The Timaru chemist who believed he might have a remedy for those severe finger problems and proved to be correct, a diagnosis that was close to the most important happening in my cricket career.

Lou Benaud: Someone who knew a great deal about cricket, legspin bowling and people. As well as developing the technical side of the game for me, he also developed in his two sons a love of cricket. In the background, *Rene Benaud* who knew how to encourage her children and, at the same time, keep their feet on the ground. *'Do your best and never give up, but don't take yourselves too seriously.'*

Jim Laker: No actual coaching here, but watching and observing Jim bowl us out in 1956 on two 'turners', at Headingley and then far more so on the one at Old Trafford, I wondered about his most economical bowling run-up and action. He was like clockwork and he certainly followed the O'Reilly dictum of developing one ball and concentrating on it. My run to the crease in 1956 was relatively long, around 12 paces, and I decided if I were to become more balanced and methodical in my approach and delivery stride, I should try something along Laker's lines.

This happened after the match we played in Karachi which had produced the slowest day's play on record, and we then went to Madras for the first of three Tests against India. We had one day's practice before starting this match and it was here I decided to work on the shorter run. You might think that is no big deal but when you have had one style of run-up for several years, taking up 12 paces, and you decide, as I did, to reduce it to six paces, then balance is the key. At the point of delivery there is no sense in feeling you have arrived too soon, or too late for that matter, and I needed someone to keep an eye on me in the nets.

In December, 2004, Jason Gillespie, the splendid Australian fast bowler, gave a perfect explanation of why he had shortened his run-up to the bowling crease, yet was still able to bowl as fast, or even faster. He had realised that when he was six or seven yards from the stumps at the non-striker's end, he was actually ready to bowl!

In Madras, Neil Harvey took the job of watching me bowl in the net and it involved saying what he saw as he was standing in the same spot as for a right-hand batsman. Did it all look smoother, slightly more stuttery, hesitant, rushed, anything that would be of assistance in making a judgment? Neil started by standing behind me at the bowling end in the net, then moving to each side and, finally, he went down to the batting crease.

His verdict was: *'It looks better but I can't be sure why. I think it's probably because you're now running only six paces that you are also running a little slower, which means you are balanced when gathering yourself for the delivery. The other way you may well have been running through the crease.'*

The big thing for me was that it felt smoother and more balanced, so I tried it on the opening day of the Test against India, having had a nervous night's sleep after making the decision to do so. I had done in a day what I had been thinking about for a month from the end of the recent Test series in England. It was successful beyond my wildest dreams. My final figures that day were 7/72 and they remained my best bowling figures in Test cricket.

There were some feisty characters in Australian cricket when I was growing up in the game. They needed to be because it was a tough school and some of the Sheffield Shield matches were played with all the humour and steel normally associated with Test match cricket. Generally, the ones most likely to provide a confrontation or two were the games between New South Wales and Victoria, very little quarter offered or given, always with the proviso that the discussions could be carried on in the dressing-room after the day's play over a cold beer or an iced lemonade, depending on your preference.

Jack 'Snarler' Hill from Victoria was a legend in his own lifetime in this regard and he toured with two Australian teams, Lindsay Hassett's team to England in 1953, where I was also a participant, and Ian Johnson's team to the West Indies in 1955. You were never in any doubt with Jack that you were a lucky little bugger, even if you had just smashed him through mid-on which, in other circles, might have been deemed the shot of the day. He was also a very good bowler: the surprise to me was that he didn't do better on the tour of England where I was certain he would have made the ball grip a little more. He was essentially a topspin bowler who gained great pace off the pitch, even though the scientists will tell you that is impossible. It just seemed that way! Jack gained his place when Jack Iverson decided he would not be available for the tour.

Fast bowlers, more often than not, would be the ones who gave plenty of 'lip' out on the field, in the main because they knew they always had the opportunity to get back at you with a few bumpers if you had stepped out of line. Slow bowlers were generally more reticent, although one, born in New South Wales and destined to play for Queensland, was as feisty as they came.

Colin McCool and Ivan James are mentioned a little earlier in this chapter and they go well together, one who knew what it was like to have ripped spinning fingers and the other how to fix the problem.

Colin was a legspin bowler who played in the first Sheffield Shield match after the Second World War. It was played at the 'Gabba and he had made the decision to move from Sydney to Brisbane, partly because of Bill Brown's influence and partly because he could see that with left-hander Ernie Toshack and leg-spinners Jack Pettiford, George Powell, Ken Grieves and Fred Johnston in the Sydney club competition, selection might be tough.

In his first game for Queensland he played against Arthur Morris, and Ray Lindwall and others, and two years later I was on the field for NSW making my debut against Queensland at the SCG. Not that I did anything at all and Queensland were beaten in effect in three days. It was straight after this that I went to Melbourne and suffered a fractured skull trying to hook Jack 'Dasher' Daniel and didn't play again that season. By the time we were all lining up as 'desperates' trying to make the tour to England in 1953, I'd had a very interesting match for NSW against Queensland with Colin in the opposition. He was a splendid allrounder, apart from being a

Test cricketer who only ever played in a winning side for Australia. Quite a performer!

This was at the time the South Africans were touring Australia and in the end they drew the series with us but, in that first match of the summer, NSW played a high-scoring draw with Queensland at the 'Gabba. Colin made 100 and 88 with the bat and I bowled 60 overs and took five wickets. At the end of the game we were sitting around in the weatherboard corrugated iron-roofed dressing-room, having a cooling drink in the 90° temperature, no air-conditioning at the 'Gabba in those days where the administrators only just recognised the players, rather than welcomed them.

I was talking to Colin and trying to learn as much as I could from him about bowling and it did no harm that he and my father had played against one another, Colin for Paddington and my father for Cumberland. During the chat he was showing me how he bowled his skidding topspinner and, when I took the ball and saw his ripped spinning fingers, I winced as I showed him what had happened to mine during the 60 overs. 'Son,' he said, 'find some bloody way to fix those or you'll have an extremely short career . . .'

I did the logical thing and asked what he used to try to solve his own problem but he was unable to come up with any kind of remedy. Methylated spirits was said to be good for hardening the skin, friar's balsam for softening it. Liquid plastic was just coming into vogue at the time but that didn't work either because the stitches of the ball readily tore it off the knuckles. The short answer was, in November 1952, as I was preparing to put forward my case for selection in the Australian side, no one had any kind of remedy and McCool said to me that it was simply a matter of bearing the pain, otherwise I might just as well stop playing. He did add that there was always the incentive to become a better batsman, but that he doubted the selectors would be looking at me in that light, far more the case that they would be hoping for a bowling allrounder to help solve their problems.

He added that never for one moment, on any day since he had made his club debut with Paddington in the Sydney competition, had he stopped trying to find a remedy. Nor had he ever thought for an instant of giving up despite the pain. Two years later McCool's words were more significant because the NSW side, on their way to Brisbane, played a match at Lismore and I ripped open my spinning fingers. Keith Miller and Arthur Morris called the selectors in Sydney to say they felt they needed an additional player and my club-mate, Jack Treanor, was put on the plane that afternoon. Jack was a quickish legspinner and took a hat-trick on his first morning in first-class cricket, an extraordinary debut. I took 0/87 and then batted at number three and made 125 against Ray Lindwall and the rest of the Queensland attack, Ray having moved from Sydney to captain the northern state.

It wasn't until early 1957 that I found the remedy and it was one of the best but more bizarre things that happened to me in the game of cricket. We had returned from the tour of England at the end of 1956, having won the Second Test match at Lord's and then been bowled out at Headingley and more so at Old Trafford when Jim Laker proved too much for us on a slightly unusual pitch. We then went to Karachi to play a Test and had three more in India, arriving home in Sydney by air from Calcutta on the night of 7 November, 1956.

The arrival was so late in the year that the NSW players were unable to take part in the traditional opener against Queensland at the 'Gabba and our first game was against Western Australia at the SCG. My fingers were okay for this match and I bowled NSW to a win after we had been behind on the first innings. That was one good thing, the other not so good was that I was suffering from dengue fever contracted in Bombay a few weeks earlier.

This was only a very short time after television had started in Australia and although I had no real hope of doing anything in that part of the media then, I was certainly hoping to be allowed to switch from the counting house to the editorial department of *The*

Sun newspaper. This happened and, at the same time, Sir Donald Bradman, in a conversation with Alan Davidson and me, made it quite clear that, when the selectors settled down to choose their team to tour South Africa, they would be taking very close note of performances on the Australian tour of New Zealand which had been slotted in to the programme straight after the Sheffield Shield season finished. At this time I was on a course of sulphanilamide tablets which were the one thing that seemed to be any good in countering the effects of the dengue, which several times had me 'blacking out' during the Australian summer.

We played three unofficial Tests on that New Zealand tour, I did well enough to be happy with my performances and, small though the tour may have seemed in the bigger scheme of things, it was for me the turning point of my career.

I met Mr Ivan James.

Of all places, that happened in a little town, as it was then, called Timaru. We were set to play Combined Minor Associations in a two-day match and the first day was completely washed out. It wasn't a good start because in the previous game, in Dunedin, I had ripped open the calluses on both my spinning fingers . . . and it was cold. Not that being cold made the fingers worse, but it certainly didn't make them any better.

If I say I was in a slightly churlish mood, that wouldn't be putting too fine a point on it, and I was wandering around in the small room I was sharing trying to think of something constructive to occupy the time. In the end it was just for something to do that I decided to walk down to the small chemist shop I had seen in the main street and obtain the next lot of 'sulpha' tablets from the prescription my Sydney doctor, Jack Jeffery, had given me before I left for New Zealand. It was as much to get some exercise in the open air as anything.

I suppose the lucky thing really was that I gave the prescription with my right hand to the man in the white coat behind the counter. He asked casually what the matter was with the fingers holding the prescription and I told him it was because of them being ripped about by the stitches on the cricket ball. We chatted about the Dunedin match where his favourites had done well, Frank Cameron 6/95, Alex Moir 4/89, Bert Sutcliffe 54, and he asked me what I would use to heal the fingers quickly enough to be able to bowl the following day. 'No such thing,' was all I could say, which was perfectly true. There was nothing I had ever used that healed the knuckles quickly and, as I said to him, I reckoned I'd tried everything known to man.

'Well, you never know about these things but I have something that might be a help. I have a lot of ex-servicemen coming in, particularly some who are suffering the after-effects of being gassed and have leg-ulcers. I've found it very beneficial as a treatment.'

I told him I'd be happy to give it a go and mentioned to him what Colin McCool had said to me five years earlier. 'Never let a day go past without trying to find a remedy . . .' He said he remembered McCool as one of the Australian team which had played the first Test at Wellington after the end of the War, not that the allrounder had a great deal to do because New Zealand were bowled out for 42 and 54 in what was Bill O'Reilly's final Test match. McCool took the last wicket of the match but bowled only two balls in the whole game. At any rate he was the catalyst for my constant efforts to find a finger remedy and here was a chemist in New Zealand telling me he might have some kind of an answer.

It would be a gross exaggeration to say I held out any real hopes of success, but anything was worth trying. Not that this was likely to test the vast areas of the medical world because, when he gave me the ingredients and carefully wrapped them, declining to take any payment, they didn't seem earth-shattering; mundane would be closer to the mark.

There was a small, wide-mouthed bottle about two inches high, and it said on it: OILY CALAMINE LOTION BPC '54. The '54 was part of the formula signifying the year it was listed in pharmaceutical books. Then there was another small container and the sticker on that said: BORACIC ACID POWDER. Mr James wrote on a piece of paper what I had to do and it said:

> Rub the lotion into the wound and then dab off the oil that comes to the surface. Gently rub into the wound some boracic acid powder so it forms a waxy filling.
>
> Keep doing this as much as possible and definitely when there is a recurrence of the skin tearing. Make sure you keep the waxy substance filling the hole *all* the time.
>
> Carry some fine sandpaper with you and, before you use the remedy, sand off any little bits of dead or torn skin.

I walked back to the hotel and, because I had nothing better to do, I gave myself the first treatment and, to keep the waxy bit in the wound, I stuck a bit of sticking plaster over it. Did I wake up the next morning with a flawless finger? No, I woke up with a piece of sticking plaster over some waxy stuff in a hole in my spinning finger and it looked the same as the previous evening.

It only took me a couple of days though to realise that something, in fact, was happening and, as we were just about to play the three games against New Zealand, quaintly titled 'Representative Matches', I wondered if I might be moving into some kind of new cricketing venture.

I was nervous and I think justifiably so, having no idea what might be the outcome. Although I know it's an over-used word, I always refer to Ivan James as a genius. His remedy allowed me to bowl successfully in South Africa 1957–58, against England 1958, in India and Pakistan 1959–60, against West Indies 1960–61, in England 1961, in the domestic Australian summer 1961–62 and through to the end of my career in 1964.

'Cowps' and I finished up agreeing on several points about legspinners in Australia, one of which was the number of them around at the moment. It is for both of us a thorough disappointment that, despite the coaching programmes instituted in Australia to reap total benefit from the success of Shane Warne and Stuart MacGill, they are in very short supply.

Almost non-existent in fact.

In theory, legspinners should abound in Australian cricket in 2005. Not a bit of it. I'm assured there are scores of brilliant 13- and 14-year-olds out there awaiting the chance. I certainly hope so; otherwise it will have been one of the most wasted campaigns in the history of Australian cricket.

11

THE SEASON

C ASTING my mind back through seasons to celebrate over a 15-year career, the first thing that comes to mind is that they were all memorable though not all were totally pleasant. Life isn't like that. Making a debut is always pleasant, failing is not. I had my most memorable Australian domestic season in 1961–62, the year following the Tied Test series between Australia and West Indies. In one way it would have been an anti-climax had it not been a splendid summer and it would have been a let-down for the hundreds of thousands of cricket followers who, in a sense, expected the excitement of Frank Worrell's tour automatically to be continued.

The four-year lead-up to the 1961–62 summer had in fact been one of almost unbroken success and a bit of fairytale stuff as well. It started with finding the finger remedy, which changed my cricketing life and approach. That was in 1957. Then followed the tour of South Africa in 1957–58. The fairytale bit was somehow becoming captain of Australia and, for that to happen, Ian Craig sadly was stricken with hepatitis and had to pull out of the summer after only a couple of games. The situation was that Craig had been made captain of NSW in October 1956, and of the Australian team to tour New Zealand, after that, South Africa. Then for me, as captain, came the first official tour of India and Pakistan, the Tied Test series and the series in England in 1961 where Neil Harvey captained the side to victory at Lord's and we won at Old Trafford on the last afternoon of the Fourth Test and retained the Ashes.

That was all Test cricket, the 1961–62 summer was purely domestic. It would therefore be a stern challenge to play cricket of the kind that would not necessarily be uplifted by overseas stars in a touring team, although three of the states had engaged brilliant West Indian players to represent them in the Shield competition. Rohan Kanhai was with Western Australia, Wes Hall with Queensland and Garry Sobers settled in South Australia.

Because this season followed immediately after the 1961 tour of England, the NSW players from that touring team knew exactly what our tactics would be. They would be the same as we had set out in the press conference at the start of that tour and carried on throughout: trying to make a lot of runs on the first day if we batted, quick bowling of overs, no wasting time. It was a traditional style Australian programme, with NSW first of all playing Western Australia in Sydney, and just sneaking first-innings points in a match marred by rain for two of the four days. We made 218 and then bowled WA out for 176, of which Rohan Kanhai made 81 of the most brilliant runs you would ever wish to see. Then it was to Brisbane for the game against Queensland and this turned out to be one of the best matches I had played between the two states. Because of the circumstances it underlined the way we would be trying to play for the remainder of the summer. We won the match by 48 runs, having set Ken MacKay's side 274 to win after a declaration on the third evening.

The declaration itself was interesting and humorous in that 'Slasher' Mackay, Neil Harvey, Alan Davidson and I were having a couple of drinks in the NSW dressing-room at the close of play and 'Slash' remarked to me he thought they could just about make the 274 needed if I closed now. Neil looked at him and said, 'Not as long as your backside points to the sun, Slash.' Then he looked at me and murmured, 'We'll walk it in.' I followed with, 'Why don't we find out? . . . Okay Slash, I've declared at 245/6.' Everyone burst out laughing and the reaction in the media the next morning was along the lines of the NSW captain either having taken leave of his senses, too many cold beers at the end of the day or he had spent too much time without a hat in the hot Queensland sun.

Queensland started well and, with Peter Burge unbeaten with a half-century to go with his first-innings century, they looked to be good things. It all changed around quickly though, Alan Davidson finished with 4/14, left-arm spinner Johnny Martin picked up three and I had two. Harvey turned out to be 'spot-on'. 'Slasher' kept saying he couldn't believe it and although he finished with 58 not out the rest of the batting had fallen in a heap. He then contented himself with saying, 'We'll be after you in Sydney.' Prophetic words. Davidson's performance in this 'Gabba match was outstanding and was the forerunner to one of his greatest summers for NSW.

We were moving along well at that moment, with one first-innings win and one outright and the next game, against Victoria, to be played at the MCG over the Christmas-Boxing Day period. I won the toss, decided to bat and told the team I wanted to try something of an experiment and have 400 on the board at the end of the day. Now, in these modern times, that doesn't sound out of the ordinary, considering the way the Australians and others have batted in the past two or three years. In 1961, though, it was a bit over the top, even if it was in keeping with what we had endeavoured to do a few months earlier in England. It would be exaggerating a little to say everything went entirely to plan, though one aspect eventually did. We scored at the five an over required to have 400 at the close of play. The only problem was that when Alan Davidson was out at 141 after 25 overs, we had lost our sixth wicket and, although only two hours' play had been used up, the plan needed a bit of upgrading. Grahame Thomas was just a few not out at the other end and I told him we were still on target for the 400 and let's go for it.

When we were 396 Bob Cowper was bowling and I tried to reach

402 in one hit but was caught at long-on. Johnny Martin went out to the centre and also tried for a six but we fell two short and declared on 398/8 in what had been quite a stirring afternoon for the 14,000 crowd. It was holiday time in Melbourne so, after taking a first-innings lead, instead of enforcing the follow-on we batted again, set Victoria a target and still won the match with time to spare. It was all very entertaining for the good crowds at the MCG and local hero Bill Lawry made a half-century and a century, but NSW were on a roll.

Now we came to the return match against Queensland, this time at the SCG, with Ken Mackay already having stated this was to be Queensland's match to make up for the earlier defeat at the 'Gabba. We won the toss and made 354/7 the first day at five an over and they replied with 351. Our closure came at lunch on the final day and we set them 273 to win in four hours at about three and a half runs an over. A reasonable challenge and 'Slasher' played a 'blinder'. He had thrashed 96 in 89 minutes when he cut Davidson down to Frank Misson at third man, turned for two at the Paddington End but was blinded by the sun in trying to see the fielder. Misson's fast, flat throw was a beauty and suddenly 229/3 gave us a slight chance. With Davidson and Misson using the second new ball, the last seven wickets went down for only 14 in 22 minutes and we had another extraordinary victory by 31 runs in what was developing into a very exciting summer.

It was also a summer where the crowds were responding, not only to what NSW were doing but in other centres as well where the cricket had been equally good with captains and players chasing victory rather than thinking about safety. The attendances for our game in Melbourne had been very good for a Shield match and the game against Queensland at the SCG provided record Sheffield Shield takings for the NSW Cricket Association. However, assume nothing. Was it going to be possible to keep up the impetus, or would we fall at whatever hurdle we might find in our way? It certainly wasn't to happen in the next match which was against South Australia, also at the SCG. Les Favell was captaining South Australia and 'Favelli' was game for anything on the cricket field providing it was exciting. My sports editor at *The Sun*, Con Simons, was so enthused by what had been happening that he promised me as much publicity as I wanted for the SA match in the five-day lead-up to the game. We had the lead story every day, in the main concentrating on the battle between the young left-arm spinner David Sincock, who turned the ball more than anyone else I had ever seen, and the rampaging NSW batting side.

It turned out to be an astonishing win for NSW, even though the entire third day of the match was lost through rain. Les Favell won the toss and batted and, from 55 overs, SA had 250 with Ian McLachlan making a superb 109. The Saturday produced a crowd of more than 17,000 people who came in to watch the battle with Sincock. David took three wickets, Bob Simpson, Ian Craig and Neil Harvey, but we hit 140 off his 20 overs and made 443 all out from only 82 overs of wonderful entertainment for the spectators. We had made 401 on the second day and SA were 17/1 at the close. It was as good as you could get for your attendance money. On the last day we bowled SA out for 229 and needed to score a brisk 37 to beat a storm sweeping in from the west.

Alan Davidson had been having a very good season and in the next game against Victoria, the return match at the SCG, he turned in a wonderful performance. When you look at the scores on paper it seems to be a comprehensive victory for NSW, which was the case. How it was achieved is another matter. We lost three for 25, recovered slightly, again found problems and then Davidson was joined by wicket-keeper and number eleven, Doug Ford. 'Davo' was 48 at the time. He reached his half-century from the next ball, kept the strike and then reached his century almost before the Victorian bowlers had time to think about containing him. The pair made 59 in 25 minutes, or rather Davidson did because Doug remained not out without scoring. I was easy on 'Davo' when Victoria batted again and spin wrapped up the innings and the victory, and now we needed to beat Western Australia in Perth to win the Sheffield Shield. After that we had to take on South Australia and Sobers in Adelaide. First though Perth, where the local side were always a vastly different proposition from when they played in the eastern states, particularly at the SCG.

Although Davidson had been in good form throughout the summer, we needed a special effort from him in this coming match. We received it too, but not quite in the way we imagined. Batting first and scoring at almost six an over, it might have been that we were a little over-confident but, more to the point was that Hugh Bevan and Laurie Mayne bowled superbly to have us 38/6 when I walked out to join Davidson. We put on 61 before I was out and then 'Davo' did it again with the bat, hitting a magnificent 108 out of the 180 added while he was in the centre.

Barry Shepherd was captain of Western Australia and he made a splendid 59 in the WA first-innings reply. We struggled again in our second time at bat and at the close of play on the third evening, needing only 174 in all to win, WA were 84/4 and Shepherd was going well. Davidson had claimed three of the wickets to fall. The odds were all on WA but NSW on the final morning took their last six wickets for only 17 and the Sheffield Shield was ours. It had been a magnificent summer to date, unbeaten, but then there was always Sobers to come.

He had started in the South Australian side when they played Western Australia in the first match of the season at the Adelaide Oval. He made 32 and 80 and took wickets as well, but for the WA side Rohan Kanhai played a blinder, with 31 and 135 run out, and that was followed by a 37-run partnership for the last wicket between Keith Slater and Hugh Bevan to see WA through to victory. Garry didn't make a century until the last game of the season, which was against NSW, and he certainly made up for lost

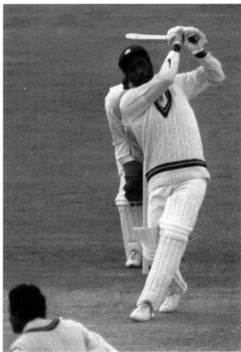

hree great West Indian cricketers in action. Malcolm Marshall (*above left*) was a real handful
or batsmen. He had a quick run to the bowling crease and gave the impression sometimes
hat he was running through it. He was part of an outstanding line-up of West Indian pace
owlers after Clive Lloyd thought about why he had been beaten in Australia in 1975–76.
ivian Richards (*above right*), the Master Blaster of his time in the game, was one of the most
onderful entertainers cricket has seen. One of Wisden's 'Five cricketers of the Century', he
as there alongside Garry Sobers (*below*) whose skills had him listed as the greatest allrounder
ver to walk on to a cricket field.

Australia and England have always had fine competitive wicket-keepers. Australia's three best in recent times have been Ian Healy (*above left*) Adam Gilchrist (*above right*) and Rod Marsh (*below*) in an unusual role, opening the batting for Australia against John Snow at Headingley in 1975. This was the Test where the final day was abandoned because vandals damaged the pitch overnight. Healy was an outstanding cricketer with 366 victims and 4356 runs in 119 Tests, Marsh 355 and 3633 in 96, Gilchrist 287 and 4452 in 68. Three great champions in a span of 35 years.

Adam Gilchrist had to leave NSW to play for Western Australia as wicket-keeper so he could then find his way into the Australian team. He is a splendid all-round cricketer.

Missing an aeroplane most times is one of the more boring aspects of life. Catching an aeroplane in Antigua these days has become an experience not to be missed. Daphne and I spent a delightful day with Tony and Joan Lewis, at the end of ITC's Barbados-Antigua work-experience week, at the Sticky Wicket, a mere hundred yards from the departure gate of the airport. It is the brainchild of a wealthy Texan. He has turned what was virtually wasteland into a delightful cricket ground with a good pitch and splendid outfield, where matches are played and the onlookers have boarding passes in their hands. The pavilion was a delight, food was good, wines very good and showing discreetly in the background was a constant menu of videotaped cricket matches from the past, or those being played somewhere in the world that day.

At the Colony Club, Barbados, with good friends Bernard Lawton (*middle*) and Ian Wooldridge (*right*). It was the occasion of delivering the Frank Worrell Memorial Address, with Australia having demolished West Indies in three days at Kensington Oval. And that was way back in 1995!

It's okay, Lindsay, all is forgiven by our two great West Indian friends, Pat Contant (*left*) and Michele Kennedy-Green (*right*). They are all pictured with Daphne at the SCG Walk of Honour ceremony where, in 2000, plaques of prominent sportsmen were unveiled on a specially designed path at the Sydney Cricket Ground. Lindsay Kline, good cricketer and great team-man, was one of two batsmen not out in the Fourth Test of the Tied Test series in Adelaide. He and Ken ('Slasher') Mackay defied West Indies for 100 minutes after Australia's ninth wicket had gone down and defeat seemed inevitable. Instead, it was a pulsating draw.

Above: A typical Greg Chappell stroke, forcing the ball away off the back foot through the cover region. Perfect balance. When you see a batsman play a stroke in that fashion, with the balance just right, it always seems as though he has more time at his disposal than other batsmen.

Below: Watching from the commentary box, there were four great allrounders to observe as a group in the late 1970s and through the 1980s. Imran Khan (*below*) was first on the scene in 1971, followed by Richard Hadlee, Ian Botham and Kapil Dev. Most times, microphone in hand, you're lucky to see one great allrounder in a decade, four provided riches beyond belief.

eft: Dennis Lillee made his Test debut in Adelaide in 1970 and took five wickets at the first me of asking. An unbroken future of fast bowling success beckoned, and 31 wickets in the rawn series with England in 1972 did nothing to dispel that theory. Assume nothing. Back roblems surfaced in the 1972–73 series against Pakistan in Australia and he played only the pening Test against West Indies in Jamaica a few weeks later, and then not again for another 0 months. During that time he was in a plaster cast and receiving treatment from Dr Frank yke in Perth. He played on as a champion until retirement on 6 January 1984 when he, ireg Chappell and Rodney Marsh left Test cricket.

eft: One of the best attacking leg-break owlers in Test cricket, Abdul Qadir, kept the t going through the late 1970s and 1980s at time when pace bowling was predominant. owling defensively was never in his mind-set id he had the whole armoury of deliveries. metimes he used them all in the one over, id he was wonderfully entertaining.

Above: There was no holding Ian Botham in 1981. Botham's match at Headingley, then 5/1 in 28 balls at Edgbaston, at Old Trafford in the Fifth Test, five wickets in the match and a century from only 86 balls faced, with England in trouble at 104/5 when he arrived at the crease. It was, for him, an astonishing summer!

The Coronation Lawn at Lord's is a delightful spot for lunch. Daphne and Simon Hewitt, the cricket lover who was responsible for me accepting the position of Patron of France Cricket.

Photographed here with my younger brother, John, who captained NSW, later became chairman of the NSW selection committee and was one of the Australian selection committee in 1989 when Australia started their extraordinary run of never having lost a series to England since Mike Gatting's triumph in Australia in 1986–87. John made a century in his last Test innings in Australia, 142 against Pakistan at the MCG in 1973.

time, hitting 251 and taking 6/72 when SA won by 130 runs. NSW won the Sheffield Shield with a record 64 points and attendances lifted dramatically, perhaps the best examples being those two NSW v South Australia matches. The first, in Sydney, was where the excitement was intense and then the match outlined above where, astonishingly, the total attendance was 24,827, a record at the Adelaide Oval in the 15 years of Sheffield Shield matches since the end of the Second World War.

There was no doubt the decision to invite the three West Indian stars to take part in the Shield had a great effect on the interest in the season and the boost in attendances. In addition, it was of great benefit to the local players in the three teams for which they played and all the others opposing them. Not everyone had been able to get to the grounds to watch the five Tests in the Tied Test series and Australian sports television was in its infancy then. The good fortune to have a close-up look at players of such quality was of immense benefit to more than 70 other Australian cricketers. I had been playing 12 years in Sheffield Shield cricket before that 1961–62 summer and it was worth waiting for. It was a wonderful season where excitement and flair dominated the five months, my favourite season of all from the Australian domestic cricket point of view.

12

WELL BOWLED

Alec Bedser, Trent Bridge 1953–7/55 and 7/44

The Australian selectors gave Lindsay Hassett a new-look side for the 1953 tour of England. In it were three very young allrounders, Ron Archer, Alan Davidson and Richie Benaud. The opening batting situation after the First Test was such that Lindsay had to move himself up and go in first with Arthur Morris, Graeme Hole dropping down to the middle order where he batted well. The problem for everyone was Alec Bedser who was at the height of his powers and he was a wonderful medium-fast bowler. That England didn't win the opening Test at Trent Bridge was due to the weather, but Alec's bowling performance was magnificent and he finished with 14/99 for the match. Tall and strong, he always hit the pitch hard with a high-class bowling action. In our second innings the light deteriorated markedly just as the sixth wicket fell at 81 and Don 'Deafy' Tallon was quickly on his way out to the centre. Lindsay called out loudly, *'It's very dark, give it a go, Deafy.'* Not for nothing was Don known by that nickname and he smashed 15 off the remainder of the over and then was caught trying to hit another six. 'I thought you meant *throw the bat,'* was his explanation on returning to a ropeable captain.

Alec was very good in our first innings and outstanding in the second where the ball was really gripping on the soft pitch for his leg-cutter. His controlled swing made life very difficult and, in all, it was one of the greatest exhibitions of bowling of that type I ever came across in my time in the game. I watched him bowl very well in other Tests on that tour, notably at Lord's, Old Trafford and Headingley, where he took another 22 wickets. In the final Test at The Oval, England won the Ashes for the first time since the Bodyline series in Australia in 1932–33.

Jim Laker, Old Trafford 1956–9/37 and 10/53

Australia won the Second Test at Lord's on a good pitch by the handsome margin of 185 runs. It was known as 'Miller's Match' because he bowled magnificently and took ten wickets in the Test. Old Trafford was known as 'Laker's Match' because he took 19 wickets, the most ever in a Test match. There was no point in thinking about anything else Jim had done on the cricket field after Manchester 1956 where he took those nineteen. Earlier on the tour, in the game against Surrey, Jim had a 'practice net', taking all ten Australian first-innings wickets. The extraordinary thing about that, in the light of the later Old Trafford happenings, came in the first-innings bowling analyses of Jim and Tony Lock in that game at The Oval.

Laker: 46–18–88–10   Lock: 33–12–100–0

'Lockie' took seven wickets in the second innings, but those of us not playing at The Oval wondered how one bowler could take all ten and the other take none. We were to find out two months later. Jim bowled wonderfully well at Old Trafford and, as I mention in another chapter, I benefited by watching him closely and then, a few weeks later in India, changing my run to the crease and my bowling attitude. I doubt if 'Lockie' changed anything because, in the second innings at Old Trafford, he beat the bat three times as often as Jim without taking a wicket. On the last afternoon at Old Trafford, with rain threatening, and indeed falling on either side of the ground but not on the ground itself, we fought hard, having not done so in the first innings. I batted for an hour and a quarter up to tea on the final day, and then beyond, but in the end Jim was too good for us. It was an extraordinary performance and an unpalatable loss, one that Neil Harvey and I vowed to reverse the next time we toured England.

Fred Trueman, Lord's 1963–6/100 and 5/52 Edgbaston 1963–5/75 and 7/44

1963 was the first year I worked for BBC Television and what a year to start. The cricket was exciting and, by the time the Third Test had been decided, the England v West Indies series stood 1–1, West Indies having won the First at Old Trafford by ten wickets with a day to spare and England the Third at Edgbaston by 217 runs. The Second at Lord's was a draw but full of excitement and drama, with Colin Cowdrey going out to bat at number eleven with his broken arm in plaster after being hit by a short-pitched delivery from Wes Hall. David Allen played out the final over and any of four results were possible when the last ball was bowled by Hall. This was a remarkable time for that outstanding bowler, Fred Trueman. At Lord's he showed wonderful control of swing and length and he seemed to be as lively at the end of the day as the beginning. He had started playing for England against India in 1952 and then was in the 1953 side against Australia at The Oval when the Ashes were regained. The England-West Indies game at Lord's was one of the best matches I have ever seen; Fred was magnificent, so too the rest of the team members. In the next Test at Edgbaston, England still one down in the series, squared it all up and Fred followed his 11/152 at Lord's with 12/119 in the match at Edgbaston. In the second innings he routed the very strong West Indian batting line-up. When he came back on to bowl for his second spell he quickly took the last six West Indian wickets at a cost of an edged boundary, and it took him only 24 balls in which to end the innings. Fred eventually became the world's highest wicket-taker; though 18 others have since gone past his figure of 307 wickets which he took in only 67 Tests.

Bob Massie, Lord's 1972–8/84 and 8/53

When Bob Massie took his 16 wickets on his Test debut it was confirmation that swing bowling was alive and well. The Australians had already lost the opening Test against England at Old Trafford, even though there had been a late batting flurry from Rodney Marsh. Massie didn't play in that game because he was recovering from a groin strain and one of the aspects of his bowling at Lord's, to come around the wicket to both right- and left-handed batsmen, was as a result of practising that way in the Old Trafford nets, bowling to team-mate Ross Edwards. When it came to the Lord's Test match selection, the Australians brought in both Edwards and Massie and the latter turned in one of the more astonishing efforts I've seen in a debut at Test level. In Australia he was always known as a very accurate bowler and he came from a long line of good medium-pace and fast bowlers from Western Australia. Bowlers there are taught how to swing the ball and to swing it late and in the early days, when I played Sheffield Shield, WA had bowlers like Charlie Puckett and Ray Strauss, prodigious swingers of the ball. Massie had an additional attribute which he used at Lord's; he was able to bowl outswing and inswing without any easily discernible change of finger or wrist action. It was not uncommon, in the Tests and matches against counties on this 1972 tour, to see the English team on the players' balcony using binoculars to try to pick the direction of swing the instant *before* the ball left Massie's hand. Massie had less success as the tour went on and his career lasted only six Test matches after he lost the ability to bowl the inswinger. One great benefit he had in the Lord's Test was that the man bowling at the other end was Dennis Keith Lillee who gave a magnificent exhibition of bowling for no just reward.

Michael Holding, The Oval 1976–8/92 and 6/57

After the problems the West Indians had in Australia in 1975–76, a 3–0 victory over England in 1976 would have been very sweet. Holding, completely recovered from the injuries he sustained on that tour of Australia, had increased his pace and improved his control and, to make it more difficult for the batsmen, he was now a thinking bowler as well. He had introduced a very good yorker to his repertoire and the occasional slower ball, although that change of pace still seemed to be fairly swift. The Oval in August most times comes up with a very good batting surface and it was the case in 1976. The selectors had given Tony Greig, the England captain, a bowling attack of Bob Willis, Mike Selvey, Derek Underwood, Bob Woolmer, Geoff Miller, Chris Balderstone, Peter Willey and Greig himself. Plenty of numbers, but what about the penetration? Viv Richards took care of all that with his 291 and there were four brisk half-centuries as well from Roy Fredericks, Lawrence Rowe, Clive Lloyd and Collis King. Dennis Amiss hit a splendid double-century for England. Nothing though in those perfect batting conditions was better than the bowling of Michael Holding who bowled fast, kept his speed up throughout his 53 overs and gave one of the greatest pace bowling exhibitions it's ever been my pleasure to watch. Michael went from there to become one of the finest fast bowlers from any country until his retirement in 1987 and there were few batsmen around who didn't regard him as one of the best.

Dennis Lillee, MCG 1977–6/26 and 5/139

The Centenary Test Match at the Melbourne Cricket Ground was one of the more extraordinary games of cricket ever played. The first Test at the same ground, known then though as the Richmond Paddock, resulted in a victory for Australia by 45 runs. The Centenary Test, played in the same week of March 100 years later, resulted in a victory for Australia by 45 runs. There was a lot of grass on the pitch surface and it was damp at the start of the match. First the England bowlers and then Lillee took full advantage of this. Australia were bowled out for 138, but then Dennis took 6/26 from 13.3 eight-ball overs to reduce England to 95 all out. Having dispensed with the preliminaries, the batsmen got to work with Australia's Rod Marsh hitting an unbeaten century, a feat to be followed by Derek Randall whose 174 was a marvel of skill, orthodoxy and some extraordinary strokeplay and by-play. When Randall was on 161, Marsh dived forward and to the side to take a catch and Randall was given out by umpire Brooks. Marsh instantly called that he had not held the ball cleanly and Randall was recalled. Lillee bowled better in the second innings than in the first, taking into consideration that the pitch had settled down to be an absolute 'belter'. When Alan Knott was the last man dismissed, Lillee was carried from the field on the shoulders of his team-mates. I have seen him bowl wonderfully well on many occasions, but never better than in this match which was played in very hard, but fair, fashion. Lillee was to continue until early 1983 and became Australia's greatest wicket-taker, with a figure of 355 that has now been passed by Shane Warne and Glenn McGrath in Australian cricket. Dennis was a wonderful bowler, a great character and a very courageous cricketer.

Bob Willis, Headingley 1981–0/72 and 8/43

Discard the 0/72 as an aberration because, after the Botham heroics in that game, it needed someone to bowl out the Australians in their second innings for a very modest total. Kim Hughes had enforced the follow-on and, when England won the match, it was only the second occasion in the history of cricket that a team had won after being made to go in again. At one stage in England's second innings they were still 92 behind Australia and only had three wickets in hand. With the Australians batting last, things altered dramatically when Bob Willis changed ends to bowl with the breeze at his back, and he came steaming in from the Kirkstall Lane End in a manner that indicated he and Brearley believed the match could still be won. At this point the Australians, not without some problems, had made their way to 56 for the loss of Graeme Wood. Sometimes the small targets can be easy, sometimes though they can be very difficult as the pressure mounts. Chris Old played his part as well as Willis. He was needed to bowl at his best and did so, taking the crucial wicket of Allan Border who made most runs for Australia on the tour, most runs in the Tests and also was on top of the batting averages. Old bowled him for a duck to make Australia 65/5 and then Willis crashed through again to take the remaining five wickets.

This match remains for me the number one as regards television commentating and I have a lot of very good matches to stack up against it. The amount of effort Willis put into his bowling was extraordinary. I can still see him racing in and hurling himself, wild-eyed, at the bowling crease and, I guess, at the figure at the other end as well. It was all drama and one of the greatest bowling performances in a seemingly lost cause ever to pass through the pages of Test match history.

Malcolm Marshall, Adelaide 1984–85–5/69 and 5/38

This was the Centenary of Test match cricket at the Adelaide Oval and it was quite an occasion, with 22 captains who had led their country being present at the ground. In the searing heat the performance of Malcolm Marshall was something that has always remained in my mind; no Australian batsman was ever comfortable against him on a pitch that was made for batting. Marshall, with his distinctive style, almost running through the bowling crease at the batsman, keeping an immaculate length and swinging the ball and moving it off the seam, was in terrific form throughout the game, taking 10/107 overall. At a critical time for West Indies in the first innings he dismissed Allan Border and David Boon and then, with a changed batting order in the second, he quickly removed Border and Kim Hughes. To me he always looked a difficult bowler to face because of his method which often had the ball skidding at the batsmen. That's not to say he couldn't bowl a devastating short ball because it had a similar skidding effect for the batsman who was often late with the stroke. Clive Lloyd had great faith in him as a spearhead of the bowling attack and Marshall never let him down.

I saw Malcolm bowl very well at other times, notably in England in 1988 where, in the five Tests, he took 35 wickets and West Indies won four of the matches with the other one, the First at Trent Bridge, drawn, after he tore a rib muscle just before close of play on the fourth evening. England finished with 301/3 and saved the match. Ten wickets in the next Test at Lord's had Marshall back on track and he remained a splendid bowler and coach until retirement and his untimely death, aged 43, in 1999.

Shane Warne, the 'Gabba 1994–95–3/39 and 8/71 MCG 1994–95–6/64 and 3/16

Two consecutive Test matches ten years ago provided the kind of cricket watching all old legspinners should be allowed. The matches were a month apart and I doubt if Shane Warne has ever bowled better, though I have seen him in top form in the 15 years I have watched him in action. This was Mike Atherton's tour and Michael had in his team two former captains, Mike Gatting and

Graham Gooch. The Australians were led by Mark Taylor and this was at the beginning of Taylor's brilliant Test captaincy career. It was a good toss for Taylor to win in Brisbane, Australia made 426 and then Craig McDermott took 6/53 and Warne 3/39 from 21 outstanding overs. No batsman for a moment looked comfortable against him. When England faced 11 hours of batting to save the game Warne was irresistible. In his second over he bowled Alec Stewart with a wonderful 'flipper', the ball hitting the stump as Stewart was half way through his stroke. Then, in his next over, a quicker leg-break accounted for Atherton; it was a beautifully concealed change of pace. In all he bowled 50.2–22–71–8 and it was some of the finest over-the-wrist spin bowling I have ever seen. Warne then warmed up for the Boxing Day Second Test by bowling well in a Sheffield Shield match at the WACA and five days later, at the MCG, England won the toss and sent Australia in on an overcast day and with the pitch damp. That Australia's 279 was enough for a first-innings lead was due to fine batting from the Waugh brothers and then there was more superb legspin bowling from Warne, 27.4–8–64–6. In the second England innings McDermott was too good for the England batsmen and Warne took the hat-trick of Darren Gough, Phillip DeFreitas and Devon Malcolm to round off ten wonderful days of Test match bowling, and a useful Christmas present as well.

Glenn McGrath, Lord's 2001–5/54 and 3/60

Australia have produced a number of fine fast bowlers over the years and Glenn McGrath is one of the best I've seen from any cricketing country. I was there for his debut when he walked on to the WACA ground in Perth to bowl against the New Zealand opening batsmen Mark Greatbatch and Blair Pocock. There was no hint that the then spindly paceman with a serviceable delivery stride and bowling action would go on to the heights he has reached 12 years later. His first Test wicket was Greatbatch and, in the same innings, Craig McDermott in dismissing Ken Rutherford reached the 200-wicket mark, thus providing something of an incentive for McGrath. Over the years I have watched McGrath he has always been improving. There are bowlers of all types where that is a natural thing, but McGrath, in keeping with the very best performers, is a deep thinker on bowling. He has two hauls of eight wickets at Test level, one at the 'Gabba against West Indies and the other against Pakistan at the WACA in Perth, where it all began.

The one that most impressed me though was at Lord's in the Second Test of the Ashes series in 2001. Australia had just won the First Test with an exhilarating display after putting England in to bat at Edgbaston. They sent them in again at Lord's and McGrath proceeded to provide a Master Class of pace bowling in 43 overs of brilliance. In the first innings he dismissed Atherton, Butcher, Thorpe, Stewart and White, all either caught at the wicket, slip, gully or lbw, which is a reminder of McGrath's method. 'Keep it simple' has never been better used by a pace bowler; he swings the ball a little either way, moves it a touch off the seam just about half the width of the bat. All this is done in such a way that the batsman is compelled to play at almost every ball which hits the pitch where the batsman would least like it to land. When England fought back in the second innings McGrath took 3/4 in eleven balls. It was a superb and memorable performance from a splendid athlete.

13

THREE GREATS

Arthur Morris, Keith Miller and Ray Lindwall

MORRIS, Miller and Lindwall were everything any young cricketer could want as mentors, at a time when there was intense competition for places in an extraordinarily strong New South Wales team in the late 1940s. That strength continued through the 1950s and early 1960s with the Sheffield Shield being won 12 times in 14 years. Those three brilliant and experienced cricketers always had time for the younger players and they knew precisely what would be of assistance to them in improving their all-round games. All-round doesn't just mean batting, bowling and fielding, but thinking came into it as well. Sitting in the dressing-room after the day's play was always a great experience. It was a case of listening more than talking, though there were always questions to be asked and answers to be remembered. All this was priceless for any youngster lucky enough to be in the NSW team at that time.

When I was chosen in the NSW team to go to Queensland for the traditional opener of the season in 1951, Ray was the opening bowler. The pitch at the 'Gabba was always magnificent for batting, but we contained Queensland to 316, with Ken Archer making a magnificent 106. Lindwall's bowling figures were 26.1–7–45–7 and it was one of the greatest exhibitions of pace bowling I had ever seen to that time. He bowled fast, had perfect control of swing and movement off the seam and his changes of pace constantly had the batsmen in trouble. In the second innings his figures were 13–5–

23–2 and again he bowled magnificently. Facilities at the 'Gabba in those days were rather ordinary and the two teams had their dressing-rooms side by side. The flooring was of weather-beaten timber, scarred over the years by the long spikes of the players as they walked around and did their loosening-up exercises. Don Bradman's spikes had left their mark on the floor when he had made his Test debut 23 years earlier.

Ray was a splendid footballer as well as a great cricketer and he was always super-fit, always looked after himself. Before bending and stretching became fashionable in the modern game 'Lindy' was doing it, but without the aerobics! He always finished up with running on the spot, something that was almost unnoticed in other dressing-rooms around the world, but not at the 'Gabba where the timber floor allowed the noise to bounce across and off the walls and then up to the corrugated iron roof where it doubled in sound in our room and trebled in the Queenslanders' room. He only ran on the spot for one minute but it must have seemed more like an hour to the two batsmen next door padded up and ready to open the innings.

Ken Archer was a fine cricketer, one of the more brilliant fieldsmen ever to play for Australia and a very good opening batsman. More credit to him this day then for having held out against Lindwall, caned the other bowlers, including me, and made his century. When NSW batted Arthur Morris, the skipper of the side, made 253 out of the 400 innings total, an innings to be matched with anything I had seen in Sheffield Shield cricket. The third member of the group, Keith Miller, missed out with both bat and ball in the game which was eventually drawn, but he had other great all-round performances in the past and there were certainly more to come at the 'Gabba in the future.

Lindwall had made his debut in first-class cricket against Queensland at the 'Gabba in November 1941 and I watched him bowl in a match at the SCG that year which was shortly before Japan entered the Second World War, and then I watched him play in some Services' matches when he came back to Sydney from the jungles of New Guinea. He bowled against one of my Central Cumberland team-mates, Bert Alderson, who was an opening batsman and had been chosen to play for NSW in one of those games. Bert, who had been a champion schoolboy cricketer, was also a very heavy scorer in club cricket and for many years was at the top of the first-grade batting figures at our club. It was quite an experience for him batting against Lindwall because he had a slightly unusual grip of the bat, with the index finger of his left hand resting on the back of the bat, down the spring. Ray, bowling at blistering pace, yorked him but not before he had severely jarred that index finger through the ball thumping into the blade.

Test cricket resumed in Australia in the 1946–47 season and, although Ray was a certainty for the opening Test against England at the 'Gabba in 1946, he contracted chicken-pox and had to miss the Second Test in Sydney which was the first Test match I ever watched and in which Don Bradman and Sid Barnes each made 234. Ray's absence from this Sydney match was a great disappointment to me but he was back in the next Test in Melbourne, taking three wickets and making a century. Although Ray was always listed as a fast bowler in any tour guides, he was in fact a fine allrounder, one of the best ever produced by Australia. He is one of only four Australian players to take 200 wickets and score 1,000 runs in Tests. He went on in that first series after the war to take six wickets in the Fourth Test in Adelaide and nine in the final game in Sydney.

At the same time Miller was hitting a half-century and a century and Morris hit three successive Test centuries at the top of the order, so the heart of a 16-year-old was able to beat a little faster. Ray and Keith had developed into a feared pace bowling combination, Ray already being spoken of as the finest fast bowler since Jack Gregory and Ted McDonald in their prime. I played under Lindwall's captaincy in 1956 in Bombay, as it was then called, in the series we played on the way back from England, and then he played under my captaincy on the first-ever official tour of India and Pakistan in 1959–60, as well as in the series against England in 1958–59 when he went past Clarrie Grimmett's Australian Test wicket-taking record of 216.

Ray always produced plenty of apprehension among opening batsmen and some of his greatest tussles were with Len Hutton, the great England opener. I can still remember the stunned silence with which the Yorkshire crowds twice accepted their hero being bowled by Lindwall for a duck. His bowling arm was slightly lower than normal but this gave him the opportunity to bowl a very dangerous outswinger, even if it did restrict the inswinger which he eventually developed when playing in the Lancashire League, where he found the snicks were not easy for the fieldsmen to hold.

Lindwall was a model for all young cricketers, fast but very rarely furious, and a role model for the acceptance of umpires' decisions and attitude. That attitude was do your best on the field but, whether you've made a duck or a hundred, make sure you are still in the dressing-room of the opposition team at the close of play saying 'well played' or 'thanks for the game.'

Lindwall was as much responsible as Benaud for what happened at Old Trafford in 1961 when I went around the wicket on the last day, England collapsed and Australia won the game by 54 runs. During the second-last day I had been looking at the footmarks on the pitch and thinking of whether, in certain circumstances, it might be worth bowling at England's left- and right-handers from the around-the-wicket angle.

In those days it wasn't something that Australian legspinners ever did and I hadn't actually practised the manoeuvre. The thought process came about because of what I had seen left-arm spinner Tony Lock do to the Australian XI side in Sydney in 1958 where, from over the wicket, landing the ball in deep footholes, he was close to unplayable for right- and left-handers. Here at Old Trafford, in 1961, there were deep footmarks at the Warwick Road End which had been made by Jack Flavell, Ted Dexter and, to a lesser extent, Fred Trueman, who had also created the ones for 'Lockie' at the SCG three years earlier. Ray was in the Lancashire committee room when we went across for a drink after play concluded on the fourth day and I pulled him aside and put the proposition to him. 'Might it work?' We talked it through and he said, 'It will be worth trying if you're in trouble, but you'll need an extra man on the legside to the right-handers and you'd better make sure you do it properly or they'll kill you, and don't forget it can only be effective if the batsmen are attacking. You won't be able to get a right-hander lbw if they are defending.' It is a measure of the high regard I always had for his cricket brain that I made a beeline for him as soon as I arrived in that committee room.

He produced admiration from cricket followers and victories for captains, sometimes those for whom he was playing. On this occasion it was for one of his former captains who was in a bit of trouble at the time.

I first met Arthur Morris at the back of the old Members' Stand at the Sydney Cricket Ground when I went with my father to see a match before the Sheffield Shield restarted after the war. I had read a great deal about this left-hander, described as one of the best and most elegant players Australia had produced, and had also been following his name after his record-breaking debut in first-class cricket in 1941. The last of the Sheffield Shield games had been played in the 1939–40 season and the games between then and the resumption had been mainly between NSW teams and Services' sides.

My father knew him because of having bowled to him when playing for Central Cumberland against St George which was the very strong team captained by Bill O'Reilly in the Sydney grade competition. I had been mentioned a few times in the newspapers as a promising Parramatta High School cricketer who had played in schoolboy representative games in Sydney and Newcastle. When introduced I said very politely, 'Hello, Mr Morris', as one did in those days, and, after chatting for a minute or so, he said he hoped my cricket continued to go well and he went up to the dressing-room to get ready for the day. It would be a better story if I had vowed that I would one day play in the same team as him but, although that actually happened a few years later, I was more interested at that moment in going to watch the players practise in the nets which used to exist on the old SCG No 2, just 20 yards away.

I played in Cumberland second grade and then was promoted to the first-grade team in 1946 so I had the chance to play against NSW players Ernie Toshack and Bill Alley, plus Jack Pettiford and 'Ginty' Lush when Cumberland played Gordon. The latter was captain of the club side and had captained the NSW side as well before Sid Barnes, and then Arthur, became captain.

In October 1948 NSW and Queensland revived the Interstate Colts match which had been a feature of contests between the two states in the pre-war period. NSW had a very strong line-up and two of the players who were successful in the match at the 'Gabba, Jim Burke and Alan Walker, opening batsman and left-arm fast bowler respectively, were soon included in the Sheffield Shield team, Walker for the first game of the season at the 'Gabba and Burke for the second in Perth. In his first two innings Jim made 76 not out and then 69 against Victoria in Melbourne and Walker was taking wickets, so the state selectors had derived plenty of pleasure and praise for their decision to use that Colts match as a selection yardstick. I'd had a reasonably good Colts game, without having reached the heights of Walker and Burke, and I was starting to wonder if the selectors might keep on with their planning.

When NSW played Victoria in Melbourne in the Boxing Day match at the MCG, Morris and Ron Moss were the opening batsmen but Moss, who was also Arthur's opening partner at St George, made nought and five. At lunchtime during the third day of that match I had gone out of the accountant's office where I worked, bought a newspaper to read the cricket stories and there was the announcement that Moss had been left out of the team for the New Year's Day game against Queensland at the SCG. Jim Burke would open with Arthur Morris and I had been chosen as the replacement in the twelve. This was high excitement, made more so when I arrived back at Parramatta after work and my parents were just as delighted and probably even a touch more nervous than I was.

In the lead-up to this game the three players I was watching closely from a distance were having a brilliant start to the season. Arthur Morris had hit three centuries, Keith Miller a century and a half-century and Ray Lindwall was taking wickets and, judging by the newspaper and radio reports, was bowling very well. I was about to move into exalted company.

It turned out to be a most unusual match. Arthur welcomed me into the team but the rain that had started before the toss kept drizzling and there was no play on the opening day. When we assembled the next morning the rain had stopped, the pitch was grassy and very green. Arthur won the toss and sent Queensland in to bat and they were bowled out for 202 after having been 38/5. Our bowling attack was Lindwall, Miller, Alan Walker, Vic Emery the offspinner, Fred Johnston, a very good legspinner, and Benaud, supposedly an allrounder who also bowled legspin. Queensland bowled us out for 180 with their outstanding pace bowler Len Johnson taking 6/51 and I was one of the six.

We then bowled them out for 120 and I was fielding down at fine-leg when Alan Walker was waltzing through the Queensland line-up, taking 6/20 in ten overs of fierce pace bowling. NSW needed 143 to win and Jim Burke made 29 of them while Arthur hit a magnificent 108 for a ten-wicket victory. On paper it looked easy, not losing any wickets in the chase for a win, but I knew at the end of the three playing days I had moved up a level and that the other 21 players in the game were far more accomplished performers.

It doesn't need Einstein to work out that in such a tight match, and with a first-innings deficit, I was unlikely to have been in the forefront of Arthur's thinking as a bowler when we were in the field, but he was kind enough to apologise for not having been able to bowl me. I was very happy to have been part of a winning team and a week later it seemed that it might have been not only my debut but also my last game in first-class cricket. It was in the week following the NSW-Queensland match that I was hit in the forehead trying to hook a bouncer at the MCG and played no more cricket that summer. After an operation and two weeks in Royal Prince Alfred hospital in Sydney, it was also suggested that I might never make it back into the NSW side, although the medical people said they could see no problem, just try not to be hit in the head again.

They added that I shouldn't play any cricket for the remainder of the season, so I was left with the one appearance and the chance to watch the remaining two matches at the SCG, one against Victoria and the other against South Australia. George Powell, the Randwick legspinner, took my place in the first game and then the selectors chose pace bowler Dave Hanlin for the South Australian game where I was again an interested spectator.

The next summer, 1949–50, had the Australian Test side in South Africa, but a glaring omission was the dropping of Keith Miller which meant he would be captaining NSW in the Sheffield Shield. No one seemed able to fathom the fact that he had been dropped and it later transpired all three selectors, in private conversations, indicated they had voted for him, not against him. A slightly bizarre sequence of events. At any rate, it meant that two of my cricketers, Morris and Lindwall, were in South Africa, the other, Miller, was in Australia, though that was soon to be changed because Bill Johnston was injured in a road accident in South Africa and Miller was flown over as the replacement player.

He had captained NSW to a stirring 15-run victory over Queensland at the 'Gabba in the opening match of the summer, making 80 and taking six wickets, and, in grade cricket with Cumberland, I had made a good start to the season which included 160 against Gordon at Lidcombe Oval. I had been retained in the NSW practice squad and after making those runs I was included in the twelve for the game at the SCG against Western Australia, carrying the drinks successfully and very happy to be back again. When Miller left for South Africa, the selectors made Ron James captain of the state team for the southern tour which meant I was about to play my second game of first-class cricket, something of a relief after the predictions that I might not play again.

The selectors also included Alan Davidson, the former left-arm over-the-wrist spinner from Gosford High School who was now playing with Northern District in the Sydney club competition and had changed himself into a left-arm pace bowler, genuinely quick and with wonderful control of swing. It was an inspired selection. 'Davo' took the wicket of Bob McLean with his first ball in first-class cricket and had such a good summer with the ball that the Australian selectors named him in the Australian team to make a short tour of New Zealand under Bill Brown's captaincy. The team was to be named at the conclusion of the NSW-South Australia match at the SCG and Alan and I both had reasonably good matches. He took six wickets and I made 93 but I'd found wickets hard to come by. I was a chance for selection in the line-up for New Zealand but, when I looked at the final touring party nominated, I could see clearly I had yet another level to climb. I might have been promising, and certainly I had made something of a comeback after serious injury, but it was a case of translating promise into something more concrete when the Sheffield Shield was at full strength with all the Test players available.

1949–50 then was a summer of considerable learning, but it was also a summer without Miller, Morris and Lindwall, all of whom had a successful tour of South Africa, even though Lindwall was dropped for the final Test there, despite having had match performances of 5/32, 3/47 and 4/89. Morris hit two centuries and Miller, although not making a century, turned in excellent all-round performances. Not least of the mysteries was that the man for whom he was sent as a replacement player, Bill Johnston, was far and away Australia's best bowler with 23 wickets in the series, having made a very quick recovery once Lindsay Hassett and his tour selection committee had ensured Miller would be on the next aeroplane! One of the more devious and clever Hassett and Morris moves to circumvent an originally poor selection.

It was great to go to the NSW Sheffield Shield squad practices the following summer starting in October 1950, and meet up with the six players who had returned from South Africa. Alan Walker, Jack Moroney and Ron Saggers were back in the team, as well as Morris, Miller and Lindwall. The one thing patently obvious to all the players from the previous Australian summer was that it was going to be very difficult to catch the selectors' eyes and, having done that, performances would need to be at a peak to remain in the side. I scrambled in as 12th man for the first two games against Queensland at the 'Gabba and then the SCG. In the game at the 'Gabba, 'Davo', who beat me for a place in the final eleven, excelled with 7/49 from 20 overs in the Queensland first innings. The second match produced the extraordinary Melbourne Cup broadcast declaration. NSW went on to win that game after Don Tallon declared the Queensland innings so that all players could listen to the Cup and Morris and Miller then opened the innings and hit an astonishing 225 off 29 overs to win the match. Each of them had already made a century and a half-century in the game in Queensland and Lindwall took wickets in both matches. I might not have made it into the final eleven, but it was just as fascinating in 1950 to hear the three of them discussing tactics and advising the young players in the dressing-room or at the dinner table, moving salt and pepper shakers around to illustrate the advice and make a point.

I was an avid listener and I was also doing well enough in the grade cricket matches to retain my place in the twelve for the southern tour, with the first match to be played at the MCG. Selection was so tough that Alan Davidson was made 12th man for that game, and the subsequent one in South Australia, though he returned to the side when the First Test was being played in Brisbane and the top players were out. It was a tough summer! In the Melbourne game I made 55 and took 3/46, the latter including Lindsay Hassett lbw. I'd like to be able to say I dismissed the Australian captain and great player of over-the-wrist spin with a beautiful delivery, dipping and spinning, but, in fact, it was a topspinner which landed on one of the famous cracks in the Melbourne pitch and ran along the ground, hitting Lindsay on the foot.

I had caught the eye of the selectors to the extent that I had been named in the Australian XI team to play England at the SCG, so too Jim Burke who made a century and then gained a place in the Test side. I couldn't play because I had broken a bone in my right thumb fielding the last ball of the day in a club match the Saturday prior to the Australian XI fixture.

The summer of 1951–52 was no easier as regards selection. The West Indies were touring after their triumphant series in England where they beat England for the first time. When NSW played West Indies at the SCG immediately after the First Test in Brisbane, I put on 100 in an hour with Ray Flockton. West Indies had put NSW in to bat and, when I walked out, the green pitch and some spirited West Indian pace bowling had us 96/7. Flockton was an outstanding schoolboy cricketer and, when given the chance, did very well in the state team. In one later season, 1961–62, he played in the first two matches and then was 12th man in all the others; such was the strength of NSW that year that only 12 players were used in the summer where the Sheffield Shield was again won.

In that West Indian year Sid Barnes, who captained the team when Miller and Morris were on Test duty, gave me two great opportunities with my batting. He batted me at number six in the game against South Australia in Adelaide and I made 117 and then he put me up to three in the return game against them at the SCG and I made 93. I was lucky to have the chance. In the first of those matches the century gave me an inside berth to the Test team if the selectors were intending to make any changes for youth. It didn't appear likely.

The Test rubber was still alive when West Indies seemed certain of winning in Melbourne, having set Australia an interesting challenge. With Valentine, Ramadhin and Worrell taking nine wickets, it looked highly unlikely that the Australians last-wicket pair, Doug Ring and Bill Johnston, could make the 38 needed for victory. They did it with a mixture of swashbuckling batting and adventuresome running between the wickets which completely demoralised John Goddard and his team. It was at this moment, with the series won, the selectors decided to experiment and they brought in Colin McDonald, George Thoms and me, leaving out Arthur Morris, Jack Moroney and Ian Johnson, none of whom deserved to be omitted but it was something the selectors were looking at for the future. It was George Thoms' only Test. He decided to stay in the medical profession, which was a full-time job, and he became one of Australia's leading gynaecologists.

It was a safety decision to retire from cricket. Surgeons cannot afford to take risks with injuries to do with the hands. Colin McDonald became one of Australia's finest opening batsmen and a great thinker on the game, and I moved along in the all-round sphere for another 12 years.

It was in the next summer that I derived the full benefit of the assistance Morris, Miller and Lindwall were providing. It was when the South Africans toured Australia and drew the series, the summer where the Australian team to tour England in 1953 was to be named on the afternoon the Fifth and final Test concluded in Melbourne. I had been 12th man in the opening Test in Brisbane and then played in the next four, doing enough to gain a place in the touring party and, with all three of them certain to be in the touring side, Morris, Miller and Lindwall were keen for me to make it as well. Although one, Morris, was a batsman and the second, Miller, a fast bowling allrounder and Lindwall a fast bowler and allrounder, they each knew about every aspect of the game, including spin bowling. They all played it very well. Morris, alongside Neil Harvey, made up the best two I ever played with or against as far as slow bowling was concerned. It was in the footwork, always at least close to perfect, most times brilliant and certainly always attacking.

I made the team and at Worcester, in the first match on tour, I batted with Miller who was quick to point out that while English pitches were slower and less bouncy than those in Australia, good footwork was still necessary and most times you would play forward more often to nullify the movement of the ball off the seam. Then, at Bradford in the third match, I batted with him on a greenish 'seamer' and made 97, and he helped me along with advice when I was in real trouble early on against the moving ball. The three young allrounders on that tour, Ron Archer from Queensland, Alan Davidson and me from NSW, all benefited greatly from their advice and they didn't mind how often we asked. One of the things from which I had derived great benefit was playing under Morris first of all as NSW captain and then Miller, after Arthur was mysteriously removed from the captaincy at the end of the season when the West Indies toured. I assume the actual decision must have been made closer to the start of the 1952–53 summer when the South Africans were about to arrive. Such a momentous sacking could hardly have remained a secret for six months in the corridors of power at the New South Wales Cricket Association. I was pleased for Miller, though I had no idea at that stage what sort of captain he would be. I just knew he had a splendid grasp of the game and was, like Arthur, wonderful at imparting information and giving assistance to young cricketers.

In typical Australian cricket administration style, no one had the gumption to walk up to Arthur and tell him what was about to happen and why it was going to happen. NSW had enjoyed a wonderful run of success under his captaincy and we had again won the Sheffield Shield easily in the previous summer when the West Indies were touring. Arthur, as captain and opening batsman, made over 700 runs in very fast time at an average of better than 50 per innings.

It's difficult to believe the selectors thought that could be improved. Under his quiet exterior Arthur had a very good tactical mind and also willingness not to kow-tow to cricket administration, something that wasn't widely approved of by the general administration in the state. With a system of choosing delegates based on two per club, rather than the 24 best, there was a lot of jockeying for positions within the clubs. Bill O'Reilly was one who served for a short time as a St George delegate, before being told that he'd already had his fun and derived the benefits from the game of being a player representing Australia. It was time for him to step back and let someone else have the glory of being an administrator. Don't worry about the skill O'Reilly could have imparted to the administration of the game.

Arthur was in Hong Kong playing with Jack Chegwyn's XI when the story of his sacking appeared in the newspapers and on the radio. It was said to be coincidence that they had waited until he was out of the country to announce his sacking, though they did try to make the excuse that no one knew he would be away. Believe that and you'll believe anything as the Cricket Association had to approve the tour, and the names of the players! A refusal to be subservient to administrators and always being fashionably dressed was looked on with suspicion in those days.

It made no difference to his attitude towards young cricketers. He was every bit as observant and helpful, so too Keith in the two tours of England I made alongside him, 1953 and 1956, with the tour of the West Indies in between where Keith was vice-captain to Ian Johnson. Arthur retired after that 1955 tour and Keith after the one to England in 1956. The two of them, alongside Ray Lindwall, remain the bench mark for me in the manner in which they played their cricket and responded to the needs of youngsters. It may seem something that might be done automatically but it is not always so. When it does happen it is priceless for the beneficiaries.

14

SIX AUSTRALIAN INNINGS

Don Bradman

It is another aspect of being a selector that one is free to nominate batting and bowling performances over the years and I have been able to choose six Australian batting performances over a period of 69 years. The idea started when I was commentating for Channel Nine in Hobart in the Australian summer of 1999–2000 and I watched Adam Gilchrist and Justin Langer share a partnership in the fourth innings of the Test against Pakistan. When they came together at 126/5, with another 243 needed, it was a forlorn chase; almost a case of pack your bags and check to see if there are any seats on the early flight back to Sydney. When the winning runs were hit and I was eventually back in Sydney, raising a glass and thinking about the batting, I reckoned Gilchrist's innings was one of the best I had ever seen. Then I wondered if I could find a few more I liked, or had been told about, and the answer is that I found a dozen and decided in the end to cut the list to six. One of them I heard as a six-year-old, all of the others I saw from the dressing-room as a player or was working on the match as a commentator.

The first was Don Bradman. In 1936 I was at Jugiong where my father was a schoolteacher at the small public school which was attended by only 23 pupils. During the day I might attend a class early in the morning, then go to the concrete-walled storeroom which my father had cleaned out and I would bowl a tennis ball against the wall and, when it bounced back, I would hit it with the

193

small cricket bat my father had made for me. He had shown me how to play a forward defensive shot, a backward defensive shot and a straight drive if the ball bounced back off the wall and landed just in front of me. My father had given me a book, *The Australian Team in England 1934*. It had in it drawings and some blank scoring pages, and he had filled in the names of the England and Australian cricketers who were taking part in the 1936–37 series. Apart from my 'Test' matches in the storeroom in Jugiong, there was this proper Test series being played between Australia and England. I had been told about the 'Ashes' and that England and Australia played for them, and that Australia currently held them because they had won that series in England in 1934.

The Test matches were being broadcast. We heard them from the very tall piece of furniture in the corner of the living-room, a Kreisler wireless, and through 2CO Corowa I could listen to the booming voice of the ABC's cricket commentator Mel Morris and others describing the five Test matches. There was no good news in the early part of that series for a young Australian lad because England won both Tests, the First in Brisbane by 332 runs and the Second in Sydney by an innings and 22 runs. The pitches were uncovered in those days and in each game the Australians were caught on a 'sticky' after overnight rain had softened the pitch. Going into the Melbourne Test the Australians, with Don Bradman, captain for the first time in a series, were in a must-win situation if the series itself was to go to Australia. They could retain the Ashes by drawing one of the three remaining games and winning the other two.

Rain had been forecast for the MCG game so tactics would play a big part in the eventual outcome. Bradman had made 80 in the Second Test but had three other low scores, and the Australian Board of Control delegates had summoned four of Bradman's team for some reason never properly explained, possibly a 'pep talk'. In the end they panicked, poured them a drink, said goodbye, but never told them why they had been invited, or perhaps 'summoned' was closer to the mark. It was rumoured they wanted to ask if the players were giving the captain full support, but didn't have the courage to get the words out past their tightly-pursed lips. All Bradman wanted was a victory. To achieve that he desperately needed to win the toss so that if the rain did come he would be in a position to dictate terms.

The rain came all right and the Australians, 181/6 overnight, declared at 200/9 and, on a pitch made treacherous by overnight rain and then sunshine, Morris Sievers, a tall, strongly-built, fast-medium bowler, took 5/21 and Bill O'Reilly 3/28. The trick at that time, with the weather forecast for the following day very good, was not to get the England batsmen out too quickly otherwise the early Australian batsmen would also have to bat on a bad surface. Walter Hammond and Maurice Leyland played superbly for England but, despite the clever Australian tactics, England did close their innings before stumps. It was, however, a tardy closure by 'Gubby' Allen, their skipper, after England had lost their last six wickets for eight.

The Australians were thankful he had delayed it so long but it did force Bradman into a change in the batting order. He sent in Bill O'Reilly and 'Chuck' Fleetwood-Smith to open and put legspinner Frank Ward in at number three. When Fleetwood-Smith asked why he was opening the batting for Australia, the answer was to the effect that even on a good pitch he had great trouble laying bat on ball; on this one there was no chance of him being caught. He did survive until stumps but still made a duck on the second morning. With the pitch flattening out under the heavy roller the next morning, Keith Rigg and Bill Brown were the batsmen to come in after the tailenders had gone, then Jack Fingleton and Bradman put on 346 for the sixth wicket and Australia totalled 564. Bradman was at his very best in grabbing the chance he had been given by the weather. His innings was less flamboyance and more grit and determination to achieve this one win in the series.

Another in either Adelaide or Melbourne would retain the Ashes. Bradman made 212 in Adelaide and Fleetwood-Smith bowled Hammond on the last day with a wonderful delivery, left-arm over the wicket, drifting away towards the slip fielder and spinning back sharply between bat and pad. England began that day at 148/3 with Hammond 39 but the great batsman didn't add to his overnight total. The Ashes were still with Australia after that Adelaide victory. Then, at the MCG, Bradman's 169, and brilliant centuries from McCabe and Badcock, were instrumental in winning the series 3–2. It was the only time in the history of the game that a team had come back from a 0–2 deficit to win a Test series. Massive crowds watched the matches, interest around the country was intense and people say Bradman's 270 in the Third Test at the MCG was his greatest innings. I'm not surprised they say that because of the circumstances where, if that Melbourne game hadn't been won, it would have been oblivion for the Australian team.

Neil Harvey

Neil Harvey made many centuries for Australia and was one of the greatest cricketers ever to walk out in Australia's colours. His team members tell me that his century in Durban in 1950, when the Australians had been caught on a wet pitch, was one of the finest seen in the past 60 years, but I watched an innings in 1959 that was the best I ever saw from him. It was played on a matting pitch against the greatest modern-day bowler on matting, Fazal Mahmood of Pakistan. Batting on matting over clay is no fun. Australians play a lot of their cricket on matting pitches but the base is almost always concrete, the surface is hard and the ball comes off with pace and bounce. There was a time in country areas of Australia where ant bed, rolled hard, was occasionally used as a base with what were known as 'Kippax mats' on top. Coir matting was thick and woven, Kippax was softer and more like thin carpet, or jute. It needed to be stretched very tightly and captains were permitted to inspect the matting to make certain that was done.

In Pakistan, where the soft clay is watered and rolled each morning, the amount of 'cut' off a mat only *'softly'* stretched is extraordinary. Apart from Fazal Mahmood, Pakistan had another great matting bowler in Khan Mohammad, against whom we played in 1956 on our way back from England. He was outstanding but, when we went there three years later, he had retired and Israr Ali, a left-arm medium-pacer was the other opening bowler. We had three tactics devised for the match. The first was that if we won the toss we were going to send Pakistan in to bat so we had a good idea of how the pitch would play. The second was that, although we had Ian Meckiff and Ray Lindwall in the bowling attack, our main bowlers were going to be Alan Davidson, Ken Mackay and me. Ken Mackay? There were plenty of eyebrows raised by that, I can tell you, but I had a good ally in my vice-captain, Neil Harvey, who had stood with me watching Mackay bowl in Brisbane a few weeks earlier when on four consecutive mornings we had matting pitch practices on a closely-mown and rolled section of the outfield at the 'Gabba.

This was at a time when the Australian Board of Control had promised us that all three Tests in Pakistan would be played on turf, but there was something quietly jangling away at the back of our minds saying, 'assume nothing.' Confirmatory messages from Pakistan were light on the ground. Hence the insistence on practising on what might be termed makeshift matting pitches in Brisbane during our four-day stopover on the way to Dacca (now Dhaka). The best bowler at all of those practices was 'Slasher' Mackay who bowled at medium pace, was very accurate and moved the ball off the seam a considerable amount. He was to be our surprise, but it came as no surprise to him. Our third tactic was unusual, but we knew it was vital. We used two buses to go to the ground each day but just one to return to the hotel at the close of play.

Originally one person was to travel in the first morning bus, Lindsay Kline. He was not only 12th man but he was the Australian team supervisor for pitch-tightening as well. As you might have gathered, letters had never arrived to say we were playing on turf, so our team-meeting thinking now came into play. We had decided the mind-set would be that we would make the best of whatever conditions we found in India and Pakistan and that we would have a happy tour. No one would complain but our manager, Sam Loxton, and I would do our best to ensure Pakistan cricket did the sensible thing with pitches and make them all turf so the country could eventually take its proper place in world cricket.

When Kline travelled to the ground on the first morning we actually had one other player go with him so they could compare notes which they would then give to me when we arrived on the second bus. Kline's brief was to have the matting stretched to its tightest point, area by area, all the way down the pitch. Then, having made the notes of how that was done, he was to make certain it was exactly the same each morning so that neither team derived any extra benefit.

When the toss was made on the opening morning I called correctly, put Pakistan in to bat and they made a few more than we wanted. Duncan Sharpe was run out but Davidson, Mackay and I picked up the nine wickets to fall to bowlers and, in all, we kept them to just under two an over. It was a tough, tight start, but now we had to negotiate Fazal Mahmood.

It was Neil Harvey who did it, even though he had spent most of the previous night being ill after a bout of dysentery and food poisoning which left him very badly dehydrated. He was out in the centre almost immediately because Les Favell was dismissed by Israr Ali and 'Harv' then made a brilliant 96 out of 151. He was back-cutting Fazal, pulling him and even dancing down the pitch to hit him over the top of the infield, no mean feat against a champion bowler who was about the same pace as Australia's

Michael Kasprowicz. Endeavouring to play the latter shot yet again to reach his century, he was bowled by the Pakistan captain but he had given a wonderful exhibition. He had also needed to go off the field half a dozen times for running repairs but had refused to contemplate not continuing his innings. He knew how important it was for Australia to gain a first-innings lead. Wally Grout, batting at nine, hadn't scored when Harvey was out at 151, he then smashed a stunning 66 while Ray Lindwall and Ian Meckiff stayed with him, making four and two respectively, and there were two sundries. Australia had a 25-run first-innings lead which was invaluable. It was time now to put into practice what we had planned for this situation, that Mackay, Davidson and I would make runs as scarce as gold nuggets for Pakistan.

The bulk of the bowling was to be done by 'Slasher' and me, depending of course on circumstances, possibly the Pakistan batsmen deciding on all-out attack, as they had seen from Harvey and Grout, although somehow that didn't seem likely. More likely was that they would try to grind us down, get a lead of around 200 and then try to bowl us out. From our point of view we wanted runs to be scarce. 'Spinner' Kline had done his job and, when we had entered the ground each morning, we could hear his cries of 'pull you bastards, pull' as the sweating ground staff pulled at the leather flaps and then drove the metal spikes into the turf alongside the pitch to ensure the matting was tight. The groundsman and his staff took great pride in what they were doing because it had been carefully explained to them that they were ensuring the surface would be good for both teams.

I bowled Hanif with the score at 32 but Pakistan had got away to the start they wanted. However, suddenly 'Slasher' bowled Ijaz Butt and Saeed Ahmed in the space of only five runs and we were in for the kill. I had four wickets at the end but our trump card, Ken Mackay, finished with 45–27–42–6 to give him ten wickets for the match. His bowling was a triumph in an astonishing victory the cricket world thought could never happen, but it was Neil Harvey's innings that set it up for us. In all the circumstances, it was one of the greatest innings ever played for Australia.

Bill Lawry

The start of the 1961 Australian tour of England produced one of the most desperate personal times I had known after I tore the fibres off the tendon in my right shoulder in the opening game at Worcester. In the end it turned out to be a great tour, but there were times when I wondered if I would be able to get back on to the field and bowl at all, and life seemed to be on a never-ending medical trail.

The match at Worcester was played in very cold weather. I then managed to play in the First Test at Edgbaston and, at one point, we looked as though we were in with a chance of winning until Ted Dexter gave us a fearful hammering in the second innings and my shoulder collapsed again.

As we came towards the Second Test at Lord's, it became apparent I had little chance of being fit to play as a bowler and there was no thought I would play merely as a batsman. Perhaps on my form as a batsman four years earlier in South Africa, where I had hit two Test centuries, it might have been a consideration, but my batting and place in the side had changed completely in those four years where, as captain, I had moved down the list so that Alan Davidson and I could bat either side of Ken Mackay. I wanted to make sure if 'Slasher' was in for a considerable time, runs could come quickly from the other end. It was therefore simply a case of get fit as quickly as possible, but don't think about playing at Lord's in the Second Test. This is the most disappointing thing that can happen to any captain of an Australian side; that he doesn't lead his team at the home of cricket but, after I'd had a net at the Nursery End the day prior to the Test, we announced that Neil Harvey would be captaining the team.

He had just led the side in a very exciting encounter against Kent at Canterbury, a game which was a perfect illustration of the way we had said we would play on this tour, with Neil twice declaring and setting Kent in their second innings a target of 291 to win from something like 60 overs. Colin Cowdrey, who was captaining England at this time, with Peter May in the team but returning from illness, had a wonderful match with the bat making 149 and 121, the first occasion any Australian team playing in England had a century scored against them in each innings of a game. The boys, when they returned to London, said he had been in magnificent form and Kent were only seven runs short when stumps were drawn.

A real problem for us was that Alan Davidson had been unable to bowl in the second innings because of an asthmatic attack and we certainly didn't need anything to go wrong there, with me out of the reckoning. There was a side issue we could have done without as well. There had been an article written in *The Sun* newspaper in Sydney, quoting me on my shoulder problems and with a big headline, 'I'll bowl till I drop.' The words naturally didn't appear in the text. Bradman phoned Syd Webb, our manager, to let him know about it and Syd came to me and said Don had told him he, Syd, was to take over all future public announcements, I was not to talk to the media, and that was what he was going to do, starting from that moment. I thought at the time it was a strange thing for Don to say because he could have rung me just as easily to ask what was going on. At any rate, Syd applied the 'gag' as it was known and it was first put into action on the Sunday of the game against Kent when, after having had treatment on my shoulder, I was driven down to Lord De L'Isle's home, Penshurst Castle, where the team were being entertained at an official function for the day.

The Australian journalists came to see me as my car pulled up and all wanted to know the latest news on my shoulder, was it improving, etc., and, to the first inquiry which was from Tom

Goodman, I said, 'I'm sorry, Tom, I'm not allowed to say anything to you, you'll have to ask Syd how my shoulder is.' It was the same answer to the other journalists and the next day there was an even bigger story in the Australian papers, 'Manager gags captain.' The cartoonists had a field day, so too the writers, but it only needed a few days of this furore back home before Syd came to me and said he felt that I'd been punished enough and we would now revert to the status quo where I made all the statements to do with the cricket and anything else I wanted and Syd stuck to the administration!

Bill Lawry had been in very good form in the Kent match, making a century in the first innings, and our only selection problem was whether or not 'Davo' would be fit on the morning of the match. Neil, Colin and I knew I wouldn't be playing and we had to decide which of the bowlers would take my place. We were very lucky to have Bob Simpson fit and in good recent form with scores of 76, 35*, 65 and 41 and he also was a very capable legspin bowler. With Lord's traditionally favouring pace bowling, we made the decision to bring in the young quick bowler Graham McKenzie for his Test debut. He was only 19, about to have his 20th birthday on the Saturday of this Test, and what a birthday he had.

Cowdrey won the toss and, watching nervously from the dressing-room, I saw Peter Burge at gully put down an absolute sitter off Davidson to give Geoff Pullar a life, Bill Lawry missed Ted Dexter at short-leg off Misson and then Misson also had Subba Row dropped by Wally Grout down the legside. All in the space of half an hour. I felt for Neil skippering the side and having this happen to him because our bowlers were all over the England batsmen, particularly Davidson who was getting a great deal of bounce from a good length when he was bowling from the Pavilion End. The day ended with everyone closely examining the pitch at that Nursery End and the general consensus was that there was something wrong with it, in that it didn't seem to be level. We lost Colin McDonald and Bob

Simpson before the close of play but Bill Lawry and Neil Harvey saw us through to the end. It was, though, a very tough pitch on which to bat.

The following day I watched one of the finest innings I have ever seen in difficult circumstances, Bill Lawry played it and, apart from being skilful, it was full of courage. Bill rather liked Lord's. Earlier in the tour, in the match against MCC, he had hit a brilliant century and was 84 not out when I declared on him in the second innings, having told the team I was going to set up the last afternoon as a run chase for the opposition, as we had promised before the tour began. The target I set cost Bill a century in each innings at Lord's but was described as 'daring' in *Wisden* and I told Walter Robins the previous evening that he shouldn't miss the afternoon because of what we were going to do. Walter refused to believe me and only arrived at Lord's when we had wrapped up the game by 63 runs with 34 minutes to spare. A man of little faith.

That though had been on a very good batting pitch. This Test pitch, when Lawry walked out on the second morning, was anything but a good strip. Lawry was magnificent. He was also black and blue by the time he came back to the dressing-room, having made his maiden Test century and batting six hours and ten minutes in all. When he went, at 238, he had made 130 and although over the years he played other splendid innings, for me there was nothing to match his first hundred at Lord's. Later in the series, in the Old Trafford Test, he made 74 and 102 and was instrumental in giving us a chance of victory in what was one of the most exciting games of cricket in which I ever played. By coincidence McKenzie who, on his debut at Lord's took 5/37 and made 34 priceless runs, also had a good match with the bat at Old Trafford, sharing a 98-run last-wicket stand with Alan Davidson which allowed us to set England 256 in three hours, fifty minutes.

There was still a final twist to the Lord's Test, with Australia needing only 69 to win, because suddenly we had lost our first four wickets for only 19. Tony Lock just failed to hold on to a difficult chance from Peter Burge off the last ball before lunch or it would have been 35/5. Neil sent 'Burgie' out after lunch with instructions to play his natural game, which was all aggression, and he finished with 37 not out, a small but heart-stopping innings.

Lawry made 2,019 runs on that 1961 tour and was the only player to pass the 2,000 mark, with the highlight of his career the maiden Test century at the home of cricket on a pitch which later was found to have a 'ridge' at the Nursery End. A team of experts announced, after examining this area, that there were several depressions in the surface. I would have thought this automatically meant there were also several 'hills' which would have had batsmen being hit so often and finishing bruised and in pain. That certainly applied to Lawry, but the great thing about him was that he wasn't beaten until he had fought through more than six hours of battering.

Greg Chappell

The season of 1972 in England was a watershed for Australian cricket. Bill Lawry had been sacked by the Australian selectors towards the end of the Australian season of 1970–71 when Ray Illingworth was in the process of regaining the Ashes for England. Ian Chappell had been handed the captaincy, the game in Sydney to end the series was a close-fought affair, but England won and took the kudos and the Ashes urn. The South Africans had been scheduled to tour Australia in 1971–72, but that tour was called off and, instead, a Rest of the World team played five unofficial Tests prior to the team being chosen to tour England in 1972. Australian cricket was going through interesting times and there were some good cricketers around though it was accepted that England would be hard to beat. What Australia did have was potentially the finest fast bowler in the world in Dennis Lillee, who had bowled well in the games against the Rest of the World, and an interesting swing bowler in Bob Massie who had the ability to swing the ball both ways, and late. John Gleeson, the unusual fingerspinner was there as well and Rodney Marsh, a fine wicket-keeper and hard-hitting batsman, was likely to be very valuable down the batting order. There was a feeling this might be the time the Australians would give a very good account of themselves and so it proved when Ian Chappell's side won the Second Test at Lord's and the final one at The Oval. England won the First at Old Trafford and the Fourth at Headingley on an appallingly-prepared surface, the Fusarium pitch, so the series was squared 2–2 with the Third Test at Trent Bridge drawn.

When Chappell's team arrived at Lord's they were already that one match down in the series, England having won the first encounter at Old Trafford by a comfortable 89 runs. That Australia got as close as they did was due to a brilliant innings of 91 from Rodney Marsh who came in to bat with Australia 120/6 in the second innings, needing 342 in all for victory. His 91 came from 130 added while he was at the crease, and he hit Norman Gifford for four mighty sixes after Illingworth had brought the slow bowler on to try to buy his wicket. This game, played on a pitch with a very green look about it, produced a fine battle between two top-class fast bowlers, John Snow of England and Dennis Lillee on his first Ashes tour. Each took eight wickets and, in their own individual styles, looked very impressive and exciting. Neither was done any favours at Old Trafford by the catching of the two teams. On four bitterly cold days in early June several catches were put down by both teams and all bowlers had cause to be aggrieved. The Australians at Old Trafford were without Bob Massie, which meant Lillee was partnered with the new ball by David Colley who was brisk medium pace and didn't mind testing the batsmen on their ability and willingness to play the short ball. Tony Greig made a half-century in each England innings, as did Keith Stackpole for

Australia, but basically it was a case of the ball being on top for most of the match and England's winning margin was a true reflection of the way that opening Test unfolded.

Two Australian players who weren't fit for the Old Trafford match were Ross Edwards and Bob Massie and, when I was off a commentary stint, I went to the railing just above the practice nets where these two were batting and bowling. When they'd arrived the bowling foothold, right-arm over-the-wicket, was too soggy to use, so Massie bowled around the wicket in the net. It was fascinating to watch and I made a mental note that if he were chosen at Lord's he might well cause the England batsmen many problems because, in this hour-long net session, he was beautifully accurate, swung the ball both ways very late from around the wicket and looked a high-class bowler. What was even better was that there seemed no discernible change in grip of the ball or arm action between outswinger and inswinger. One problem in the Australian camp was definitely in finding a proper opening batting partner for Keith Stackpole. In a selection that defied common sense, both Lawry and Redpath had been left behind by the selectors who preferred Bruce Francis, Graeme Watson and Ross Edwards to be used in the role.

In 1970 I had seen Greg Chappell hit a century on his Test match debut at the WACA ground in Perth and in England he had a splendid tour, with his experience of having played county cricket with Somerset doing him no harm at all. In the Second Test of this 1972 series he made a wonderful century and, although he made another at The Oval when Australia squared the series, the one at Lord's is the best I ever saw from him in his brilliant career. The match became known as 'Massie's Match' because of the eight wickets he took in each innings where his match figures were 60.1–16–137–16. It seems incredible even now, looking back 33 years on the whole thing. Certainly Massie was more difficult for the batsmen when he bowled around the wicket and had his inswingers angling towards first slip then coming back very sharply into the right-handers. The pitch was well grassed and the heavy atmosphere seemed to aid Massie in his swinging of the ball. After Massie and Lillee had taken all ten wickets between them, Australia lost their first two wickets for seven and Greg Chappell came out to join his brother Ian, who was batting aggressively but who was dismissed by a brilliant low, running catch at deep square-leg with the score only on 84. Greg batted for the rest of the day and there is no doubt he summed up the situation perfectly; that it was necessary for him to be there, if not at the end of the innings, then certainly close to it. It was an innings of technique and refusal to be disconcerted by the amount of movement of the ball either in the air or off the seam.

John Snow bowled superbly to him and Chappell was all elegance and fierce concentration in repelling him. Snow's first-innings bowling figures of 32 overs, 5/57, were a fair reflection of his skills and the fact that Australia gained a slender lead of 36 showed what a tough, tight game it was. Having reached his century just before stumps on the second day, Chappell batted for another hour and a half on the Saturday when the gates had been closed with more than 30,000 spectators in the ground. Rod Marsh did the job again with the bat for Australia, hitting a forceful half-century, and David Colley hit out well at the end of the innings and was last man out.

The value of Greg Chappell's innings, and his reading of the match, was shown by the fact that Lillee and Massie soon had five England batsmen back in the pavilion and that first-innings deficit hadn't been wiped out. One of the unlucky batsmen was Geoff Boycott who shouldered arms to Lillee only for the ball to hit his body, loop over his shoulder and drop on to the bails. Lillee bowled with great pace and aggression throughout the match and was of great assistance to Massie. Eleven days later Boycott suffered a badly fractured middle finger of his right hand when hit by a sharply-lifting delivery from Bob Willis in a Gillette Cup match. It was six years before Boycott and Lillee met again on a cricket field.

Greg Chappell was a wonderful stroke-player, an exciting batsman. The knock at Lord's wasn't one of his fastest because he had batted for three hours before he struck his first boundary. He then hit another 13 during his innings which was played specifically to ensure the Australians would not face a daunting task batting last in the game. At the time I thought it close to the most flawless innings I had seen and I still believe that to be the case. It was beautifully elegant with wonderfully executed strokes, great technique and it exhibited a deep knowledge of what was needed to square the series. All that added up to a memorable experience.

Steve Waugh

This was a freakish happening. I was able to watch one of the great innings of modern times, played in Jamaica, West Indies, simply because it rained for a week in the United Kingdom. A word of explanation. The Test match was between West Indies and Australia and West Indies had won the previous Test in Port-of-Spain by nine wickets, on a ridiculous pitch which could not be distinguished from the outfield. We watched the First Test in Barbados because I was there to deliver the Frank Worrell Memorial Address, which I did, but only after that opening Test had been completed in three days. A new boy on the block, Glenn McGrath, took eight wickets in that game and the reason he played such a prominent part was that Australia's two opening bowlers, Craig McDermott and Damien Fleming, were injured prior to the start of the series and took no part in the four matches. McGrath stepped up to the plate when Mark Taylor was devising and explaining the tactics he intended to employ; that it was basically to be a series where, with the Australians short of bowlers, the West Indian batsmen were to be denied run opportunities. They were, in bowling terms, to be strangled. Taylor's tactics throughout the series were impeccable and it was one of the best exhibitions of captaincy in Australian cricket history because of the success of regaining the Frank Worrell Trophy.

Although I have nominated Steve Waugh as one of the six batsmen of my group, it needs to be underlined that this was a series where poor pitches and dominance of ball over bat meant runs were hard to come by. More credit then that Waugh and his brother Mark were the only two batsmen to average 40 in the four-match series. Mark Taylor and Ian Healy were averaging 25 when the last ball was bowled and the bowlers themselves had a great time. One of the things that interested me at the time, after those two Australian pace bowlers were declared unfit for the series, was that Glenn McGrath, as legitimate a number eleven as there had ever been, said at the team meeting he intended to bounce the West Indian fast bowlers because he was certain they would do the same to the Australian tailenders. McGrath took 17 wickets in the four matches and Paul Reiffel, always an underrated bowler and cricketer, took 15, as did Shane Warne. This was the real start of McGrath's proper bowling career where he stood up and made a commitment to the team and challenged the West Indian pace bowlers. He has finished up as one of the greatest bowlers ever to represent Australia, one of the finest the cricket world has seen.

When we flew out of Barbados and into London and beyond on 27 April, 1995, the weather was good everywhere but in the United Kingdom. In immigration at Heathrow we were told it had been throwing it down for days and, when we arrived at our final destination and switched on the television, the weather men said it was still throwing it down and would continue to do so. However, as every sports event in the UK other than swimming and synchronised diving, one of the great spectator sports, had been cancelled because of completely waterlogged venues, we were informed we would be able to watch every ball for the five days of the West Indies v Australia Fourth Test match at Sabina Park, Jamaica. That could hardly have been better news!

It's not just because I work in television but this seemed something not to be missed. It turned out to be so. Mark Taylor, who had called many of the shots on the tour to date, only batted once in this match and Australia's first three batsmen made 52 between them after West Indies first innings had produced 265, with Richie Richardson making a level 100 before Reiffel had him lbw. West Indies lost 7/77 but, to fall back on that, they always had the thoughts of Andy Roberts who, a trifle disdainfully, had once said, 'No matter for how few they bowl out our batsmen, we'll bowl them out for less.' That was the way Courtney Walsh and Curtly Ambrose began as well, Mark Taylor, Michael Slater and David Boon being back in the pavilion very quickly. It was a battle to get through to stumps for Steve and Mark Waugh but they were unbeaten, if not unbruised, at the close of play. When he was 42 Steve gave an unaccepted chance to Courtney Browne, the wicket-keeper, but that apart he played in typical Steve Waugh fashion, nose on the pitch, refusing to be unsettled by the short-pitched bowling which umpires Liebenberg and Bucknor seemed not to notice in the centre of the ground. He played his trademark drives and strokes through the offside and mid-wicket with great skill. The key to Australia's success lay in the fact that the brothers, together at lunchtime, then got through to the tea interval with courage and a wonderful appreciation of the right ball to hit. Although they were hit many times they didn't play too many false strokes and it was possible to sense the West Indians wilting in the field, with Steve and Mark taking seven an over off them in the hour after the luncheon interval. They then stayed together until late on the second evening when Mark was caught off Carl Hooper. From where we were watching this was regarded as a sadness because of the high levels of skill attached to the partnership with both players realising that, weather permitting, there was a real chance of regaining the Worrell Trophy after an absence of 17 years. It was a combination of skill, courage and clear-minded appreciation of how to go about their batting, with victory the ultimate goal.

Mark Waugh's dismissal, not far short of the close of play on the second evening, meant Australia had a lead of only 56, but they had six wickets in hand. This was by no means a really comfortable position and it needed Greg Blewett, unbeaten on six at stumps, to step up now and stay with Steve. He had made a century on Test debut but he never played a greater innings than at Kingston in this nerve-wracking situation. He made 69 out of the 113-run partnership, and it was an outstanding contribution.

One of the things about making a choice of outstanding innings is that you can find yourself caught up in having to make a selection from several innings the same individuals have played over the years. Such was the case with Steve Waugh, as well as the others, Bradman, Harvey, Lawry, Chappell and Gilchrist. My problem with Waugh was that I have always had at the top of the list the two centuries he made against England at Old Trafford in 1997, after Mark Taylor had made a great decision to bat on an initially awkward pitch. That captaincy decision was so that Warne could bowl at England in the fourth innings and it needed the batsmen to do the right thing. Steve Waugh did just that by hitting a hundred in each Australian innings, two of the great knocks I have ever seen.

The circumstances of the Kingston effort though were such that I opted for it as being one of the best single performances I have seen, Steve batting for more than ten hours and withstanding early spells of great fast bowling, then dominating with both bat and mind. It seemed to me that only Courtney Walsh stood up to Steve Waugh and when the Australians were finally dismissed, with Waugh last man out for 200, it left the West Indians something like an hour to bat on the third evening. They didn't enjoy it at all. Once again Paul Reiffel lifted his bowling and knocked over Stuart

Williams, Richie Richardson and Brian Lara and that basically was the end of it with showers restricted to the rest day on 2 May. It was a wonderful win by a team originally deprived of their leading pace bowlers, a great team effort with outstanding captaincy from Taylor and an innings that will always be at the forefront of my memory of television watching.

When Kenny Benjamin was last man out at 213, and Australia had won by an innings and 53 runs, Daphne and I raised a glass *to the win*. When Steve Waugh was named Player of the Match we raised another, *to Steve*. You might think that's a lot of glasses but there was still one to go. Richie Richardson, the West Indian captain, in the speech he made when handing over the Frank Worrell Trophy after its 17-year absence, said, long-faced, that this was the weakest Australian side he had ever played against. The third glass raised was *to grace in losing*.

Adam Gilchrist

Generally cricket is a team game, though there are some individual performances without which anyone's team game could be secondary. Sometimes it might be a partnership which goes some way towards winning a match, sometimes a stand-out batting performance or a bowling spell that turns a game. The circumstances in Hobart on 21 and 22 November, 1999 were that the Australians were just about gone and forgotten, even though they had a lead of 24 on the first innings. Justin Langer, batting at number three, had made 59 very hard-earned runs but the Australians lost their last eight wickets for only 40, at a stage where they seemed likely to take a sizeable lead into the latter part of the match. Offspinner Saqlain Mushtaq did the damage, taking 6/46 in 24 very accurate overs, 6/17 in his last eight overs. Two of them had been Langer and Gilchrist, the latter not picking Saqlain's 'doosra' and being stumped by Moin Khan. Then Inzamam played a blinder with the bat, putting on 134 with Ijaz at four an over to give Pakistan a decided advantage by the close of play on the third evening, Inzamam still there on 116 not out. With Shane Warne bowling and Inzamam cutting fiercely and getting a top edge, Mark Waugh removed him first thing on the fourth morning with one of the greatest catches I've seen at slip. The ball was past Waugh when he grabbed it. Pakistan's lower order wagged well enough that, with one day to go, Australia still needed 181 to win, their eventual heroes, Langer and Gilchrist, having already added 62. Langer was 52 and Gilchrist 45.

It was a tough ask. The Pakistan bowlers would be back fresh on the final morning; in Australia's favour was the fact that the pitch was still good and that Saqlain was gaining less turn from the surface than had been the case when he ripped through Australia's first innings. Very much in the Australians' favour, if such can be said about a fifth-day run chase, was that Gilchrist had batted with his usual freedom the previous evening, scoring his unbeaten 45 out of the 62 the pair had already put on. Gilchrist is such an extraordinary cricketer that almost nothing is beyond him and his counter-attacking with the bat often has turned matches which seemed to be going the way of the opposition.

Fast forward for a moment to the New Year Test match at the SCG in 2005. Australia had already won the series but Pakistan fought back on the first day with a first-innings score of 304 that enthused spectators, and then Ricky Ponting hit a brilliant 207. Incredibly, he was third out with the score at 257, and Michael Clarke went at 318 to bring Gilchrist to the crease. He was greeted with a standing ovation, and that was only walking on to the ground rather than off it. He made 106 at just about a run a ball and provided the most wonderful entertainment for the spectators at the ground and a worldwide television audience in the vicinity of half a billion people. His innings featured some of the cleanest striking of the cricket ball I have ever seen and some of the most memorable strokes. I didn't choose that as my innings, even though it was on a pitch with the ball playing uneven heights and providing an enormous amount of turn for the spinners.

The SCG match turned out to be wonderfully entertaining and Gilchrist played a big part in what was on show but, with the series already in Australia's hands at 2–0, it was a game for pride more than anything else. However, had Gilchrist been dismissed, Pakistan could have made life very difficult for the Australians.

I decided I should stay with Gilchrist's Hobart innings which gave me the idea for this chapter, one where he dominated a situation where it looked for all the world as though Australia would be beaten, and he did it with what was certainly the cleanest hitting I had seen up to that day. The scene then on the last morning in Hobart was Wasim Akram setting his field, strangely a field that veered more towards the defensive than all-out attack. Perhaps he had been troubled through the night by visions of the manner in which Gilchrist had taken matches away from opposition teams over the past year and also the innings he had played against Wasim's team at the 'Gabba only two weeks earlier; this was Gilchrist's Test match debut.

It is never easy to supplant a local hero and that day in Brisbane, making his debut in Ian Healy's home town, would have been more tense than usual for Gilchrist. He didn't show it. When he came out to bat Australia were still 25 behind Pakistan's first-innings 367, had only five wickets in hand and Gilchrist slaughtered them, belting 80 out of the partnership with Mark Waugh, the latter going on to make a century.

I'd be surprised if this wasn't weighing very heavily on Wasim's mind when he was setting his fields for Langer and Gilchrist at Bellerive Oval; certainly they were more attacking for Langer. It made no difference. The pair both played their strokes, Langer was very good square of the wicket on the offside and Gilchrist simply blitzed them with wonderful strokes all around the ground. In all

Langer batted more than seven hours for his 127 and was dismissed only five short of the victory figure of 369. Gilchrist hit his 149* from only 163 balls, an astonishing rate of scoring considering the position of the match and the pressure that would suddenly have been brought about by the loss of another wicket. My most vivid memories of the last day are of Gilchrist hitting all the bowlers into the boundary on the offside, they were some of the best shots imaginable and the whole time his partner, Justin Langer, was exhorting him to greater things. Gilchrist hit only one six and 13 fours, which is a low ratio for some of his innings, but each time he found the boundary he made certain he also caught the eye of the bowler who was standing in mid-pitch glaring at him. Gilchrist couldn't have done it without Langer who did a remarkable job of keeping the pair of them focused on the task in hand, but that is the case with so many great partnerships in Test cricket around the world. Closer to the mark is that Australia couldn't have done it without Gilchrist who played a memorable hand.

15
AUSTRALIAN HALL OF FAME

THE Melbourne Cricket Club has always been the pre-eminent cricket club in Australia. It staged the first tour by an English cricket team in 1861–62, then the match in 1877 between a combined Melbourne and Sydney team and James Lillywhite's touring team. This game later was to be listed as the first Test match to be played between England and Australia. The club led the way in organising tours to England and receiving teams from England. It may not always have been popular north of the border around Sydney town, but there never was the slightest doubt the Melbourne Club was the leader.

On 6 December, 1996, the Melbourne Cricket Club launched the Australian Cricketers' Hall of Fame and, in my view, it is one of the best of its kind anywhere in the world. There are lots of Halls of Fame the world over, some for major sports, some for minor ones, some with hundreds of people listed as 'Famers', but the one in Melbourne has a touch of exclusivity about it. It has been in existence nine years now and there are 23 members. There have been a considerable number of cricketers who have played for Australia and that is the first of the requirements for election. In that sense it is different from some other Halls of Fame where a sport might be played inside a country, rather than internationally.

With eleven to a cricket team, it came as something of a surprise when the first intake was only ten, but the reason given was that if it had been eleven nominations it may have been assumed that it was being classed as the best team ever to play for Australia. As it was, the Melbourne Cricket Club lined up an outstanding group of ten cricketers to start the honour roll.

Jack Blackham	(Victoria)
Fred Spofforth	(New South Wales)
Victor Trumper	(New South Wales)
Bill Ponsford	(Victoria)
Clarrie Grimmett	(Victoria and South Australia)
Don Bradman	(New South Wales and South Australia)
Bill O'Reilly	(New South Wales)
Keith Miller	(Victoria and New South Wales)
Ray Lindwall	(New South Wales and Queensland)
Dennis Lillee	(Western Australia and Tasmania)

Spofforth and Blackham were in the Australian team when, in 1882 at The Oval, they beat England for the first time in England. Ponsford and Bradman were the two batsmen who dominated bowlers in the late 1920s and early 1930s, with Bradman going on until his retirement after the Invincibles tour of England in 1948. Miller was Australia's greatest allrounder and, with Lindwall, formed the most feared Australian pace bowling attack since Jack Gregory and Ted McDonald in the 1920s.

Lillee was the greatest fast bowler of the modern era in Australia, may well have been the greatest ever. O'Reilly and Grimmett carried the Australian bowling attack in the 1920s and 1930s. Each in his own style was a magnificent bowler and Trumper is the one batsman who is spoken of in the same breath as Bradman. It was a good start for the Hall of Fame.

Fred Spofforth, in that 1882 match at The Oval, was the player who, when all the odds seemed to be against Australia winning, exhorted the rest of the team, including Billy Murdoch the captain, calling out: 'This thing can be done . . .' Spofforth was the bowler England feared most. He was the leading bowler in the Australian side and, with his moustache and sideburns, looked someone to be feared by any batsman at the other end of the pitch.

When he uttered his famous rallying cry in the dressing-room there was no doubt the Australians were facing a tough task. Australia had made only 63 in their first innings, Jack Blackham top-scoring with 17, and all the batsmen were in trouble against England's bowlers on the pitch softened by rain. There had been heavy falls the night before the match began and conditions were difficult for batting almost all the way through the two days. When England batted Spofforth bowled Dr Grace for 4 and took 7/46, a magnificent performance, but England still gained a lead of 38 priceless runs. It was then the Australians had a lucky break as there was more heavy rain overnight, and then again just prior to the start of play which was delayed until ten minutes past mid-day. Now, instead of the ball biting into the surface, it skidded off. Hugh Massie, the big-hitting right-hander, again went in with 'Alick' Bannerman, smashed 55 of their 66-run partnership and was actually first out. It gave Australia a chance, even though their second innings had been restricted to 122, but England needed only 85 to win.

When they were 51/2 it seemed all over but then George Ulyett and Grace were dismissed with only two more runs added, and the game took on a new dimension with Spofforth and Boyle bowling 12 successive maidens. The last eight wickets fell for 26 and Spofforth bowled from start to finish, other than once to change from the Northern End to the Pavilion End. The sensational finish to the game gave Spofforth match figures of 64.3 overs (four-ball overs in those days), 33 maidens, 14 wickets for 90, and 'this thing' had certainly been done, and with style.

Bill Ponsford was the first great run-getter of the Australian cricket world and it was said of him by bowlers that he always seemed to be using a bat wider than anyone else in the game. Until Bradman came on the scene it seemed Ponsford would be the champion and the two of them shared some great partnerships until Ponsford retired from the game after the Fifth Test at The Oval in 1934. In that match he and Bradman each made a double-century. Dennis Lillee came on to the Australian cricket scene in the late 1960s, making his debut in late 1969 for the Western Australian Sheffield Shield team. The following year he made his Test debut against Ray Illingworth's England touring team and, from that moment, it was clear he was something out of the ordinary and not just from the point of view of skill, but courage as well. He had to overcome potentially crippling back injuries after only a couple of years in the Test arena, but he still had a magnificent career.

Clarrie Grimmett took six wickets against New South Wales in the first Sheffield Shield game I watched. It was played at the SCG and Grimmett and O'Reilly were in opposing teams, South Australia and NSW respectively. They were the greatest legspinners of their time, only surpassed in the modern era by Shane Warne who is the best I have ever seen.

In that game in 1940 NSW were bowled out for 270 on the first day where my father and I sat on the steps towards the back of the old Sheridan Stand, which is now the Clive Churchill Stand. We were part of a crowd of 30,400 spectators. At the close of play South Australia were 54/2 with Bradman 24 and R.S. 'Dick' Whitington 23. I can still see Barnes and Chipperfield stranded and off balance lbw to Grimmett's 'flipper', but naturally enough at that time I didn't know anything about the type of ball, only that they were dismissed.

Only one batsman has ever really been compared with Don Bradman and there is no doubt Trumper, like Bradman, was a batting genius. Tragically he died in 1915, aged 37, of Bright's disease, a severe inflammation of the kidneys, incurable in those days. He was mourned by cricket followers throughout Australia and England. The funeral director was Hanson Carter, the Australian wicket-keeper, and huge crowds lined the streets as the cortège made its way from Chatswood on the north shore of Sydney to Waverley on the east coast. Bradman was a hero in the Depression and beyond and filled cricket grounds in England and Australia; he made more runs faster and better than any other batsman and he slaughtered the opposition bowlers. Trumper was a stylist and a player of such skill in the golden age of Australian batting that spectators constantly marvelled at his ability.

Once that initial list had been announced, a Hall of Fame selection panel was nominated and various criteria listed to suggest to the panel the manner in which future nominees should be chosen. The criteria points were not mandatory by any means. For example, Spofforth only played 18 Test matches for Australia, but this was simply because not many Tests were played in the time he was in the game at international level.

This was the initial criteria list and it remains so today, but it is still a guideline. The selection committee needs to use their common sense, which is the way selection committees should always work.

Hall of Fame selection committee criteria:
- Minimum 20 Tests
- Minimum 1,000 Test runs
- Minimum 75 Test wickets
- Played in at least one country other than Australia

Additional matters to consider:
- Should be five years out of the international game
- Apart from statistics, an emphasis on legend status
- A significant and beneficial impact on the way the game is played
- Initially to be limited to players, rather than administrators or umpires

There have been some changes to the selection committee since 1996 but, at the time of writing, the style of committee and the participants are as follows:

Melbourne Cricket Club President or nominee	Bob Lloyd
Melbourne Cricket Club GM or nominee	Peter French
Cricket Australia CEO or nominee	James Sutherland
Former Australian captain	Richie Benaud
Australian Cricketers' Association representative	Tim May
Media representative, television	Bill Lawry
Media representative, writer	Gideon Haigh
Media representative, print	Mike Coward
Media representative, radio	Tim Lane

The Hall of Fame is permanently based at the Melbourne Cricket Club, as it should be, and I know through working with that committee it is a very strong and conscientious group. Our meetings are never short, but always thorough.

Since the original ten-strong list was published, there have been 13 added, and those after a considerable amount of discussion.

2000:

Warwick Armstrong	(Victoria)
Neil Harvey	(Victoria and New South Wales)
Allan Border	(New South Wales and Queensland)

2001:

Bill Woodfull	(Victoria)
Arthur Morris	(New South Wales)

2002:

Stan McCabe	(New South Wales)
Greg Chappell	(South Australia and Queensland)

2003:

Lindsay Hassett	(Victoria)
Ian Chappell	(South Australia)

2004:

Alan Davidson	(New South Wales)
Hugh Trumble	(Victoria)

2005:

| Clem Hill | (South Australia) |
| Rodney Marsh | (Western Australia) |

The first intake, after the original ten were unveiled, was very difficult because of the wide variety of names available and the quality of those under consideration. Warwick Armstrong was one of the most dominating personalities in the history of Australian cricket, English cricket too for that matter. He was often at odds with administrators in Australia and was never averse to letting his feelings be known about those who were running the game. Armstrong declined to tour England in 1912 when he was one of the 'Big Six' in dispute with the Board of Control. He was captain of the Australian team which beat England in Australia in 1920–21 and then again in the 1921 English summer, and his team is widely regarded as having spanned one of the finest four eras in the history of Australian cricket. The two left-hand batsmen who were alongside Armstrong in that first intake, Neil Harvey and Allan Border, were contrasting in style and method. Harvey, part of a family of cricketers, was a gifted player whose footwork against slow bowling was matched only by Arthur Morris in the time I have watched the game, though one should instantly note that I only saw Bradman from over the boundary fence in the two and a half years he played after the end of the Second War. Border was more a gritty batsman and came into the Australian side at a time when the West Indian fast-bowling juggernaut was in full cry in the period 1980–1993. He played some of the greatest back-to-the-wall innings ever seen in Australian cricket, constantly refusing to give up.

In England in 1981 he was an example to the rest of the team with his courageous batting and, in the West Indies in 1984 at Port-of-Spain, he made 98* and 100* to save a Test match for Australia, with the second-innings score at 299/9 and number eleven, Terry Alderman, also unbeaten on 21. In 1989 in England, Border as captain regained the Ashes and they have remained in Australia's hands since then.

Bill Woodfull and Arthur Morris were opening batsmen but there the similarity ends. Woodfull, a right-hander, became captain of the Australian team to England in 1930, following the controversial omission of Jack Ryder (it is said Jack refrained from further conversation with Dick Jones, one of the selectors, from the moment the team was announced), and Woodfull remained one of the most respected people in the game of cricket, having gone through the Bodyline tour of Australia as skipper. He was a tough, courageous batsman, said to be a sound tactician, and his careful choice of words to Sir Pelham Warner in the Adelaide dressing-room during that Bodyline Test has gone down in cricket history. Arthur Morris was the first cricketer in the history of the game to make a century in each innings of a first-class debut, and he became one of Australia's greatest cricketers in the post-war period and was a leading member of the Invincibles 1948 tour of England.

Stan McCabe and Greg Chappell were classic stylists with the bat, each a right-hander and a gifted stroke-player, at the same time possessing a beautiful defensive technique. McCabe was one of the inspired selections in 1930 to go to England under Woodfull's captaincy once the selectors had decided the 'old guard' of Australian cricket were on borrowed time. He had his 20th birthday on the tour. Bradman turned 22 during the tour and it was his prodigious scoring that sowed the seeds of Bodyline in the minds of the English cricket hierarchy. McCabe hadn't hit a first-class century at the time of his inclusion in the touring team, nor did he hit a Test century on that tour. At Sheffield Shield level in 1929–30, when the selectors were making their choices for the batting line-up for the tour of England, McCabe, in a short season, made six scores between 60 and 81 and that was enough for the selectors. Eventually his first Test century was played in the opening Test of the Bodyline series in Sydney. He scored 187* and it was said to be the greatest exhibition of hooking ever seen on the ground. Mind you, the England bowlers gave him every opportunity to practise the stroke.

Three of his innings are still talked about with the passage of more than 70 years, the Bodyline classic, also the game against South Africa at Johannesburg in 1935–36 when his 189 not out was played with such graceful attacking flair that Herbie Wade, the South African captain, appealed against the light because his fieldsmen were in danger as the ball flashed past them to all parts of the field. The umpires agreed with Wade and said there was a definite danger in the fading light. Then McCabe made 232 and was last man out at Trent Bridge in 1938 after England had declared their first innings closed at 658/8. The Australian batting had moved carefully to 134/2 when McCabe decided the only way to get out of the match with a draw was to launch an all-out attack. He did this with such success that Bradman called his players from the dressing-room to sit on the balcony to watch, with the words: *'You will never see the like of this again.'*

McCabe hit 232 out of the next 277 runs and, as well, shared a partnership of 77 with 'Chuck' Fleetwood-Smith while 'Chuck' made five. It was said by Bradman later to have been one of the greatest innings ever played by an Australian cricketer. He made six centuries at Test level and 13 fifties, averaging 48 per innings and thrilling the paying spectators with his attacking batting and flair for the game.

Greg Chappell was another youngster blooded by the Australian selectors, this time though in a Test match in Australia in the 1970–71 season when Ray Illingworth brought his team to Australia. Greg made 108 on his debut in the Perth Test, at a time when the Australians were in trouble, and he went on to hit another 23 centuries and 31 half-centuries in an illustrious career. Add 122 catches to that, plus 47 wickets, and his worth to Australian cricket can be easily recognised. When he played against Pakistan in

Sydney in his final Test before retirement, he passed Sir Donald Bradman's Australian Test aggregate record, a great effort even though others have since gone past his mark of 7,110. He has been headed by Allan Border 11,174; Steve Waugh 10,927; Mark Taylor 7,525; and David Boon 7,422. Chappell's batting average of 53.30 is headed only by Bradman of the players in retirement, although, of the current Australian batsmen, Matthew Hayden and Adam Gilchrist will accept the challenge and will give it a shake!

Lindsay Hassett was one of the great characters of Australian cricket, a man with an impish sense of humour who inherited the captaincy from Bradman after the latter retired following the 1948 tour of England. Lindsay was in the 1938 team to tour England and was always one of the finest attacking batsmen in the game, an attribute he reluctantly amended during the Australia v England series in 1950–51 in Australia and then when Australia toured England in 1953. The reason for that was the occasional batting collapse suffered by his players, more so on the 1953 tour where the selectors had given him a young team, inexperienced in batting on uncovered English pitches. Hassett finished up opening the batting on that tour, going in first with Arthur Morris, more was the pity because his twinkling footwork to the spinners and excellent positioning against the faster bowlers should never have been compromised. In Sheffield Shield cricket, quiet character though he was, he was feisty enough in the traditional NSW v Victoria clashes, which sometimes were played with the intensity of a Test match. In Test cricket Hassett had one of the best captaincy records in the game, something that is often overlooked because, in a sense, he was overshadowed by Bradman's retirement.

Hassett's co-inductee in 2003 was Ian Chappell, one of Australia's finest captains and the player who brought Australia back from a losing situation, first of all to draw a series against England in 1972, and then lead Australia to victory in 1974–75 in Australia and 1975 in England. In between times he had victories against Pakistan in Australia and West Indies in the Caribbean, the latter series highlighted by an astonishing 44-run win against the odds in Port-of-Spain in the Third Test to take a 1–0 lead in the series. This was compounded by an equally brilliant victory in Georgetown in the following Test, more so because Chappell had been without the services of Dennis Lillee in the series after the latter suffered stress fractures to his back.

Hugh Trumble has always been seen as one of the great figures of Australian cricket, a tall, sparely-built allrounder, who was the first man to take two hat-tricks in an innings, a feat he managed against England in successive Test series in Australia in 1901–02 and 1903–04. He was a highly-respected administrator as well once he retired from international cricket and became the secretary of the Melbourne Cricket Club, an important job in the cricket world. Alongside his name in the induction ceremony was Alan Davidson, one of the finest allrounders Australian cricket has ever produced, a left-arm pace bowler, hard-hitting batsman and one of the best fieldsmen ever to walk on to a cricket ground. I was delighted to see Alan on the stage at Crown Towers in Melbourne to accept his induction into the Hall of Fame. We toured together under Lindsay Hassett's captaincy in 1953 and then toured West Indies, South Africa and England on two more occasions and played Test series in Australia. He was a wonderful cricketer. On the international scene he won matches for Australia, saved some as well and, as a Sheffield Shield player with NSW, he was outstanding. Nothing on the Test scene was better than his bowling in the Lord's Test of 1961, when Neil Harvey captained the Australian side, and then, in the Old Trafford match, the fourth of the series, he dominated a last-wicket stand with Graham McKenzie, at a time when England all but had the game in their grasp. He hit David Allen out of the attack and he and McKenzie put on 98 to give the bowlers something at which to aim on the last afternoon of the match. 'Davo' was a great swing bowler. He had superb control of the ball, not unlike Glenn McGrath of modern-day bowlers, though Alan was slightly sharper in pace and he had an advantage against right-handers in that he was also able to slant the ball away towards the slips.

There was a time when Clem Hill held the record for the greatest number of 90s made in Test cricket, six of them in fact, but that has been superseded by some of the modern Australian players, Steve Waugh (10) and Michael Slater (9). Ricky Ponting already has five scores in the nineties and has room for more as his career has quite a time to go. When Hill started in international cricket for Australia it seemed as though he might have a very short career because he failed to reach 20 in his first seven knocks. Then he made 96 and became one of Australia's best batsmen of the early days, his career spanning a period from 1896 through to 1911 and on all types of pitches he averaged 44 an innings. He was regarded as Australia's most dependable batsman and was highly regarded by opposing bowlers of both pace and spin variety.

When Rodney Marsh first played for Australia in 1970–71 against England at the 'Gabba, it was an inauspicious beginning with not everything hitting the middle of his wicket-keeping gloves. 'Iron Gloves' was the name given him by some less than charitable English journalists on tour with the England team. By the time he had finished his Test career, in the same match where Greg Chappell and Dennis Lillee retired, he had shown the cricket world how good he was. Ninety-six Test matches produced 3,633 runs, including three centuries and sixteen fifties, and he had 355 victims behind the stumps.

Marsh was the first Australian wicket-keeper to score a Test century; that was in the opening Test match against Pakistan at the Adelaide Oval in the 1972–73 season. That was two years after the Australian innings had been declared at the MCG when he was 92 not out. His most important innings though was the 110* at the

MCG in the Centenary Test match in 1977, a performance which gave Australia the opportunity to win the game by 45 runs. He was a genuine allrounder and a fine team man; certainly a very strong character and one who, over a 13-year period, did wonderful things for Australian cricket.

16

THE ENTERTAINERS – WEST INDIES

I T'S a fairytale gone wrong. I made my Test match debut against the West Indies at the Sydney Cricket Ground in January 1952. It was an exciting match, as were many others I played against the Caribbean team. There were many to follow, featuring brilliant batting and bowling but, at the time of writing, early in 2005, West Indies cricket is in a slump. I hope that by the time of publication they are out of that slump as a preface to staging a proper and successful 2007 World Cup because there is no doubt world cricket needs a strong West Indies. World cricket also needs a strong England and that's another fairytale which has slipped a cog or two since England retained the Ashes in Australia in 1986–87 under strong leadership from Mike Gatting. The little urn might remain under close guard in England, but eight Test series played since that Gatting tour have produced more gloom than exhilaration in the shires of the United Kingdom. The just completed 2005 Ashes battle in England was rightly regarded in both countries as being a critical series.

West Indies are a different proposition. Australia and West Indies play for the Frank Worrell Trophy which was first presented to Australia at the conclusion of the Tied Test series in 1960–61. To Australians it remains a prize to be treasured and played for with every fibre of one's sporting body. I have always imagined the administrators of both countries would consider that to be the case, so it was a very nasty surprise for me when West Indies administrators announced to their Australian counterparts that they wanted to play only two matches in a series in Australia in 2004. No one was prepared to say exactly why this was so, but it seemed the West Indies Board had simply received a better offer from somewhere else. When Cricket Australia gently suggested they would prefer not to be a part of downgrading a famous contest in this fashion, and they would invite the West Indies team for Tests another year, the West Indies Board sent their team for the triangular one-day series, which included Pakistan as the third team. It seemed an odd situation, coming as it did at a time where the West Indian Players' Association and the WI Board were in acrimonious negotiations as regards player payments and a change in sponsorship of cricket in the Caribbean. This disagreement was all to do with the 2007 World Cup and the one thing administrators in cricket, and other sports for that matter, need to remember is that you can't sell what you don't own. And that means cricketers, as well as other things in life. This dispute was because administrators wanted control of the players' ability to negotiate their own financial lives.

The best thing about West Indian cricket is that there is room for improvement, though little of that was evident in the manner in which the team went down in a heap against South Africa in the April 2005 series in the Caribbean. In the heady days of the 1980s they were close to unbeatable, certainly unbeatable as regards Test series; now they are lurching from one problem to another. From 1930–31 the first four Test series played between Australia and the West Indies all went Australia's way. The first Test between the two countries was played in Adelaide when I was a month old, and there was little more publicity about the West Indian team until they went to England in 1950 and won the four-Test match series 3–1. When I was aged six in Jugiong, bowling a tennis ball against the concrete wall of the storeroom and hitting it when it bounced back, I was certainly not playing Australia against the West Indies Test matches. It was always Australia v England and Australia often won.

he Reunion (*above*) is the first photograph with some of the surviving members of the Tied
est match at the 'Gabba in 1960. The reason for it is the historic moment depicted in the
hotograph below. Joe Solomon has just hit the stumps with his throw to run out Ian
1eckiff. Frank Worrell, the West Indian captain, is in a perfect position to take the throw had
  gone to the bowler's end.

I was there when Glenn McGrath began his Test match bowling on 12 November 1993 against New Zealand at the WACA ground in Perth. Twelve years later, at the beginning of the recent Ashes battle, he needed just one wicket to reach the 500 mark. He has been a model fast bowler over the whole of that time and has improved his batting to the extent of making a Test match half-century. Possibly, by a minute margin, the bowling figures gave him most pleasure.

On 4 June 1993, Shane Warne bowled his first ball in a Test match in England, from what was then the Warwick Road End at Old Trafford. It drifted from middle and off to outside Mike Gatting's leg stump, spun about fourteen inches and clipped the top of his off-bail. In the print media it was described as 'the ball from hell'. For old legspinners, it was far more 'the ball from heaven'. Warne's portrait now hangs in the Long Room at Lords.

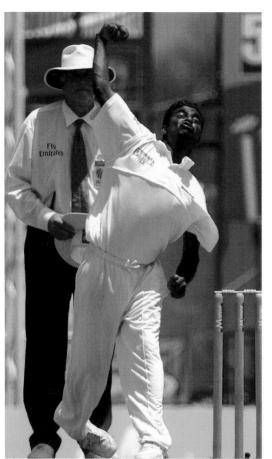

Left: Bowling has always been a fascinating part of cricket because of the new-style deliveries that are introduced. For pace bowlers, orthodox swing and then reverse swing. For slower bowlers, the Iverson style, for legspinners the leg-break and then the 'bosie', the flipper, which comes from underneath the hand, the slider from between the second and third fingers, but still looking like a leg-break. One of the more recent innovations from offspin bowlers has been named the 'doosra'. It looks like an off-break, but turns from leg to off. Muttiah Muralitharan (*left*) didn't invent it, but he and Harbhajan Singh of India pose enormous problems for the batsmen when they use it. In November 1999 at Bellerive Oval, Hobart, I saw Australia lose 9 for 55 in their first innings, with offspinner Saqlain Mushtaq taking 6/46 from 24 overs and no Australian batsman knew which way he was going.

Below: Sachin Tendulkar is one of the great batsmen the cricket world has known. This cover-drive to the boundary at Eden Gardens, Calcutta, in 2004 is close to perfect.

Mark Taylor (*above left*) was one of the finest captains I have watched and he left a good legacy for those like Ricky Ponting (*above right*) who followed him in the job. Neither had trouble with the short ball, for the most part feasting on it with the powerful pull-shot, as shown here.

One of England's outstanding batsmen over the past 20 years is Michael Vaughan. He is a fine stroke-player and made over 600 runs in the series against Australia, in Australia in 2002–03.

Before the 2005 Ashes series in England, Andrew Flintoff (*opposite*) and Michael Clarke (*above*) had never met in a Test match. They are the face of cricket of the future in both countries, with Flintoff the finest all-round cricketer England has produced since Ian Botham hung up his boots. Clarke is the most exciting youngster to represent Australia since Ricky Ponting came on the scene.

For me, two delightful and relaxing photographs. The first, a good quality white wine for Daphne and me to celebrate the conclusion of the 42nd season of commentating and writing in the United Kingdom. The second, Rene Benaud on her 100th birthday, a remarkable lady whose sound advice when we were young was 'Always do your best and never give up. And … don't take yourselves too seriously.'

When the 1975–76 Tests between Australia and West Indies concluded, with Australia winning 5–1, there had been only eight Test series between the two countries. Then suddenly there were another eight in 15 years, with West Indies not beaten by Australia in that time although the three-match series in 1981–82 was drawn 1–1. West Indies' greatest period of dominance started when Clive Lloyd went home after that 5–1 drubbing in Australia, determined he would build up a fast bowling attack to equal the one which had just caused him such anguish. Lance Gibbs had retired from Test cricket after he became the world's leading wicket-taker in the final Test of that 1975–76 series, so Lloyd had the additional problem of trying to find another spinner to replace him. In the end he didn't need to bother. The Australians in the 1975–76 series had been able to call on a bowling attack chosen from Dennis Lillee, Jeff Thomson, Gary Gilmour, Max Walker, Ashley Mallett and Terry Jenner. Waiting in the wings were Len Pascoe, Terry Alderman, Geoff Dymock, Alan Hurst, Wayne Prior and Mick Malone. West Indies had two youngsters, Andy Roberts and Michael Holding, also Keith Boyce and Vanburn Holder. Lloyd worked hard on the problem and within a couple of years the West Indian attack had Roberts and Holding, plus Colin Croft and Joel Garner, Malcolm Marshall plus Sylvester Clarke, Patrick Patterson and Norbert Phillip; Viv Richards was often used as the only spin bowler. It worked a treat though there were times when the over-rates were on the slow side of turgid. Not so the strike-rates and West Indies moved into a period of dominance in the world of Test cricket and one-dayers as well. The West Indies established a record with 11 consecutive victories, later beaten by Steve Waugh's team from 1999–2001 when they had 16 wins on the trot.

West Indies were a formidable combination and all the pace bowlers, in their individual styles, were outstanding. The one who always caught my eye, as well as the attention of the batsman taking strike in the centre, was Michael Holding. He was a former champion runner and he made his Test match debut in that 1975–76 series in the opening Test at the 'Gabba, a game won by the Australians by eight wickets. Holding made 34 and 19 with the bat, coming in at number three in the second innings but had none for plenty with the ball. Then in Perth, in the Second Test, he made a duck in a massive West Indian total but took 4/88 in a fiery exhibition of fast bowling in the Australian first innings. After the Australians had followed on Michael tore a groin muscle and had to sit out the remainder of the game which finished in only four days, and then he was unfit for the Melbourne Boxing Day Test. When the caravan moved to Sydney as part of the back-to-back Tests, Holding took four wickets in the match but, from the final ball of the first day, was hit in the face when he deflected a short ball from Greg Chappell. There was hardly a dull moment for the West Indian 'quickie' because he had Ian Chappell caught at the wicket but given not out when he started his second spell on the second day. Another strained groin muscle prevented him from taking much part in the final Test so, although he was very promising, it could hardly be said he had a totally enjoyable introduction to Test cricket.

I formed the opinion in Australia that he bowled better in the early part of the tour, but that isn't totally surprising because he was a youngster who at that stage had no experience of long Test tours and he was justifiably weary by the end of the series.

Occasionally this had him bowling too short but I reckoned all he needed was more experience. I had seen enough of him though to relish the thought of watching him bowl against England a few months later, particularly as I had kept a close eye on what West Indies did against India in their series in the Caribbean after returning from Australia.

I suppose I was playing at being a selector because I knew instinctively that here was a champion in the making, despite his figures in Australia being ten wickets at 61 apiece. That, though, was in a losing series and with injuries and, when 30 years later I talked to Michael about his fitness, he told me there were no proper medical or training facilities in the Caribbean for cricketers who might be injured on the field. Between the end of the final Test in Melbourne in 1976 and the start of the series against India in Barbados, Michael had 41 days in which to convince Clive, the West Indian selectors and himself that he was fully fit and ready to play. He said it wasn't until World Series Cricket in 1977, when West Indies had Denis Waight as their fitness supervisor, they found out what being fit really meant. Holding, though, used his knowledge of being fit for running to try to make sure he was in the best possible physical condition, and very early on that 1976 West Indian tour of England Lloyd knew he had an out-and-out match-winner on his hands. Michael's figures against India in the four-match series were 19 wickets at 19.89 and he was on his way. There were five Tests in the series in England and, with Viv Richards making 829 runs in four of them, and Holding, in four Tests, taking 28 wickets at 12.7 apiece, it was something to watch and commentate on for BBC Television.

You could hardly have a greater contrast than the grace of Holding in his run to the crease and smooth as silk delivery and Wesley Winfield Hall, also a great fast bowler. Wes was one of the wonderful entertainers and he never played a game of cricket without enjoying himself and bringing the spectators into the game with him.

We only knew of him in Australia because of newspaper stories when he made his debut in India the year before West Indies were to come to Australia in 1960–61. There was in fact more publicity about Roy Gilchrist, frighteningly fast and with a dubious action, but Wes, by the end of that tour of five Test matches on the sub-continent, had made certain he would be one of the first chosen for Australia. He took 30 wickets in the five Tests and then 16 in the three Tests which followed against Pakistan, even though the series went to Pakistan 2–1.

All that was happening at the same time as Australia were beating England 4–0 in Australia. Australia then toured Pakistan and India, along the same lines as West Indies had just done, so we were able to have some almost first-hand information about the West Indians. They said Wes was fast. They also said he was a very good fast bowler which he later showed in taking 21 wickets against us in the Tied Test series, even though there was no other genuinely fast bowler at the opposite end. Because of the balance he wanted in the side, Frank Worrell decided he would take the new ball and, although he was a good bowler, it did make life more difficult for Wes without sheer speed at both ends.

'Winfield' was such an effervescent cricketer and such a good bowler that it seems incredible he was never one of *Wisden*'s Cricketers of the Year. No one would have more deserved the honour but I guess he will have to make do with being the man who bowled the last over of the Tied Test match in Brisbane.

Hundreds of thousands of Australians listened to the thrilling final day on radio but only a few more than 4,000 were actually at the ground, though I reckon I've met many thousands who almost believe they were there. The afternoon session was televised locally in Brisbane and, with television having been going in Australia for four years, there was a sizeable watching audience in the northern capital, particularly when they knew what was happening through the radio commentary.

That final day had not started well for us and Hall was the problem, along with Alfred Valentine, a genuine number eleven who, with the big fast bowler, added 31 for the last wicket at a time when we were thinking of wrapping up the innings in quick time. When Alan Davidson knocked Wes over with a yorker the big West Indian had turned in a very useful effort with the bat, 50 in the first innings and 18 in the second. Worse for us was the fact that instead of chasing 200 to win in the fourth innings, in the whole of the day, we now had to make 233 to win in 40 minutes less than a full day. Wes was buoyant from his batting success and started his run-up for the first over at the Vulture Street End from somewhere near the sightscreen. His first six balls were by way of looseners and in his second over he had Bob Simpson caught at short-leg. Then Garry Sobers took a marvellous catch at slip, diving forward and away to his left, to dismiss Neil Harvey and at lunch we were in real trouble at 28/2. More problems followed in the second session, with Wes dismissing O'Neill and Favell, Frank Worrell bowling McDonald, and Ramadhin doing the same to 'Slasher' Mackay, and we were struggling at tea. Alan Davidson and I were looking down the barrel, needing 123 in the two hours remaining. If I hadn't run out 'Davo' in the second-last over when Sobers was bowling it would have been a piece of cake, but a combination of my bad call and Joe Solomon's great throw to hit the stumps from side on was a double-whammy. When Wes began his final over of the match, and I had Wally Grout as a partner, we needed six runs to win and we had three wickets in hand. Even now it is almost unbelievable that two of those were run out. I was the exception, caught at the wicket by Gerry Alexander trying to hook a bumper, after Frank had ordered Wes under no circumstances to bowl me anything short. Grout was the first run-out to a superb piece of fielding by Conrad Hunte, Ian Meckiff the second after Joe Solomon again hit the stumps from side on to produce the tie.

I walked out on to the field and Frank and I walked back to the dressing-room, arms around one another's shoulders, and I was able to remind him that he'd said at Mascot Airport in October we'd have a lot of fun. The two teams left the dressing-rooms at 7.30 p.m., having gone through most of the calypsos we all knew, the West Indians tunefully and beautifully, the Australians off key but trying hard.

There were a couple of postscripts to the joyful time after the tied match.

The so well-named Australian Board of Control, at the instigation of the Queensland Cricket Association delegates, issued an instruction that players should in future vacate dressing-rooms within a few minutes of the close of play. The board delegates enthusiastically approved the instruction. Bradman was the only one who voted against it.

And, as a minor matter, in a general clean-up of waste paper a few years later, the scorebooks of the Tied Test match were put through the shredder, or whatever was used for disposing of rubbish in those days.

When I made my debut in the 1952 match it was against the three Ws, Clyde Walcott, Everton Weekes and Frank Worrell, and the game was dominated by the pace bowlers of either side. That was not surprising because the curator had left an inch of lush green grass on the pitch surface and the ball moved a lot off the seam as well as a great deal in the air. Gerry Gomez and Frank Worrell bowled us out in the first innings and then took seven wickets between them in the second. Miller and Lindwall shared 14 wickets and Bill Johnston had another three for Australia, so it was all a little reminiscent of my Sheffield Shield debut on the same ground three years earlier. When I toured West Indies in 1955 the three Ws, in familiar surroundings, were in good form, although Walcott was better than that. He was dynamic, hitting five centuries against us, twice a century in each innings of a Test.

There were some extraordinary shenanigans on this tour by way of West Indian administration. The experienced Frank Worrell, a cricketer with an outstanding knowledge of the game, was vice-captain to Jeff Stollmeyer in the previous Caribbean summer when England had toured under Len Hutton's captaincy but, when we arrived in Jamaica, it was announced Worrell had been given the push and Denis Atkinson would be the vice-captain. It was the start of a chapter of incidents, the first one of which was that Jeff Stollmeyer, walking off the Wembley Ground after the West Indies practice the day before the First Test, put up his hand to stop a ball from hitting spectators and badly sprained the index finger of his right hand and instantly had to withdraw from the Test. No Stollmeyer, no Worrell to take his place as captain, but Denis Atkinson, a great bloke and good cricketer, to lead West Indies within 24 hours of Stollmeyer's accident in the all-important opening Test.

Atkinson was on a hiding to nothing and, if the West Indian cricket administrators had gone searching for something bizarre to toss at their team and their supporters, they found it first time. As well, that is, as changing the content of their national selection committee so that instead of having an independent committee, the best committee they could find, they altered the make-up of the committee to four people, one from each territory, plus the captain. There was no doubt local selections would be very much the norm, as we saw in the Second Test where Denis Atkinson was dropped and local Trinidadian 'Bunny' Butler was brought into the team. In the following Test in Guyana, the selectors dropped Collie Smith, who had made a century on debut against us in the opening Test in Jamaica, and, incredibly, also left out Ramadhin and Valentine for a game on a pitch where the ball would be turning. Instead, they brought in spinner Norman Marshall. At the last minute the West Indian selectors panicked and managed to find Ramadhin and rushed him to Georgetown, but 'Val', not surprisingly, had left his telephone off the hook! Australia won the series easily and I hit a century in the final Test in Jamaica, taking only 78 minutes, but I have no idea of the number of balls I faced as that statistic wasn't in use in those days and the scorebooks were tossed out after a year. It was a great thrill to bowl to Walcott, Weekes and Worrell. Everton hit a wonderful century and 87* against us in Port-of-Spain, then 81, 44 and 56 in later matches. He was one of the great players I have seen in cricket and that century, with brilliant cutting and hooking, was something to remember. Frank had a very ordinary time with the bat, having to withdraw owing to illness from the Second Test in Trinidad and, although it was none of his making, was embroiled in the captaincy hoo-ha around the Caribbean. That was totally to do with the fact that John Goddard had been captain for a considerable time and Denis Atkinson was lined up to be the next captain. Both John and Denis were great guys and very good cricketers, but it was clear Worrell was the man who should be captain. It was later shown to be so in the aftermath of Gerry Alexander standing down and Frank captaining the team to Australia in 1960–61 with Gerry a team member.

West Indies played poorly in Australia in early 2005 in the triangular series; they couldn't make the best-of-three finals. When Brian Lara failed with the bat, the promise of the young players couldn't make up for their inexperience. On their return to the Caribbean there were disturbing stories which pointed to the possible demise of West Indian cricket. Tony Cozier, who knows more about West Indian cricket than anyone else, was very pessimistic. I just hope he's wrong, but a gloomy picture has been painted. The West Indies Cricket Board, the Players' Association and the sponsors have a great deal of work to do, not for themselves but for West Indian and world cricket. If they don't succeed, it will be a fairytale finished, not merely gone wrong. If that happens West Indies cricket lovers will never forgive their administrators.

17

ADMIN – TAKE
IT OR LEAVE IT

ALTHOUGH Australian administrators are occasionally put through the wringer in these modern times, they are light years better than in those far off days of administrators versus cricketers. Then Australia's first-class cricketers were subservient to administration, and those in charge of it, and the administrators were not merely the gentlemen of the game but didn't mind letting you know that was the situation.

The one outstanding case in Australian administration in a file marked 'Appalling' remains vetoing the selection of opening batsman Sid Barnes in the aftermath of the Invincibles tour of England in 1948. Barnes was chosen by the Australian selectors to play in the Third Test of the series against the West Indies in Adelaide in 1951–52, but his selection was refused by the Australian Board of Control, a move they hoped and believed would remain a secret.

When the Australian team had assembled without Barnes, the twelve consisted of Lindsay Hassett (captain), Arthur Morris (vice-captain), Jim Burke, Neil Harvey, Keith Miller, Graeme Hole, Ray Lindwall, Ian Johnson, Doug Ring, Gil Langley, Bill Johnston and Geff Noblet – a good team with a balanced look about it. That idyllic state of balance lasted only until the practice the day before the game was due to start when Lindsay Hassett slightly strained a muscle in his hip and pulled out of the side on the morning of the match. The match itself involved an unusual arrangement as regards dates because it was played over the Christmas break and was scheduled to begin on Saturday, 22 December. There was no play on Sunday, 23 December, play resumed on 24 December and the match concluded on Christmas Day. The selectors chose Phil Ridings, a fine cricketer, as Hassett's replacement. However, not every single board member around Australia was able to be contacted by telephone when doing his very important Saturday morning shopping, so what did they do? Well, they did something that was unbelievable. You may think they would have had in place a method whereby a small committee, say an executive committee, would have been empowered to ratify any selection changes needed: or the chairman of the board invested with some powers, or even the selectors given the responsibility. What, for example, if three players had been injured in a car accident?

As it was, so lacking in foresight were the board that precisely the same twelve players as originally named *had* to represent Australia with what was now a very unbalanced line-up. Hassett had to be 12th man even though he couldn't field and Lindwall was batting at number six. It was a crass piece of administration. The players knew it and the public knew it, but it made no difference. West Indies won the match by six wickets.

This was the same season I made my Test debut against West Indies in the Fifth Test at the SCG and in the following summer, 1952–53, when the South Africans toured Australia, there was the famous, or infamous, court case where, as a follow-up to being vetoed out of the team, Sid sued a member of the public, Mr Jacob Raith. Mr Raith, in a letter to a newspaper, had castigated Barnes and supported the board in their vetoing of him, suggesting that they had cause to do so.

Gilbert and Sullivan at their very best could hardly have done better than the board with the ensuing events. They had started by refusing Barnes's selection but then wouldn't say anything about it and tried to pretend it hadn't happened. It later transpired that when the vote was taken it had been ten-three in favour of excluding Barnes, with Aub Oxlade, Sir Donald Bradman and Frank

Cush voting against the motion put to the meeting. Bradman had been captain of the 1948 side which included Barnes as a player; Oxlade and Cush were two of the three NSW delegates. Oxlade later lost his place as chairman of the Australian board, and Chappie Dwyer, also of NSW, his position as Australian selector. It was very much, in Australian cricket administration, the night, week and disgraceful year of the long knives.

Furthermore the board, incredibly, faked the minutes of a meeting in the most extraordinary fashion, producing a document which bore no relation to what had actually happened, and pretended there had been no discussion concerning Barnes and his exclusion.

In the court case, one of the odd happenings was that following the axing of Oxlade and Dwyer, Keith Johnson, the 1948 team manager and NSW board representative, actually retained his board place. He had voted against Barnes, had been party to the deception of the doctored minutes of the particular meeting and then, in court, agreed that in his end-of-tour review to the board, after the 1948 tour, he had given every player, including Barnes, what was termed 'a glowing report'.

Chappie Dwyer, as honest a man as you would find in or out of cricket circles, said in the witness box of Sid, 'I have a high opinion of Barnes as a cricketer and no objection to him as a man.'

When the defence had disintegrated, Raith's Counsel made a statement to the judge and the defending Counsel's words should have reverberated around the walls of Cricket House, and every other administrative room in the land, but I doubt they did so. He said, speaking of the board's actions and words, 'Seldom in the history of libel actions has such a plea failed so completely and utterly. The board has presented an awful image of the chaos and bigotry under which Australian cricket is administered.'

No such reverberating happened. If anything, the whole issue strengthened the power of the board in that it could clearly be seen that anyone who had the hide to have a dissenting voice, or even a dissenting thought, may not be absolutely sure of a continuing career in the game.

Some years later, when writing about my own and other young players' thoughts at the time, I said of the board, 'Those were the days when you spoke with a touch of reverence and a certain amount of humility to cricket officials in their navy blue suits, white shirts and strong leather shoes. Jack might have been as good as his mate in the outback of Australia in the 1800s but it took a while for the idea to permeate through to the various state associations and the Australian Board of Control.'

Prior to the start of that 1952–53 tour by South Africa, the Australian board had also been in touch with their South African counterparts expressing their grave disquiet about the potential financial horrors of the tour. In South Africa there had been some conjecture about sending the team, and the South African players were hardly given an overwhelming vote of confidence by administrators around Australia. The South African Cricket Board, put under enormous pressure by the Australian board, after the latter had repeated their disquiet in yet another letter to South Africa, secretly agreed to stand losses on the tour up to a figure of £10,000. No one on the Australian Board of Control bothered mentioning that information to the cricketing public; it was to remain a secretive agreement.

The board's 'disquiet' is probably a low-key word because those Australian administrators actually feared, and said, the tour would be a complete failure. Among them was Sydney Smith, president of the NSWCA, and he had been charged with the task of proposing the *welcoming* toast to the South Africans at a function in Sydney prior to the match between South Africa and NSW. He spent most of his speech saying how bad South African cricket teams had been over the years. It was a delightfully ironic result that this South African team, led by Jack Cheetham, finished 2–2 with Australia, after a great win in the final Test at the MCG.

Certainly the Australian board found it a difficult season. Their team had failed to win the series against a South African team rubbished by the board itself. In the Barnes' court case it had been shown that the board had falsified minutes of a meeting in order to deceive people and, because of their own back-stabbing, they had lost two good men in Oxlade and Dwyer, the latter an outstanding Australian selector.

My international career was only one year old at that stage and I can assure you there was nothing at all comforting about Australian administration at that time.

Fortunately, in 2005, all that has changed. Cricket Australia have done a great job in Australian cricket in recent years; ex-players have been brought in to help administer the game and there is a good rapport between administrators and players. This doesn't just exist right at the top, but also in the various states where the Pura Cup, formally the Sheffield Shield, and the ING Cup form a perfect structure for keeping Australian cricket healthy and strong.

In any organisation of this kind there will always be strong discussion and differences of opinion. It is to Australian cricket's benefit that Cricket Australia and the Australian Cricketers' Association subscribe to that energetic discussion and, in early 2005, came to agreement on the scope of a new contract between the two bodies.

It is a far cry from the days when Sir Donald Bradman was the ex-player on the board. Now six of the fourteen-strong board of directors of Cricket Australia have played first-class cricket, three of those, Allan Border, Wally Edwards and Mark Taylor, played Test cricket and Ian McLachlan was 12th man in a Test. Bob Merriman has done a fine job as Cricket Australia's chairman, so too the chief executive officer James Sutherland who played for Victoria. Tim May, who played for Australia, has been outstanding as the ACA's chief negotiator. He will be greatly missed now that he will be living in the United States.

Much has been achieved between Australian administrators and cricketers in the past ten years. These days there is a good blend of knowledge of what is needed to run the game in businesslike fashion and mix it with a good knowledge of what goes on in the centre of the ground.

Having seen cricket administration in Australia over fifty-seven years, the improvement is dramatic and more than welcome, as is the fact that Cricket Australia and the Australian Cricketers' Association have also taken a constructive path with the Spirit of Cricket.

The Spirit of Cricket is an initiative which started in England when Colin Cowdrey and Ted Dexter in the late 1990s were trying to find a method of reminding the players that the game had twofold aims involving playing to the Laws and also the Spirit of cricket. I was asked to deliver the first UK Spirit of Cricket Cowdrey Lecture at Lord's in 2001. I'm in good company because the next three years saw Barry Richards, Sunil Gavaskar and Clive Lloyd deliver the lectures with Geoff Boycott listed for 2005.

Cricket Australia followed the UK lead and instituted the Benaud Spirit of Cricket Awards in Australia. Around the cricket world there are many more famous cricket families but none who loved the game more, nor were more pleased to be associated with it. My father, Lou, was a fine cricketer at country and then Central Cumberland first-grade club level, my brother John played for Cumberland, NSW, then captained NSW and played Test cricket, hitting a century in his last Test in Australia. I had thirteen years at Test level and fifteen in the first-class game.

Cricket Australia in their announcement said:

Teams adjudged by the umpires as having best displayed the true spirit, traditions and values associated with cricket are recognised each season in Australia with the Benaud Spirit of Cricket awards. The awards were first handed down in 2003–04 to reflect the influence and stature of the Benaud family in Australian cricket, and they underline Cricket Australia's commitment to the spirit of cricket, a concept outlined in the recently-drafted preamble to the Laws of Cricket.

In 2003 Cricket Australia's contracted players wrote a code that represents the spirit in which they seek to play the game. It reads:

As cricketers who represent Australia we acknowledge and embrace 'The Spirit of Cricket' and the Laws of our game.

This Players' Spirit of Australian Cricket serves as a guide to the shared standards of behaviour that we expect of ourselves and the values we hold.

Our on-field behaviour –

We play our cricket hard but fair and accept all umpiring decisions as a mark of respect for our opponents, the umpires, ourselves and the game.

We view positive play, pressure, body language and banter between opponents and ourselves as legitimate tactics and integral parts of the competitive nature of cricket.

We do not condone or engage in sledging or any other conduct that constitutes personal abuse.

We encourage the display of passion and emotion as a sign of our enjoyment and pride in the game, as a celebration of our achievements and as a sign of respect for our opponents.

Our off-field behaviour –

It is acknowledged that we have a private life to lead but understand our off-field conduct has the potential to reflect either positively or adversely on us as individuals and also on the game of cricket.

We consider off-field conduct that may be likely to warrant legitimate public criticism to be unacceptable conduct.

Our team –

We take pride in our sense of the importance of the team and acknowledge the role of the team captain and our direct support staff. We demonstrate this by displaying loyalty and compassion to each other, by accepting our role as mentors and by supporting each other to abide by these values.

We value honesty and accept that every member of the team has a role to play in shaping, and abiding by our shared standards and expectations.

We strive to be regarded as the best team in the world. We measure this by our on-field achievements and by exploring ways in which we might continue to 'raise the bar' in respect of our own professionalism.

We acknowledge and follow the traditions of our game while encouraging and accepting experimentation that will enable us to create our own traditions and history. We do this in the expectation that we will leave the game in a better shape than it was before we arrived.

Our opponents –

We acknowledge and respect that our opponents may hold different cultural values and beliefs from our own, and value the diversity and richness this adds to the game.

By treating our opponents with dignity and forging bonds of mutual respect, we will overcome any cultural barriers.

Our supporters –

We value our supporters and acknowledge those who support our opponents and the game of cricket. We demonstrate commitment to our supporters by always giving our best and demonstrating leadership in everything we do.

Our family –

We value the contribution and sacrifices of our families that enable us to meet these expectations.

Respect –

We respect the governing bodies of the game, our support teams in every capacity and our players' association. We demonstrate this respect by seeking and offering frank and open communication in accordance with the Players' Spirit of Australian Cricket.

Sledging, mentioned above, has become so fashionable in modern-day cricket that it even makes it into the *Collins Concise Dictionary (Third Australian Edition)*: **sledge** (sledz) vb. **sledges, sledging, sledged.** (tr) *Austral.* to bait (an opponent, esp. a batsman in cricket) in order to upset his concentration. (*from?*)

That dictionary entry (from?) refers to the fact that apparently no one at dictionary level knows the derivation of the word. There's no problem with that. It happened many years ago at a party in Adelaide, in November 1967, and had nothing at all to do with anything that had occurred on a cricket field, or has happened on a cricket field since that evening. The New South Wales team threw the party but a couple of players had to leave to attend another function. When they arrived back at the party room it was to find a waitress, carrying a tray of drinks, knocking on the same door. The door was opened to display an almost empty room apart from a couple of players, one of whom, Graham Corling, who was at the time nicknamed '*I'll be*', looked past the waitress at his two team-mates and said, using a well known four-letter expletive, that the party was over. Another player, embarrassed at the swearing in front of a lady, said: 'Aw *I'll be*, that's as subtle as a *sledgehammer*.' In the way of Australian cricketers' use of nicknames, Corling instantly became known as 'Percy' because at that time the big song in the hit parade was 'When a Man Loves a Woman' and the singer was Percy Sledge. From that moment anyone in Australian cricket who swore in front of a lady was said to have been guilty of *sledging*.

It is a complete mystery how the media managed, in such extraordinary and convoluted fashion, to transpose that to fieldsmen or bowlers who back-chat batsmen in the centre of a cricket ground.

I played within a stretch of 15 years in first-class cricket and hardly ever had anything derogatory said to me on the field, except in NSW-Victoria Sheffield Shield matches, probably from Jack 'Snarler' Hill, but I can guarantee you I wasn't in the habit of saying anything derogatory to any opposition players. The closest I reckon I got to experiencing sledging was in Jim Laker's Old Trafford extravaganza in 1956. There were some very unhappy Australians in that match, in the main because we had the feeling we were playing on a rather unusual pitch, and we were looking at defeat, which never actually makes one happy.

Well, you would be unhappy too if you were thrashed, one of the opposition bowlers took 19 wickets in the match and the ball turned square for much of the game. Additionally, the rain fell on either side of the ground on the last day, but none fell on it. You would also be unhappy if you were the bowler who only took one wicket of the 20 little Australians to fall. Jim Burke was the generous batsman who was the victim of Tony Lock.

On the final afternoon I was engaged in some prudent 'gardening' against 'Lockie', patting down the pitch, sometimes not quite ready to face up, so much so that one prominent English administrator, sitting alongside a very prominent Australian administrator, said grimly that, because of the gardening, I should never at any time in the future hold a position of responsibility in an Australian team.

He nearly had his way too! If Ian Craig hadn't gone down with hepatitis in 1958 I would have remained as a player due to my performances in South Africa, but I would never have been captain. Out in the centre at Old Trafford, Colin McDonald and I were battling our way through to the tea interval and, in the last over, Tony bowled from what was then the Warwick Road End. I played forward firmly to a half-volley and it went to the bowler's left hand. Great fielder, 'Lockie', and a very good and accurate throwing arm in either the infield or further out. He gathered this ball and it rocketed into Godfrey Evans's left glove, alongside my left ear and, 'Tap that one down, you little bastard' came floating down the pitch.

Godfrey and I burst out laughing, it was an amusing interlude and I forgot about it the moment I turned to walk back to the dressing-room. However, the late Rev. David Sheppard had been fielding at short-leg and he was into our dressing-room very quickly to apologise for the profanity on the field. I didn't say to him I'd encountered much worse than that in my short career, particularly in New South Wales-Victoria matches, but I did have a chuckle and tell him it wasn't a problem. I added, as well, that I didn't blame 'Lockie' one little bit.

Sledging always seems to me to be such a waste of time. I came up through the game concentrating on my bowling, trying to land the ball on the right spot, endeavouring to be one step ahead of the batsman with bowling skills, trying to bowl him out rather than talk him to death. Fred Trueman had a good line in letting the batsman know he was an attacking bowler and there were others, generally fast bowlers, whose chat was occasionally interesting, though mostly boring. I can't believe, with the best will in the world, that fast bowlers of today are any more intelligent than 50 years ago. Some may be very clever bowlers on the basis of how to dismiss a batsman, though most of the time in the modern era it seems to be more a case of organising the media to do the work for them. A bowler goes out of his way to tell a media interviewer which method he intends to use to dismiss a batsman. It may have no relevance at all, it could be the direct opposite of what he actually intends to do and the media seem quite happy to do the work for the bowler. Far more dangerous though is when a batsman announces he intends to knock a bowler out of the attack, possibly out of the team and therefore, if followed to a logical conclusion, end that player's career. It might produce a headline of 'It's him or me' but it seems to me to be a very dangerous thing to do. You could for example do it with an athlete if you know you can always run or swim faster than the other person. It's easy enough to announce you will win tomorrow's race. But cricket is such a game of chance that once you have stated you intend to hit a bowler out of the attack, it only needs one little piece of ill-luck for you and suddenly you are mentally in trouble. A fielder dives two yards to take a miraculous catch, you slip on some greenish grass, can't regain your ground and are run out. The faintest inside edge on to your pad in successive innings and the umpire gives you out. Suddenly the media and general public are, if not baying for your body, certainly not patting you on the back and saying everything will be okay.

Early in 2005 one of the great sledgers of all time passed on to the sledging ground in the sky, or wherever it might be located. Peter Heine, the South African fast bowler, was never short of a word, or two or three, but he could bowl as well. He wasn't just all talk. Fast and furious, and with a very big heart, he bowled in partnership with Neil Adcock in the 1950s, having made his debut at Lord's in 1955, taking five wickets in England's first innings. Then he took eight in the next Test at Old Trafford and already his name was being mentioned in dispatches as a good bowler with plenty of chat. South Africa drew both Test series against England in 1955 and then in 1956–57, the year before we went to play SA in 1957–58. They were ready for us because they had been successful and England had made a mess of us in 1956. Peter took six wickets in an innings twice against us in 1957–58, in the First and Fourth Tests played at Wanderers' in Johannesburg; I made a century in the first innings of each match. Rule 1. Make sure your hook and pull shots were working well because the short ball and the very occasional yorker were definitely the preferred deliveries. Heine wasn't quite as fast as Adcock but he didn't like to see anyone play him off the front foot. His follow-through was down the offside of the pitch, but then he had the ability to veer towards your left ear, all the better to enable you to hear the advice he was offering. I found the best way to counter this was to decline to catch his eye, turn my back on him and shuffle around the crease so that, from the grandstand, it might have appeared we were a couple of ballet dancers in a pas de deux routine. No stump microphones and no television in those days which was probably a good idea because he was asking personal questions about my mother and father and I was offering him advice that would have made him a gold medallist in the sexual Olympic Games.

Repartee is good if it is also funny. Some of the things credited to Fred Trueman portray good Yorkshire humour, some are simply things thought up by media who regarded them as a good idea at the time. I liked Colin Cowdrey being flown to Australia as an additional player in 1974 when Dennis Amiss and John Edrich suffered broken bones in the First Test in Brisbane. In the Second Test at the WACA in Perth, Cowdrey batted number three and went in after Brian Luckhurst was caught by Ashley Mallett in the gully off Max Walker for 27, with the score 44. It was a perfect day and 16,000 spectators watched Cowdrey walk to the centre. The crowd were lively because they were watching some very fast bowling from Jeff Thomson and Dennis Lillee. No one said a word to Colin. After a couple of of overs, as 'Thommo' was walking back past the non-striker's end, Colin took a pace towards him, smiled and said, 'Good morning, my name's Cowdrey.' The ultimate disarming remark!

Sometimes you need a sense of humour. In the same game David Lloyd made 49 in the first innings and announced to his fellow players that he could play Thomson with his prick. In the second innings he had made 17 when 'Thommo' got one to rear and the ball smashed his protective box to pieces. When they had air-lifted him back to the England dressing-room his first agonising words through gritted teeth to solicitous team-mates were, 'See, told you I could.'

For straightforward repartee I've always liked David Steele, who Tony Greig brought into the England team in 1975 after he took over the captaincy from Mike Denness. When, in the first innings, Barry Wood was lbw to Dennis Lillee with the score at ten, and the very grey-haired right-hander from Northamptonshire arrived in the centre, it was to hear someone chiding Dennis for not having mentioned his father was playing in the match. It is said Steele looked straight past Rodney Marsh and muttered, 'Take a good look at this arse of mine; you'll see plenty of it this summer.' Test innings of 50, 45, 73, 92, 39 and 66, and then a century for Northants against Australia later in the summer, made it a nice little story, some say aprocryphal. Except that, for whatever extraordinary selection quirk, he never played against Australia again!

18
ONE-DAY CRICKET

I T'S always very dangerous to say one has seen it all, but I'm very close to being in the position of having seen it all in one-day cricket. Like thousands upon thousands of cricketers I played it at some early stage of my career, certainly at school, though this was a version which involved time rather than overs as the sharing point of the match. Each team may well have bowled *about* forty overs but there was no arbitrary over figure. In club cricket we played two day matches, Saturday and the following Saturday, for the most part, but the first week of October every season always saw the five teams in the Central Cumberland Club playing a one-day match on the Monday of the long Labour Day weekend. I scored 91 in a one-day match in 1946 against Randwick at Coogee Oval, just near where we now live in Sydney, and that innings was responsible for me then being chosen in the Cumberland 1st XI and it started me on my way to first-class cricket. In wartime in Sydney in the club competition there were only one-day matches, the very good reason was that soldiers, sailors and airmen on war duty could only be certain of one Saturday's leave, so the sensible thing was to bring in the one-day games. Club cricket in Sydney had never produced for the club treasurers more gate-takings, unless Bradman happened to be playing. These new-style matches drew very big crowds on the basis that, in such uncertain times, the people paying their money at the gate could be certain of seeing a result in the one afternoon.

It is for exactly the same reason that many people these days prefer one-day cricket to the longer version. I firmly believe people new to cricket watching and wanting to learn about the game, should start by watching one-day cricket and they will then soon begin to enjoy both forms of the game. Wartime one-day cricket had one beneficial effect for me as a 12- and 13-year-old. I scored for the Cumberland 2nd XI and, if a player was unable to turn up because military leave had been cancelled, I was allowed to take his place in the field. Although I was playing with fully grown men, my father had instilled into me the virtue of being a good fieldsman and never being scared of the ball, and I worked very hard on that, no matter where I was. I always dressed for the scoring role, as I would have done during the week captaining the Parramatta High School fourth-grade team in the High Schools' competition. This was restricted to boys in first and second year. I wore white cricket shirt, white shorts, white socks, white tennis shoes, or sandshoes as they were known in Australia. From the point of view of Central Cumberland second-grade team, and scoring for them, that was so that if a player was late I would be correctly dressed in white and therefore permitted by the umpires to be on the field. It was a great thrill in the one-day cricket seasons of 1942–43 and 1943–44 just to score for the 2nd XI, but even more of a thrill to be on the ground. When one player couldn't turn up I fielded and, in a match against the Petersham Club at Petersham Oval, I was last man in to bat. When I walked out from the pavilion, the batsman waiting for me at the non-striker's end was Milton Jarrett, a burly allrounder. He had been hitting the bowlers all around the ground and Cumberland needed just six to win. I had four balls to face. He said to me I should just play forward with a straight bat. Full-size bat and full-size pads, full-size fieldsmen crouched around, full-size nerves as well, but somehow I managed to push the ball on to the offside and we raced through for a single. Milton didn't fool about; he hit the next ball for a massive six. There has never been a prouder 12-year-old as I trotted off the field looking up at him.

The following summer, 1943–44, against North Sydney at North Sydney Oval, my best friend at Parramatta High School, Doug Milner, came to the match and Cumberland were two short and we were the last two men to bat. Doug made ten and I made six and the match was won. It was one of the most exciting things either of us had known in cricket. The following year Cumberland re-entered the Green Shield (Under-16) competition and Doug and I played together in that side and then we were in the Parramatta High School team which won the High Schools' competition in 1945–46.

Club officials were aware, at that stage in Australian cricket history, the only sensible basis at club level was to play competitions within a structure that involved cricketers being prepared for the next grade, which in this case was the longer version of the game, the Sheffield Shield. That wartime competition was the only one-day cricket in the early days of my time in Sydney club cricket.

The next one-day cricket competition in which I was involved was in the United Kingdom in 1960 when I was covering the England-South Africa series for BBC Radio. In those days Rothmans sponsored a Sunday one-day competition which was televised by the BBC and they were good contests, featuring current county players, ex-internationals and one or two from the entertainment industry who knew how to handle a bat and bowl as well. Then, when the England cricket authorities decided they might as well have whatever profits were accruing, they began a one-day competition between the counties in 1963 but, despite their best efforts, initially they couldn't find anyone as sponsor. It was though the start of what might be termed *proper* one-day cricket and 25,000 people crammed into Lord's for the inaugural final and one-day cricket was here to stay. Ted Dexter was the first captain to work out the right tactics and his Sussex team won close finals in each of the first two years, the first occasion by just 14 runs. Dexter reasoned that during this competition good spin bowlers might well be more valuable than an extra medium-pace trundler. In the final against Worcestershire at Lord's he included Alan Oakman and Ken Suttle to bowl offspin and left-arm spin respectively and, between them, they bowled 18 overs and took 1/17. Don Kenyon, the Worcestershire captain, was just as inventive with Norman Gifford and Martin Horton who took five of the Sussex wickets. That competition, called in its first year, 1963, 'The Knockout Competition' and, in 1964, 'The Gillette Cup', prospered over the years in England, with some wonderful finals at Lord's.

The success, noted by Australian administrators, led to the start of a one-day domestic competition in Australia, at first sponsored by V & G Insurance. It worked well but certainly wasn't easy to organise with only seven teams taking part, six Sheffield Shield states and New Zealand, and semi-finals and a final required. One of the unusual things about the start of the one-day competition in Australia was that the scoring was low; the ball was almost always on top of the bat. It took curators and administrators a season to realise the matches needed to be played on what, in effect, were two-day-old pitches, much more in favour of batting than bowling.

That first Australian one-day competition was in fact Australasian, and was won by New Zealand who were captained by Graham Dowling. Bob Cowper was captain of Victoria, John Benaud led NSW, Les Favell was in charge of South Australia and Sam Trimble of Queensland. The other two captains were Tony Lock, England's former left-arm spinner who led Western Australia and Alan Knott, England's then current wicket-keeper, captained Tasmania. The V & G competition went for two years, then Coca-Cola came in as sponsors and the first final under their sponsorship, in February, 1972, saw a great battle between South Australia, captained by Ian Chappell, and Victoria led by Bill Lawry. Chappell made 82 and Lawry a match-winning and unbeaten 108*. It still wasn't enough to persuade the Australian selectors that Lawry should go to

England with the Australian team, and the other major error they made was to leave out Ian Redpath.

The domestic one-day competition in Australia has grown dramatically in recent times and now 31 matches are played each summer, compared with six in the first Australasian summer. The competition has had several sponsors, the most recent, ING, starting in 1992–93 as Mercantile Mutual and then changing to ING in 2001–02, and they were fortunate to have for many years the services of Geoff Prenter as their cricket consultant. He was responsible for some interesting innovations in the domestic one-day game.

Cricket Australia, the national selectors and ING now use the competition as the basis for Australian cricket to do well in the World Cup. Australia, with ING as sponsors from 1992, finished runners-up to Sri Lanka in India and Pakistan in 1995–96 and then won the next two World Cups, in England in 1999 and South Africa in 2003.

On the international scene, limited-overs cricket and television have been the financial saviour of Test cricket. When the first one-day International was played at the MCG in 1971 it proved to be the forerunner of the first World Cup played in England in 1975, with the final beamed to television audiences all over the world.

Two years later, day-night limited-overs cricket was part of World Series Cricket and, in 1978, we had the remarkable day-night match at the Sydney Cricket Ground where 52,000 spectators were in the ground with the gates opened rather than closed to the public. The second and third World Cups were played in England in 1979 and 1983 and then, in 1987, India were the hosts when Australia won the Cup for the first time under Allan Border's outstanding captaincy. There is no doubt the World Cup competition has been the catalyst for the financial well-being of the game around the world and, apart from producing some excellent cricket, it has taken cricket to countries and people who might never otherwise have been part of the game.

It is a constantly evolving type of cricket, with new playing conditions, such as bonus points, being tried out at domestic level before perhaps being used at international level and then brought in to the World Cup organisation. It is possible to have a boring Test match but easier to have a boring one-day match because, if the team batting first suffers a collapse, then spectators and viewers on television will most times have a good idea of the result. Not always though. I have seen more Test cricket than most and I have, as well, seen more one-day cricket than most, though I didn't play it for NSW and Australia. More's the pity. I would have loved to be part of the tactical ploys, the big hitting, the brilliant fielding and trying to deceive the batsmen with legspin.

I've watched a lot of exciting games, with all their twists and turns, and four stand out of the pack. One of those was the first World Cup final, with West Indies the victors over Australia at Lord's. Clive Lloyd hit a century, Viv Richards ran out three Australians and Alvin Kallicharran two, and Dennis Lillee and Jeff Thomson battled hard at the end but weren't quite good enough to hold out the Windies. This was the longest day's cricket in the history of the game, lasting from 11 a.m. to shortly before 9 p.m.

In 1984 at Old Trafford I watched one of the more remarkable games I had seen to that time and the key men were Vivian Richards and Michael Holding. It was a good batting pitch but there had been enough sweating under the covers overnight to add to the cloudy morning and to allow the England attack to rip through the West Indies. Bob Willis, Ian Botham, Neil Foster, Derek Pringle and offspinner Geoff Miller were too much for the visitors and, at 102/7, Viv Richards had played a lone hand. He had some assistance from that underrated allrounder Eldine Baptiste, who helped in adding 49, but it was still tough going when Holding came in at 166/9. At least, if the last wicket fell quickly, the bowlers would still have something at which they could aim, even though the sun breaking through the clouds was going to be in favour of England.

Richards and Holding shared a partnership of 106, with Michael making 12 and facing only 27 deliveries. He showed skilful defence and a keen appreciation of how to take the quick single if Viv generously allowed him to face a ball. Viv, at the other end, was simply magnificent and those at the ground or watching BBC Television had the treat of their lives. Not out 189 from only 170 balls is what it says on paper, but that doesn't go even part of the way to confirming the dominance of one batsman over the opposition, even though he was playing beautiful strokes, rather than bludgeoning the bowlers. It was an innings I'll never forget, nor will others at the ground or watching on television, including the man who was for the most part an interested onlooker from the non-striker's end.

One of the best limited-overs cricketers ever to walk on to a cricket ground is the Australian Michael Bevan who, over the years, has done some extraordinary things in the shortened version of the game. He used to play for NSW, now he has moved to Tasmania and is still very much in the business of winning matches for his new state, though not for Australia because the Australian selectors have given him the push. He showed he hadn't lost his touch in 2004–05 when he guided 'Tassie' to victory over Queensland in the ING final at the 'Gabba with a typical decisive innings of 47 not out.

Two of the most memorable innings he has played in this form of the game were in different competitions, one against the West Indies in a Sydney match when he was still in the Australian team. This first game was a low-scoring affair in slightly damp conditions, with West Indies making 172/9 after the game had been reduced to 43 overs a side, maximum. Carl Hooper made 93 of those runs in a very good attacking innings and Shane Warne took four wickets to contain the Windies to the reasonable target. West Indies bowlers just steamrollered Australia and had them 74/7 and looking for all the world a beaten side. Then Paul Reiffel made 34 out of an 83-run partnership and another two quick wickets had Glenn McGrath coming out to join Bevan in the final over. Roger Harper was to bowl it with the score 167/9 and McGrath somehow pushed a single to give Bevan the strike. Four were needed from the last ball and Bevan, as he always did, had his areas picked out depending on where the ball pitched. It went back past Harper at a rate of knots and finished under the sightscreen to provide a magnificent victory; a typical Bevan effort, timed to perfection.

In the World Cup in 2003 in South Africa, he conjured up a win from nowhere, one that left Michael Vaughan's England side flattened by the manner in which they had snatched defeat from those well known jaws of victory. England made most of the running in this game played at Port Elizabeth on a very ordinary pitch. They did very well to make 204/8 although the Australian, Andy Bichel, turned in a sensational all-round performance of which he could be very proud. Nick Knight and Marcus Trescothick added 66 for the opening partnership, Andy Flintoff and Alec Stewart shared 90, with Flintoff making 45 and Stewart 46, but then Bichel, in an extraordinary last few overs of his permitted ten, finished up with 7/20. It didn't do the Australians much good because they quickly lost wickets until Darren Lehmann and Bevan pulled things around with a 63-run stand. Then three wickets fell for almost nothing and, when Bevan walked across to Bichel on his way out from the dressing-room, 69 were still needed.

Bichel hit 34 of those from 36 balls faced. Bevan controlled the bowlers with exquisite touches and their partnership was worth 73 and the game was won with three balls remaining. Bevan has the attribute of being able to bring mild panic to opposition teams because they know he is able to turn what seems a certain loss into an extraordinary victory. So it was this day in Port Elizabeth and it effectively put England out of the World Cup.

The limited-overs game that amused and thrilled me more than any other, though, was the 1999 semi-final at Edgbaston between Australia and South Africa. Steve Waugh had hit a century in the match between the two teams four days before the semi; that match was played at Headingley and was a high-scoring affair with Waugh being dropped by Herschelle Gibbs who was celebrating the catch before it was properly in his hands. Hence Waugh's alleged throw-away line of, *'You've just dropped the World Cup, Herschelle . . .'* The semi-final at Edgbaston was a much tighter affair than the match at Leeds, with Australia making only 213, Steve Waugh 56, Michael Bevan 65 and Shaun Pollock turned in a wonderful bowling performance of 5/36. Then South Africa several times looked as though they would make the runs in comfort. It was Shane Warne who turned it around for Australia after Gary Kirsten and Gibbs had added 48 and Jacques Kallis had made a very good 53. Warne bowled magnificently this day, but then it looked as though Lance Klusener would certainly win it for South Africa with some astonishing strokes off Damien Fleming's final over. The amusing side of things came in that final over with Klusener, having clubbed 31 from only 16 balls faced, being involved in the most extraordinary and completely unnecessary mix-up with South African number eleven, Allan Donald. This resulted in Donald being run out, still with two balls remaining in the over. Thus the semi-final was tied and the Australians, being ahead of South Africa in the Super Six table because of net run-rate, therefore went through to the final where they beat Pakistan. The run-out was on a par with me running out Alan Davidson in the Tied Test in Brisbane, no sense in it at all. On reflection, my running-out of 'Davo' was not good cricket; South Africa's run-out at Edgbaston was unbelievably bad cricket. Fleming on the other hand performed with great skill and common sense. Taking the flick throw from Mark Waugh, he made certain there could be no way out for South Africa by rolling the ball along the pitch to wicket-keeper Gilchrist.

It is true that a thrilling Test match will stay in the memory for a long time because it is played over five days and the ebbs and flows of each day, rather than one day, will make a difference. The great thing about modern-day cricket for me, though, is that you can have excitement in both Test cricket and Limited-overs cricket and that will continue to be the case around the world. Never forget as well that only 50-overs-a-side limited-overs cricket can properly prepare teams for the World Cup. Anything less than that will be worth nothing by way of preparation.

19

TWO YOUNG GUNS

Andrew Flintoff and Michael Clarke

Two of the finest young cricketers in the world had not been in opposing teams in a Test match up to the year 2005. From the countries which began Test cricket 128 years ago, circumstances have conspired to put Andrew Flintoff and Michael Clarke on the field, but playing against other countries. Clarke hasn't been in the game for very long, but he has made a striking beginning to his Test career, with a century on debut in India and then another century the first time he played in Australia. It was a remarkable performance. Flintoff has played 45 Tests but injury has meant sometimes he hasn't been able to get on to the field. Further injury during the 2004–05 series against South Africa in South Africa meant he had to fly back to England instead of playing in the Limited-overs Internationals after the Test series was concluded, where England came out on top 2–1.

Clarke is the best young batsman produced by Australia since Ricky Ponting came out of the Australian Academy with many accolades from good judges who had seen his undoubted potential. Flintoff is the best allrounder produced by England since Ian Botham came on the scene in the late 1970s, but the bad news coming out of South Africa in January 2005 was that he was to miss the one-day matches against South Africa and needed an operation on his left foot/ankle with a three-month recuperative period after going under the knife. It seemed that when he thumped his left front foot on to the pitch in bowling there were two bones which banged against one another. The medicos said it could certainly be fixed and the comfort Flintoff should have taken with him into the operating theatre, and in recuperation, was that Glenn McGrath has never bowled better since having his ankle fixed. The Australian came back too soon mind you, but once he realised that, and the medical people kept at him, he was completely cured and his form in the 2004–05 Australasian summer was outstanding.

In the splendid 2004–05 series in South Africa, when England won 2–1, Flintoff was a star with the ball despite the problems he constantly encountered with that left foot. He took 23 wickets and the runs he made sometimes came at crucial times, particularly the 77 in the first innings of the final Test at Centurion Park. In that match Flintoff took 4/44 and then, batting with that great fighter Graham Thorpe, he steered England out of trouble. Neither of the England batsmen was hampered by the South African tactics which were bewildering. It seemed to me that the South African planning had totally lost sight of the fact that there was a game there to be won. It was extraordinary to watch and impossible to understand. When Flintoff bowled he didn't look at all comfortable with his delivery stride but he certainly gave it everything, which is always the case with his cricket.

A defining moment in Flintoff's batting career was the series in England against South Africa in 2003. Particularly significant was the brilliant 142 he made at Lord's in a *losing* match. It made him hungry and wanting to play the same kind of innings in a *winning* game for England. He wanted to be there, as he was that day at Lord's, at the end of the innings when England had won a game, rather than be walking off the field with sadness predominating.

In that series between England and South Africa in 2003 I saw some of the best cricket imaginable. Certainly in the opening two Test matches the bat was on top of the ball and the South African captain Graeme Smith was right in the forefront of the batting bonanza. At Edgbaston he made 277 in the first innings of the drawn opening Test and then 85 in the second innings. Herschelle Gibbs hit a very good century, so too Michael Vaughan but, when Vaughan was caught with 89 still needed to save the follow-on, and Stewart went almost immediately, it needed Flintoff batting at number seven to hold things together with Ashley Giles. This was Flintoff in a new role, still playing with great power but picking the right ball to hit and defending beautifully.

In that Second Test at Lord's in 2003, Graeme Smith again hit a double-century, 259 this time, and with Gary Kirsten making 108 the England bowling attack was looking quite ordinary. Flintoff was certainly having trouble with his left foot. He bowled 40 overs in the South African innings and I saw enough of his movement and pain as that front foot hit the batting crease to know he was likely to need medical treatment at an early stage. But when? There is so little time between matches these days and medical treatment sometimes has to be put on the back burner. What Flintoff did in fact was come in at number seven in the England second innings and play one of the best attacking innings one could wish to see. The only problem was that it was played in a losing situation, but there is usually something good to come out of even the gloomiest happening.

There was a capacity crowd at Lord's, almost all the tickets having been sold, but the vacant seats were quickly filled by those who had been watching Channel Four and who then rushed to the ground when Flintoff started to flay the bowling. What I liked most about it was that he didn't simply hit the bowlers, he chose the loose ball very carefully and, despite hitting some of the good deliveries to and over the boundary, it was still a completely controlled performance. He came to the wicket when Stewart was out at 208 and then Flintoff scored his 142 out of the remaining 209 runs.

The lesson he was taught in that innings, apart from wanting to make runs in a winning team, was that it is very important to be there, or at least try to be there, in the centre of the ground when the innings ends. Watching him on television when England toured South Africa in 2004–05 I was very taken with the responsible batting and bowling he produced, even though he was clearly having problems with his fitness. Flintoff will be the key man during the Australian tour of England in 2005. If he fires, and the rest of the bowling attack are in top form, England have a real chance.

One of the young cricketers trying to stop Flintoff and the rest of the England team will be Clarke. Sometimes you need to see young cricketers play a few times before they make any real impact on your mind, but Clarke looked good the first time I saw him on the field which was in a Limited-overs International against England in Adelaide in the Australian season of 2002–03.

England certainly will remember his debut because this was a low-scoring game with England making 152 and Clarke taking his first international wicket, that of Ronnie Irani. Then, when the Australians were in trouble with the bat, he made 37* and Australia won the match. Here at first sighting was a young cricketer who had class written all over everything he did. I wasn't particularly interested in his left-arm spin bowling, though it might be handy for him to have it as another aspect to his game. His real problem though was that the Australian side was so strong he couldn't just walk into the squad. He had eventually made it into the Australian one-day side, but it was impossible to find a place for him in the Test team despite some outstanding innings in the Pura Cup matches (formerly the Sheffield Shield).

When Clarke made his debut in first-class cricket for NSW, he peeled off 65, 29, 73, 75, 45 and 58 to bring him to the notice of the Australian selectors. Then, in 2000–01, Clarke made 106, 111, 132, 134 and 129 and it was a matter of how soon he would play Test cricket, though he did need to keep making runs in the one-day matches. What made life even more awkward for him was that he had been left out of the final eleven of the one-day side after his very sound debut and he didn't play again until the Australians were in the West Indies and he forced his way into the match at Gros Islet in St Lucia. He had successive scores of 75*, 55* and 39 before Darren Lehmann came back into the team and made a century in the final match.

To emphasise how difficult a task it was for Clarke to force a place in the Australian Test side, it didn't happen until the captain, Ricky Ponting, broke a finger. Ponting was unable to play at the start of the tour of India and Adam Gilchrist had to take over as captain for the first three matches of the series. There was a considerable amount of nonsense talked at the time, with some players suggesting someone in form should or would stand down from the side in India to allow Clarke to make his Test debut. Fortunately nothing as ridiculous as that actually happened and the selectors made their own decision which worked out wonderfully well with Clarke hitting a magnificent 151. One player I was pleased to see retain his place in that match was Simon Katich who was at the crease when Clarke walked out on to the field in Bangalore. He is a calm influence on the team when there is trouble around and, when Clarke joined him, the innings was in some bother at 149/4 with Lehmann just dismissed. It wasn't a case of Katich completely guiding Clarke through early dramas, Clarke simply played magnificently and his partnership with Katich produced 107. And then came Gilchrist. Often the Australian wicket-keeper walks out on to the ground and turns a game. Here in Bangalore he certainly did that, making 106 brilliant runs. Together he and Clarke put on 167 in an astonishing partnership and Clarke kept going until the Australian score had reached 471.

Australia won that match, the Second at Chennai (Madras) was abandoned on the final day and Australia's Nagpur victory gave them an unbeatable 2–0 series lead. Ponting came back for the final

Test in Mumbai, a game played on a quaint surface which did no credit at all to the game of cricket. Clarke, with his left-arm spin, took 6/9 which is a fair reflection of the strip of dirt on which the game was played.

When Clarke came back to Australia there were five Tests to be played, two against New Zealand, who generously came to Australia after West Indies had decided they couldn't be bothered playing a three-match series, and also there were three Tests against Pakistan. Clarke walked out in the first Test against New Zealand, at the 'Gabba in Brisbane, and played another wonderful innings of 141 and again it was Gilchrist who was in with him, sharing a stand of 216. It was a high-scoring summer and Clarke was very much the young star in an Australian team which continued to play in magnificent fashion.

One of the highlights of the Australian summer is the Allan Border Medal Dinner. Part of this evening is the induction of former players into the Hall of Fame. The function is hosted by Australian television presenter Eddie McGuire and I am there as co-host. The main part of the evening is the awarding of the Allan Border Medal to the outstanding player of what is generally the calendar year; that though depends on the programming of the international season.

Awards are made to the One-day Cricketer of the Year, State Cricketer of the Year, the Bradman Young Cricketer of the Year, the Test Player of the Year, and the Allan Border Medallist is the player judged to be the best cricketer in all areas. In January of 2005, this black tie dinner was televised around Australia and players, their partners and a 1,000-strong guest list of celebrities and cricket followers saw Andrew Symonds listed for the One-day game, Andy Bichel for the Pura Cup, Michael Cosgrove of South Australia won the Bradman award and Damien Martyn, who had a wonderful year, was the Test Cricketer of the Year. Every match played by Australians is rated by the team members in a voting system, then media and umpires' votes are taken into account and there is a weighting system to cover the fact that there are more one-day matches played than Tests. It was a very tight count all the way through and then the Allan Border Medallist was announced as Michael Clarke.

It was an announcement greeted with great enthusiasm by those present at the dinner, a vast television audience, media and, I would suggest, most people interested in cricket around Australia. It isn't every week of the year you have the chance to salute, in whatever way you wish, one of the brilliant new talents in the game of cricket. For me, it was a very good night. I had watched Clarke on television as he made his century in Bangalore, commented on Channel Nine on his century against New Zealand in Brisbane, but I had never met him before this evening. As Daphne and I arrived at the venue we met him for the first time, talking to Shane Warne outside the dining-room. Three hours later I was interviewing him as the winner of the Allan Border Medal for 2004–05. It was one of the more enjoyable things I have done in many years because of not seeing a great deal of the players due to the very hectic television and general work schedule we have. At the grounds around Australia Ian Chappell, Tony Greig, Mark Taylor and Ian Healy do most of what might be termed the outdoor work concerned with pitch reports, the toss and interviews with players, plus presentations. I am based more in the studio with Simon O'Donnell and Bill Lawry, and the same system applies in England with Channel Four. I might have gone through the summer without meeting Clarke at all but, on that particular night, it was a great pleasure to meet him twice. I was able to think back to the time I had some success in cricket, when I was around the same age as Clarke and had first made it into the Australian team to play West Indies at the SCG, and then was chosen for my first tour of England in 1953.

I have no doubt the England camp also followed his progress

with great interest and Clarke's success will have had them making plans to curb his brilliance. He has played some cricket with Hampshire and his strengths, and possible weaknesses, will have been very carefully noted, as has been the case with opposing bowlers and captains over the years. They will make life very tough for him which is the way it should be. He is a fine young cricketer, a very good batsman and an outstanding fieldsman whose style of play is, for me, close to that of Norman O'Neill who came on to the Australian cricket scene with NSW in 1955–56, the last summer in which Keith Miller captained the state. O'Neill was very good. He was a wonderful driver of the ball off the front foot, but no one played his back-foot shots with more power and skill than O'Neill. Clarke is from a similar mould and I believe he will be one of the stars of Australian cricket over the next ten years. I'm hoping that he and Flintoff have already made the 2005 Ashes battle one to remember.

No matter what happens in the Ashes battle in England, you can be certain Australia will face a tough series against South Africa over the 2005–06 summer. Under Graeme Smith the South African team is starting to play good cricket and they have some fine emerging players in their squad.

20

POTPOURRI

SOMETHING FOR ADMINISTRATORS TO PONDER

Twenty20 Cricket: There are only three things that matter about
Twenty20 Cricket.

1. If 20,000 spectators *continue* attending cricket matches and enjoy
   themselves, then that is great for the game.
2. Will Twenty20 techniques be to the benefit of Test cricket, as has
   been the case with 50-overs-a-side limited-overs cricket over the past
   28 years?
3. Winning the World Cup every four years can only be based on
   50-overs-a-side matches and 50-overs-a-side skills; 40 per cent won't
   work.

An interesting statistic on no-balls in Test cricket: Between
1876–77 and 1968–69 there were fewer than 5,000 no-balls in
Test cricket under the back-foot Law.

Between 1968–69 and 2005 there were more than 27,000 no-balls
in Test cricket under the front-foot Law. Two questions for the ICC:

1. Is there any common sense associated with that?
2. Do those figures mean it is a good Law of cricket?

The white ball: Limited-overs cricket and the World Cup have
brought untold riches to administration and worthwhile increases
in income to players. Is there a reason no money has been spent on

producing a proper white ball? Is it just laziness, couldn't care less, can't be bothered, or because the easy way out is just to use two balls an innings?

Polishing the ball: ICC regulations make sure that in this era match referees and umpires keep a close eye on the ball to make certain no one is handling it in illegal fashion. In fact, all the ICC need to do about any form of ball-tampering is bring in one simple Playing Condition, with an eye to making it a Law of the game.

Allow only the bowler to shine the ball.

At the end of each over toss the ball to the umpire, who will look at it to make certain nothing has happened in the previous over, the umpire tosses the ball to the new bowler who has precisely six balls in which to work on it legally. The remainder of the fielding team are banned from doing anything to it. What could be simpler?

It has become a fetish with teams who have completely bluffed the ICC into not doing anything about it. If the ICC want to do something constructive about time-wasting for spectators then this is one matter they could attend to straight away, and then look into the really important question of match referees paying proper attention to Test matches starting at the stated time, which they do, and then finishing at the stated time, which they don't.

On the time-wasting with ball-polishing, paying spectators are ill-served by what goes on. Just think of the ridiculous posturing and polishing that goes on at the moment. The ball is returned from the 'keeper to gully, who polishes and then tosses it to cover, who polishes and then sends it to mid-off, who polishes madly, sometimes going through contortions that most times would be produced by someone stricken by a muscular affliction.

The latest addition to this is that teams have a 'master polisher'.

He is the one who is said to polish the ball better than any other in the team. Have you ever heard anything more nonsensical? Perhaps the game in some respects has gone bonkers, if so this is certainly one of them. The players thumb their noses at the match referees with this Playing Condition of the game and, when they're not doing that, they're laughing at them because they know no referee has the fibre to invoke the penalty clause that a captain can be banned for a match or even two for time-wasting and late finishing of match days.

In April 2005 the laughter became a little more muted.

The 15 degree bent arm in bowling: Now it has been established that the waiting legal people were the ones who brought the new throwing Law into being, is there anything else in the game being hidden from us that might be a big issue with legal threats in the future?

AT THE DOUBLE – OVER THE YEARS

Test Match Double

Order of reaching the Double of 2,000 runs and 200 wickets

Season	Name	Runs	Wkts	Tests Played	Double Achieved in Test No
1963–64	Richie Benaud	2,201	248	63	60
1970–71	Garfield Sobers	8,032	235	93	80
1981–82	Ian Botham	5,200	383	102	42
1982–83	Kapil Dev	5,248	434	131	50
1983–84	Imran Khan	3,807	362	88	50
1984–85	Richard Hadlee	3,124	431	86	54
1997–98	Wasim Akram	2,424	383	91	78
2000–01	*Shaun Pollock				56
2001–02	*Shane Warne				100
2003–04	Chris Cairns	3,050	202	62	58
2004–05	*Chaminda Vaas				82

* Still playing Test cricket

Australian Sheffield Shield Double

Order of reaching the Double of 2,000 runs and 200 wickets

Richie Benaud	v Victoria	23–28 December, 1961
Alan Davidson	v WA	2–6 February, 1962
Johnny Martin	v WA	19–23 February, 1965
Terry Jenner	v WA	25–28 October, 1974
Ray Bright	v Tasmania	22–25 February, 1985
Peter Sleep	v Tasmania	18–21 November, 1988
Ken MacLeay	v NSW	2–5 March, 1990
Greg Matthews	v Tasmania	12–15 December, 1991
Tony Dodemaide	v Queensland	29 Feb–3 March, 1992
Tom Moody	v Queensland	16–19 January, 1999
Brendon Julian	v Victoria	15–18 October, 1999
Shaun Young	v SA	15–18 March, 2001

RICHIE BENAUD BIOGRAPHY

Name: Richard (Richie) Benaud

Born: 6 October 1930

Wife and date of marriage: Daphne, 26 July 1967

Family links with cricket: Lou Benaud, my father, a legspin bowler and allrounder, was an outstanding country cricketer in NSW in the 1920s and early 1930s. He then played in Sydney first-grade club cricket for many years. When I made my debut in Central Cumberland's 1st XI in 1946, he was in the team. My brother John played for NSW and Australia, was an Australian selector from 1988 to 1993 and also was chairman of the NSW selection committee.

Education: Parramatta High School.

Career outside media: With Daphne as Benaud and Associates Pty Ltd, International Sports Consultants.

Other sports played: Tennis and soccer until aged 21, since then golf.

Other sports followed: Golf, horseracing, soccer, Rugby Union, Rugby League, Australian Rules.

Relaxations: Golf, horseracing, reading and the occasional glass of Montrachet or Lynch-Bages.

Broadcasting career: BBC Radio 1960. BBC Television 1963–99. Channel Nine Television 1977–. Channel Four Television 1999–2005.

Newspapers and magazines: Journalist with *The Sun* (Sydney newspaper) 1956–1969, *News of the World* 1960–. Freelance journalist 1969–

Books published: *Way of Cricket* (1961); *A Tale of Two Tests* (1962); *Spin me a Spinner* (1963); *The New Champions* (1965); *Willow Patterns* (1969); *Benaud on Reflection* (1984); *The Appeal of Cricket* (1995); *Anything but . . . an Autobiography* (1998); *My Spin on Cricket* (2005).

As a player: Right-hand bat, legspin bowler. Played for NSW (1948–64) and Australia (1952–64). The first cricketer (1963) to complete the 'double' of 2,000 runs and 200 wickets in Test cricket. The first Australian (1961) to complete the 'double' of 2,000 runs and 200 wickets in Sheffield Shield cricket. One of ten Australian cricketers to have scored 10,000 runs and taken 500 wickets in first-class cricket.

1st class 100s:	23
1st class 5w in innings:	56
1st class 10w in match:	9
1st class catches:	254

Overseas tours: Australia to England 1953, 1956, 1961 (captain), West Indies 1955, Pakistan 1956–57, 1959–60 (captain), to India 1956–57, 1959–60 (captain) to South Africa (1957–58).

Extras: Captain of Australia 1958 63 (28 Tests). Awarded the OBE 1962. One of *Wisden*'s Five Cricketers of the Year 1962. In excess of 500 Test matches as a player, watcher and commentator.

Best batting: 187 Australians v Natal, Pietermaritzburg, 1957–58.

Best bowling: 7/18 NSW v MCC, SCG, 1962–63.

First-class and international career performances:

	M	Inn	NO	Runs	HS	Avge	100	Ct	Runs	Wkts	Avge	Best	5wI	10wM
T	63	97	7	2,201	122	24.45	3	65	6,704	248	27.03	7/72	16	1
FC	259	365	44	11,719	187	36.50	23	254	23,371	945	24.73	7/18	56	9

EPILOGUE – PEOPLE CRICKET CAN'T DO WITHOUT

A cricket match is a contest and as I found, aged 12, when I scored for Central Cumberland 2nd XI, the scorer is one of the most important people at the cricket match. There are some people who are dispensable in cricket, even though they might also be delightful, but the scorer is indispensable. Think for a moment what would have happened at the 'Gabba in 1960 had the scorers not been giving the game their full attention, particularly as some of the players weren't certain for a few moments which side had won before they realised that neither side had done so. In the outback of Australia the scorer, or scorers if there are two, will keep their carefully-written records in a large scorebook. The one I used as a youngster when scoring unofficially was the small *Pocket Unrivalled Scoring Book*. When scoring for the Cumberland 2nd XI I had the larger version of the *Unrivalled*, the same as used in club, Sheffield Shield and Test matches in the early days in Australia.

It was a great compliment from there to be asked in 2000 and 2004 to write the forewords to Tom Smith's *New Cricket Umpiring and Scoring* book, the internationally recognised and definitive guide to the interpretation and application of the Laws of cricket and of scoring.

In the television commentary boxes these days a far more sophisticated system is used so that a record is able to be kept of every ball bowled. For Channel Nine in Australia Max Kruger is an excellent scorer-statistician. For Channel Four in the United Kingdom Jo King does an outstanding job; Malcolm Ashton, thoroughly professional, preceded her and he was also the BBC Television scorer for many years. Irving Rosenwater was, and is, a brilliant cricket historian, as well as a scorer and statistician, and Wendy Wimbush, apart from doing an extraordinary amount of work for the Cricket Writers' Club, splendidly handles the scoring in media centres around the UK. BBC Radio nowadays relies on Bill Frindall who produces, as well, printed records of every Test match played and every statistic known to the game. He was preceded at the BBC by Arthur Wrigley, Roy Webber and Jack Price. All of the modern scorers use the same basic system mentioned above which allows the whole match to be replayed. I have always thought this to be one of the best scoring methods I have seen in any sport and I was even more intrigued some years ago to learn how it came about.

The information came because during a BBC telecast at Headingley in early August 1994, in the course of the England v South Africa Test, we showed a youngster sitting in the crowd. He was avidly watching the cricket and keeping, in very neat fashion, his own scorebook of the match. I remarked that I had done the same as this lad when I was his age and I hoped he might one day go on to be a good cricketer and enjoy the game as much as I have done.

A week later I received a letter from Ken Pendlington, enclosing a newspaper cutting dated 16 January, 1914 noting the death of his grandfather. The story it told was that Mr John Atkinson Pendlington, a great lover of cricket, when reviewing on a winter's evening the important contests as reported by Lillywhite and *Wisden* thought it should be possible to devise a scorebook to record the result of every ball bowled in a match. He soon had it worked out and took the score at Scarborough in Lord Londesbrough's match against the Australians in 1893 (Mr C.I. Thornton's XI). This record showed, for all time, the number of balls each batsman received from each bowler, and what runs he made from them. It caused much amusement and pleasure to Dr W.G. Grace who was at Scarborough and was presented with the authentic document.

John Atkinson Pendlington was born in South Shields in 1861 and he and his son played for Benwell in the Northumberland League. He was noted as a Shakespearean scholar and a good conversationalist and he founded the Tyneside Supply Company which later became the British Electrical and Manufacturing Company of Newcastle and London. Once asked his religion he is said to have answered 'I am neither heterodox nor orthodox, but just a paradox.'

It seems a nice way for me to say goodbye to British Television because Pendlington, and those dedicated scorers who followed him over the past 112 years, are among the people cricket can never do without.

INDEX

ABC television (Australian
　　Broadcasting Commission) 9–10
aboriginal pioneers 104, 105
ACA *see* Australian Cricketers'
　　Association
ACB *see* Australian Cricket Board
Abdul Qadir 108, 122
Adcock, Neil 114, 250
Adelaide Oval 7, 12, 32, 167, 174
Agnew, Jonathan 85–6
Alderman, Terry 117, 222, 231
Alderson, Bert 180
Alexander, Gerry 235, 238
Allen, David 170, 226
Allen, 'Gubby' 112, 195
Alley, Bill 183
Alliss, Peter 90–91
Ambrose, Curtly 210
Amiss, Dennis 172, 251
Anderson, James 30
anti-siphoning list 13–14
Archer, Ken 145, 178–9
Archer, Ron 168, 190
Arlott, John 48
Armstrong, Warwick 124, 141, 221–2
Ashes (1882) 23; (1936) 196; (1953)
　　169; (1961) 161; (1972) 204;
　　(1987) 229; (1989) 116, 223;
　　(2001) 177; (2005) 14, 229, 270

Ashton, Malcolm 277
Atherton, Michael 58, 61, 93, 175–6
　　ball tampering incident 94–7
Atkinson, Denis 88, 236–8
Australia
　　1999 World Cup 35
　　aboriginal pioneers 104–5
　　important cricket moments 103–5
　　team of the century 107
　　v England (1877) 21, 216; (1882)
　　　22–3, 217; (1905) 141; (1908)
　　　110; (1926) 66; (1930)110;
　　　(1936) 194–6; (1948) 48, 223;
　　　(1952–3) 3, 65, 145, 153, 225;
　　　(1956) 55, 67, 169, 247–8;
　　　(1959) 7; (1961) 72, 74, 181,
　　　200–4, 226; (1970–1) 8; (1972)
　　　15, 204–7; (1975) 9; (1981) 117–
　　　18, 174; (1997) 211; (2002–3)
　　　266
　　v India (1980) 110–11; (1991–2)
　　　116; (1999) 35; (2004) 28, 30–1
　　v New Zealand (2000) 35; (2001)
　　　268; (2004–5) 75
　　v Pakistan (1959) 196–200; (1972–
　　　3) 227; (1976–7) 120; (1999–
　　　2000) 35, 193, 212–15; (2005)
　　　213
　　v Rest of the World 204–5

v South Africa (1935–6) 224;
(1949–50) 145; (1952–3) 240;
(1957–8) 250; (1997–8) 32–4;
(1999) 261; World Cup 35;
(2000) 35; (2005) 270
v Sri Lanka (1995–6) 257; (2004)
28–9
v West Indies (1951–2) 188–9, 229,
236, 239–40; (1955) 88, 153,
236; (1960–1) Tied Test 7, 8,
113–14, 124, 161, 229, 234–6;
(1975–6) 9, 12, 115, 231–2;
(1978) 13; (1991) 87; (1995)
210–12; (2004) 230; (2005) 238
Australian Academy 263
Australian Board of Control 6, 9, 72,
194, 197, 235, 239–43
Australian Broadcasting Commission
see ABC
Australian Broadcasting Control
Board 9
Australian Cricket Board
and Hansie Cronje 34
payment to players 10
Australian Cricket and Cricketers 22
Australian Cricketers' Association 58,
243–4
Australian Cricketers' Hall of Fame
216–28, 268
Australian team of the century 107
The Australian Team in England 1934
194

Bacher, Dr Ali 36–7, 39, 43
Badcock, Jackie 196
Bailey, Noel 15
Bailey, Trevor 30, 65, 109
Balderstone, Chris 172

Ballesteros, Seve 90
Bangladesh 19
Bannerman, 'Alick' 218
Bannister, Jack 58, 60–2, 84, 86
Baptiste, Eldine 258
Barber, Bob 142
Bardsley, Warren 124
Barnes, Sydney Francis (England) 108,
110, 119, 123–5, 151
Barnes, Sidney George (Australia)
112, 140, 180, 183, 189, 219,
239–41
Batchelor, Denzil 48
Batohi, Shamila 42
BBC Radio 5, 255
BBC Radio Five Live 42
BBC television
televising cricket 15, 78–92, 94
training course 4–5, 14, 90
Beal, Charlie 22
Bedser, Alec 65, 111, 118, 122, 129,
168–9
Bell, Ronnie 101
Bellerive Oval, Hobart 214
Bell's Life 22
Benaud, Daphne (wife of RB) 1–2,
126, 269
Benaud, John (brother of RB) 244,
256
Benaud, Lou (father of RB) 3, 24–6,
121, 127, 151, 193, 244
Benaud, Rene (mother of RB) 152
Benaud, Richie
BROADCASTING 275
BBC television training course 4–5,
14, 90
sports commentator 5, 13–17, 104
television broadcasting 4–5, 79, 275

EDUCATION, school cricket 24, 183, 275

LIFE
biography 79–80, 275–6
This is Your Life 134

PLAYER
captaincy 221, 276; (1953) 3; (1958) 45, 113; (1960) 7, 67; (1961) 100, 114, 161
selection for Australia 188, 190, 269
Spirit of Cricket lecture 244

WRITING
biography 275–6
Benaud Spirit of Cricket Awards 244
Benjamin, Kenny 212
Berry, Darren 104
betting on cricket 43–4
Bevan, Hugh 166
Bevan, Michael 259–61
Bichel, Andy 260, 268
Bird, Dickie 95
Birmingham Post 60
Blackham, Jack 217–18
Blewett, Greg 211
Bligh, Hon.Ivo 22, 23
Bocelli, Andrea 3, 17
bodyline bowling 38, 105, 122, 223
Boon, David 175, 210, 225
Border, Allan 58, 61, 85, 91, 107, 174–5, 221–3, 243, 257
   Allan Border Medal 268–9
   runs 174, 225
Bosanquet, Bernard 45, 140–3
Botham, Ian 30, 108, 117–18, 258, 263
bowlers 168–77, 249
bowling 21, 29, 30, 58–73
   bodyline 38, 105, 122, 223
   bosie 45, 140

doosra 60–1
fast bowlers 122
finger problems 151, 155–9
finger remedy 158–9
flipper 148–50
googly 56, 140
lbw 54–7
leg-theory 55–6
legspin 121, 135, 139–60
run up 152
throwing 58–73
Boyce, Keith 231
Boycott, Geoff 82, 84, 207, 244
Boyle, Harry 218
Bradman, Sir Donald 16, 47–54, 64, 69–70, 73, 106–13, 121, 125, 157, 193–6, 217, 222, 236, 240, 243
   captain 127, 194–6, 225, 241
   runs 110, 180, 196, 219, 220, 223, 225
Brangwyn, Frank 45
Bray, Charles 48
Brearley, Mike 118, 174
Brightman, Sarah 3, 17
Brooks, Reginald 23
Brooks, Shirley 23
Brooks, Tom 173
Brown, Bill 48, 154, 186, 195
Brown, Freddie 144
Browne, Courtney 210
Bucknor, Steve 76, 210
Buller, Syd 67, 70–71, 101
Burge, Peter 55, 95, 148, 163, 202, 204
Burke, Jim 144–5, 183–4, 188, 239, 248
Butcher, Mark 177

Butler, 'Bunny' 237
Butler, Frank 68

CA *see* Cricket Australia
Caine, C.Stewart 22
Cameron, Frank 158
Cape Times 40
Carlson, Phil 7
Carter, Hanson 219
Cave, Harry 70
Centenary Test 7, 172–3, 228
Central Cumberland Club 24, 26
Champions' Trophy 31
Chandrasekhar, Bhagwat 115
Channel Four 4, 15, 74–5, 81, 83, 93–
    4, 265, 269, 277
Channel Nine 4, 9, 10–12, 32, 78–9,
    81, 83, 88, 91, 94, 116, 193, 277
Chappell, Greg 107–8, 113, 115, 204–
    8, 221, 223–5, 227, 232, 256
Chappell, Ian 15, 33, 82, 204, 207,
    221, 225–6, 232, 269
Chauhan, Chetan 111
Cheetham, Jack 242
Chegwyn, Jack 146–7, 191
Chester, Frank 64–7
Chicago White Sox, v Cincinnati
    Reds 39
Chilvers, Hughie 47
Chipperfield, Arthur 140, 219
Clark, Belinda 104–5
Clarke, Michael 31, 213, 263, 266–70
Clarke, Sylvester 231
Coca-Cola 256
Colley, David 205, 207
Collins, Herbie 66
Compton, Denis 14–15, 91
Condon, Sir Paul 41

Cooke, Col 7
Corling, Graham 247
Cornell, John 10
Cosgrove, Michael 268
County Championship 18
Coward, Mike 221
Cowdrey, Colin (Lord Cowdrey of
    Tonbridge) 14, 55, 66, 170, 201,
    244, 251
Cowper, Bob 139, 159, 163, 256
Cozier, Tony 238
Craig, Ian 113–4, 150, 161, 165, 248
Crawford, Pat 55
Crawley, Aidan 15
cricket
    Australian administrators 239–52
    Australian team of the century 107
    balls 271
    betting on 43–4
    club cricket 18
    day-night cricket 10, 13, 52, 257
    Five Cricketers of the Century 106
    Laws 21, 52, 54–62
    limited-overs cricket 18
    match fixing scandal 36–43
    matting 196–7
    one-day cricket 9, 14, 253–62
    schools cricket 24–7
    scoreboard 12
    scorebook 278
    scorers 277–8
    sledging 245–50
    Spirit of Cricket 244
    statistics 30
    throwing controversy 56–64, 273
    time-wasting 65, 71
    umpiring 21, 34, 62–77
    walking decisions 98–102

Cricket Australia 230, 243, 244, 257
  Benaud Spirit of Cricket Awards 244
  contract strictures 31
  players' code 245–6
  sponsorship 18
Cricket Writers' Club 277
Croft, Colin 231
Cronje, Hansie 32–43
Cush, Frank 241

Daniel, Jack 'Dasher' 154
Davidson, Alan 27, 55, 146, 151,
      157, 162, 166, 168, 188, 190,
      199, 200, 203, 221, 226, 235,
      261
  bowling 163–4, 186, 197–8, 227,
      234
day-night cricket 10, 13, 52, 257
De L'Isle, Lord 201
de Lotbiniere, Seymour 16
DeFreitas, Phillip 176
Denness, Mike 251
Depeiza, Clairmonte 88
Dexter, Ted 13, 15, 182, 200, 202,
      244, 255
Dickens, Charles 103
Dilley, Graham 118
Donald, Allan 261
Dooland, Bruce 141, 142, 148–51
Doshi, Dilip 111
Dowding, Alan 66
Dowling, Bill 69–70
Dowling, Graham 256
Dravid, Rahul 28
Drysdale, Russell 45–6
Dujon, Jeffrey 120
Dwyer, Chappie 241, 243
Dymock, Geoff 231

ECB (England and Wales Cricket
      Board) 97
Edrich, Bill 112
Edrich, John 251
Edwards, 'Banna' 26
Edwards, Bert 129
Edwards, Ross 171, 206
Edwards, Wally 243
electronic scoreboard 12
Elliott, Herb 67
Emburey, John 30
Emery, Vic 184
England
  v Australia (1877) 21, 216; (1882)
      22–3, 217; (1905) 141; (1908)
      110; (1926) 66; (1930) 110;
      (1936) 194–6; (1948) 48, 223;
      (1952–3) 3, 65, 145, 153, 225;
      (1956) 55, 67, 169, 247–8;(1959)
      7; (1961) 72, 74, 181, 200–4,
      226; (1970–1) 8; (1972) 15, 204–
      7; (1975) 9; (1981) 117–18, 174;
      (1997) 211; (2002–3) 266
  v New Zealand (1994) 84; (1999)
      35; (2004) 29–30
  v South Africa (1955) 250; (1960)
      67; (1994–5) 174, 278; (1998)
      34; (2000) 39; (2003) 28–9, 260,
      264; (2004–5) 28, 29, 263–4, 266
  v West Indies (1963) 5, 14, 170;
      (1976) 116, 233; (1984) 258–9;
      (1994) 113; (2004) 28, 29
England and Wales Cricket Board see
      ECB
Evans, Godfrey 120, 129, 248

Farquharson, John 67
Faulkner, Aubrey 141

Favell, Les 165, 198, 235, 256

Fazal Mahmood 196–8

Fender, Percy 16

fielding 53

finger remedy 157–9

Fingleton, Jack 64, 195

    Brightly Fades the Don 47–8

Five Cricketers of the Century 106

Flavell, Jack 182

Fleetwood-Smith, 'Chuck' 140, 195–6, 224

Fleming, Damien 208, 261

Fleming, Stephen 98

Flintoff, Andrew 30, 260, 263–6

Flockton, Ray 188

Ford, Doug 165

Foster, Drew 1–2

Foster, Neil 258

Fox Sports 14

Francis, Bruce 206

Francke, Malcolm 7

Franses, Gary 15, 81

Fraser, Neale 67

Fredericks, Roy 172

Freeman, 'Tich' 142

French, Dick 104–5

French, Peter 221

Frindall, Bill 278

'Gabba, the 7, 91, 154–5, 179, 197, 277

Gardner, Fred 86

Garner, Joel 231

Gatting, Mike 85, 127, 175, 229

Gavaskar, Sunil 108, 110–11, 125, 244

Gibb, Paul 70

Gibbs, Herschelle 40–1, 261, 265

Gibbs, Lance 127, 231

Gifford, Norman 206, 256

Gilchrist, Adam 28, 30–31, 98–9, 108–9, 120, 125, 193, 211–5, 225, 261, 267–8

Gilchrist, Roy 233

Giles, Ashley 30, 265

Gillespie, Jason 31, 152

Gillette Cup one-day cricket 9, 256

Gilmour, Gary 115, 231

Gleeson, John 140–1, 146–8, 205

Goddard, John 189, 238

Gomez, Gerry 236

Gooch, Graham 176

Goodman, Tom 128, 202

Goonesena, Gamini 140

Gosford High School 26

Gough, Darren 176

Gover, Alf 70

Gower, David 1, 97

Gower, Thorunn 1

Grace, Dr W.G. 80, 110, 218, 278

Grafton High School 24

Greatbatch, Mark 176–7

Greenfield, George 67

Greenidge, Gordon 108–9

Gregory, Dave 21

Gregory, Jack 122, 180, 217

Greig, Tony 30, 33, 172, 205, 251, 269

Grieves, Ken 154

Griffin, Geoff 70–1

Griffiths, Alan 79, 83–5

Grimmett, Clarrie 112, 121, 127, 132, 137, 140–2, 148, 181, 217, 219

    Grimmett on Getting Wickets 135

Grout, Wally 199, 202, 235
Gyngell, Bruce 4

Hadlee, Barry 117
Hadlee, Dayle 117
Hadlee, Sir Richard 108, 117
Hadlee, Walter 117
Haigh, Gideon 221
Hall, Wesley 88, 162, 170, 233–5
Hammond, Wally 108, 111–2, 140,
    195–6
Hanif Mohammad 199
Hanlin, Dave 185
Harmison, Steve 30
Harper, Roger 260
Harvey, Neil 65, 100, 107, 145–6,
    152, 161–3, 165, 170, 190, 196–
    204, 211, 221–2, 226, 235, 239–
    40
Hassett, Lindsay 3, 55, 65, 86, 128–
    30, 140, 143–5, 148, 153, 168,
    187–8, 221, 225–6, 239–40
Hayden, Matthew 28, 113, 225
Headley, George 108, 111
Healy, Ian 107–8, 120, 209, 214, 269
Heine, Peter 114, 250
Hemmings, Eddie 119
Hill, Clem 124, 222, 227
Hill, David 11
Hill, Jack 146, 153–4, 247
Hirwani Narendra 119
Hobbs, Robin 140
Hobbs, Sir Jack 66, 106, 108, 110,
    124–5
Hodge, Brad 31
Hogan, Paul 10
Hoggard, Matthew 30
Holder, Vanburn 231

Holding, Michael 172, 231–3, 258–9
Hole, Graeme 145, 168, 239
Hollies, Eric 86, 140, 142
Hooper, Carl 210, 259
Horner, Norman 86
Horton, Martin 256
Hudson, Robert 14
Hughes, Kim 118, 173–5
Hughes, Simon 75
Hunte, Conrad 235
Hunter, Nick 15
Hurst, Alan 231
Hutton, Sir Leonard 65, 108–9, 181,
    236

ICC *see* International Cricket Council
ICC Code of Conduct
Ijaz Butt 199, 213
Illingworth, Ray 8, 30, 95–7, 204–5,
    219, 224
Imran Khan 108, 117, 119–20, 125
India
    v Australia (1980–1) 110–11;
        (1991–2) 116; (1999) 35; (2004)
        28, 30–1
    v South Africa (2000) 35
Indian Central Bureau of
    Investigation 42
ING 257
ING Cup 243
Insole, Doug 69
International Cricket Council (ICC)
    anti-corruption investigator 41
    bowling actions 58–64, 71
    fracas in Zimbabwe 19
    umpiring 74
Invincibles tour (1948) 217, 223
Inzamam-ul-Haq 212–13

Irani, Ronnie 266
Israr Ali 197–8
Iverson, Jack 140–7, 154

Jackman, Robin 117
Jackson, 'Shoeless' Joe 39
James, Ivan 151, 154, 157, 159
James, Ron 143, 145, 186
Jarrett, Milton 254
Jeffery, Jack 157
Jenkins, Roly 140
Jenner, Terry 231
John Fairfax Pty Ltd 67, 128
Johnson, Ian 55, 65, 88, 144–5, 148, 153, 189, 192, 239
Johnson, Keith 241
Johnson, Len 184
Johnston, Bill 143, 145, 186–7, 189, 236, 239
Johnston, Brian 5, 14–15, 68, 85–6, 91–2
Johnston, Clive 144
Johnston, Fred 154, 184
Jones, Dick 223
Jones, Simon 30
Jordaan, Alan 32–3

Kallicharran, Alvin 258
Kallis, Jacques 33, 126–7, 261
Kanhai, Rohan 162, 166
Kapil Dev 108, 111, 117–9
Kasprowicz, Michael 33, 199
Katich, Simon 267
Kelleway, Charlie 124
Kenning, David 13, 15
Kenyon, Don 256
Khan Mohammad 197
Kilburn, Jim 48

King, Collis 172
King Commission 39–43
King, Jo 277
King, Mr Justice 39–43
Kippax, Alan 132
Kirsten, Gary 261, 265
Kline, Lindsay 8, 198–9
Klusener, Lance 261
Knight, Nick 260
Knott, Alan 120, 173, 256
Kruger, Max 277

Lakeland, Ray 14
Laker, Jim 13, 15, 65, 127, 140, 152, 156, 169–70, 247
Lane, Tim 104–5, 221
Langer, Justin 193, 212–15
Langley, Gilbert 66, 239
Langridge, John 70
Lara, Brian 28, 87, 108, 113–14, 212, 238
Larwood, Harold 108, 122
Laver, Rod 67
Lawrence, Charles 104
Lawrence, John 140
Lawry, Bill 34, 164, 200–4, 206, 211, 221, 256, 269
Laws of Cricket 71
Laws of cricket Bradman 64
  lbw 52, 54–7
  throwing 58–62
  tossing 52
Lawson, Geoff 120
Laxman, V.V.S. 28
Lee, Brett 104–5
Lee, Frank 65, 70
Lee, Jack 45–6
Lehmann, Darren 260, 267

Lewis, Joan 1
Lewis, Phil 14
Lewis, Tony 1, 78, 81–2, 84, 86, 94, 97
  Taking Fresh Guard 78
Leyland, Maurice 195
Liebenberg, Karl 210
Lillee, Dennis 104–5, 107–8, 111,
    115, 119, 122–3, 125, 172–3,
    204–8, 217, 219, 226–7, 231,
    251, 258
Lillywhite, James 21, 104, 216, 278
limited-overs cricket 18, 52–4, 261–2
Lindwall, Ray 55, 107–8, 116, 122,
    145, 154, 156, 178–92, 197, 199,
    217, 236, 239–40
Lloyd, Bob 221
Lloyd, Clive 115, 118, 172, 175, 231,
    233, 244, 258
Lloyd, David 251
Lock, Tony 65, 70, 140, 169, 181–2,
    204, 248–9, 256
Londesbrough, Lord 278
Longhurst, Henry 5, 68, 90
Lord's Taverners 91
Loxton, Sam 145, 198
Luckhurst, Brian 251
Lush, 'Ginty' 183

Macartney, Charlie 26, 124
McCabe, Stan 48, 112, 127, 196, 221,
    223–4
McCool, Colin 133, 141–2, 144–5,
    151, 154–6, 158
McDermott, Craig 176–7, 208
McDonald, Colin 100–1, 148, 189,
    202, 235, 248
McDonald, Ian 144
McDonald, Ted 122, 180, 217

MacGill, Stuart 33, 142, 160
McGrath, Glenn 28, 61, 108, 120,
    122–3, 173, 176–7, 208–9, 227,
    260, 264
McGuire, Eddie 268
Mackay, Ken 'Slasher' 8, 146, 162,
    164, 197–200, 235
McKenzie, Graham 202–3, 226
Mackenzie, Keith 82–3, 86–7, 89, 94,
    96
McLachlan, Ian 165, 243
McLean, Bob 186
McMillan, Brian 33
McMillan, Craig 98, 120
Mailey, Arthur 45–9, 133, 141–2
  10 for 66 and All That 45
Malcolm, Devon 97, 176
Mallett, Ashley 104, 231, 251
Malone, Mick 231
Mandela, Nelson 41
Marsh, Rod 108, 120, 171, 173, 205,
    207, 222, 227–8, 251
Marshall, Malcolm 174–5, 231
Marshall, Norman 237
Martin, Johnny 163–4
Martin, Jonathan 82
Martyn, Damien 268
Marylebone Cricket Club *see* MCC
Maskell, Dan 5, 68, 90
Massie, Bob 171–2, 205–7
Massie, Hugh 218
May, Peter 55, 201
May, Tim 58–60, 63, 221, 243
Mayne, Laurie 166
MCC (Marylebone Cricket Club)
    illegal bowling action 3, 69
MCG *see* Melbourne Cricket Ground
Meckiff, Ian 7, 197, 199, 235

Melbourne
  Age 103
  Melbourne Cricket Ground (MCG)
    6, 9, 110, 172, 188, 194–6, 257
  St Kilda ground 6–7, 12
Melbourne Cricket Club 104, 216
  Australian Cricketers' Hall of Fame
    107, 216–28, 268
Menzies, Right Hon.R.G. 48
Mercantile Mutual 257
Merriman, Bob 243
Miller, Geoff 172, 258
Miller, Keith 55, 66, 107–9, 116, 122,
    124–5, 143, 145, 156, 169, 178–
    92, 217, 236, 239, 270
Milner, Doug 255
Misson, Frank 164, 202
Moin Khan 212
Moir, Alex 158
Moody, Clarence, *Australian Cricket*
  and Cricketers 22
Morelli, Brian 11
Moroney, Jack 145, 187, 189
Morris, Arthur 65, 107–9, 116, 145,
    154, 156, 168, 178–92, 221–3,
    225, 239
Morris, Geoff 88
Morris, Mel 112, 194
Moss, Ron 183–4
Mudge, Harold 140
Muralitharan, Muttiah 71
Murdoch, Billy 217
My Greatest XI (*DVD*) 103–25, 139

Nagle, Kel 67
New Cricket Umpiring and Scoring 21
New South Wales
  Colts match 183

Sheffield Shield 162–7, 178, 185–9,
  191, 219, 225
  v Queensland 162–4, 178, 184–6
  v South Australia 165–7, 189, 219
  v Victoria 6–7, 48, 163–5, 183–4
  v Western Australia 162
New South Wales Cricket Association
  (NSWCA) 47, 191, 242
  and Bradman 50
  Sheffield Shield takings 164
  TV fees 7
New Zealand 256
  v Australia (1999) 35; (2001) 268;
    (2004–5) 75
  v England (1994) 84; (1999–2000)
    35; (2004) 29–30
News of the World 1, 37, 68, 93–6
Noblet, Geff 239
NSWCA *see* New South Wales Cricket
  Association

Oakman, Alan 101, 256
O'Donnell, Simon 269
Old, Chris 174
one-day cricket 9, 14, 253–62
O'Neill, Norman 101, 235, 270
O'Reilly, Bill 'Tiger' 48, 107–8, 111–
    12, 121–2, 126–42, 148, 151,
    158, 182, 191, 195, 217, 219
O'Sullevan, Peter 5, 68, 90
Oxford University, v Australia (1953)
  66
Oxlade, Aub 240–1, 243

Packer, Kerry 10, 11
Pakistan
  v Australia (1959) 196–200; (1972–
    3) 227; (1976–7) 120; (1999–

2000) 35, 193, 212–15; (2005) 35
v South Africa (2000) 35
Palmer, Arnold 67
Pardon, Charles F. 22
Pardon, Edgar S. 22
Pardon, Sydney H. 22
Parish, Bob 10
Parr, George 103
Parramatta
  Burnside School 24
  High School 24, 254–5
  Richie Benaud Oval 80
Parry, Laurence 1
Parry, Val 1
Pascoe, Len 231
Paul, K.K. 36–7, 42–3
Pay Television 13–14
payment to players 10
Patterson, Patrick 231
Pendlington, John Atkinson 278–9
Pendlington, Ken 278
Penrith Waratah v St Mary's 24, 25
Pepper, Cecil 112, 140, 148
Pettiford, Jack 154, 183
Phillip, Norbert 231
players
  code of conduct 245–6
  contracts 31
  match fees 10, 230
Pocock, Blair 176
Pollock, Graeme 108, 113, 114–15
Pollock, Peter 114
Pollock, Shaun 37, 61, 261
Ponsford, Bill 48, 107, 217–19
Ponting, Ricky 19–20, 28–31, 54, 98–9, 213, 227, 263, 267–8
Powell, George 154, 185
Premier Media 14

Prenter, Geoff 257
Pretoria High Court 42
Price, Jack 278
Pringle, Derek 258
Prior, Wayne 231
Prudential World Cup 12
Puckett, Charlie 171
Pullar, Geoff 202
Punch 23
Pura Cup 18, 243, 266, 268

Qayyum, Justice Malik Mohammad 38
QCA (Queensland Cricket Association) 236
Queen's Park Oval, Trinidad 87
Queensland
  v South Australia (1977) 7
Queensland Cricket Association *see* QCA

Raith, Jacob 240–1
Ramadhin, 'Sonny' 55, 189, 235, 237
Randall, Derek 173
Randell, Steve 95
Ransford, Vernon 124
Rapotec, Stan 45–6
Redhu, Ishwar Singh 35–6
Redpath, Ian 206, 257
Reiffel, Paul 209–11, 260
Rhodes, Wilfred 30, 66
Richards, Barry 244
Richards, Sir Vivian 106, 108, 115–6, 125, 172, 231, 233, 258–9
Richardson, Richie 210, 212
Ridings, Phil 240
Rigg, Keith 195
Ring, Doug 131, 189, 239

Rixon, Steve 104–5
Roberts, Andy 210, 231
Roberts, Ron, Cavaliers 114
Robertson, Austin 10
Robertson-Glasgow, R.C. 'Crusoe' 16,
    48
Robins, Walter 142, 203
Robinson, Ray 48
Rosenwater, Irving 277
Rothmans Sunday one-day cricket 9,
    68, 255
Rowe, Lawrence 172
Roxby, Ted 26–7
Rutherford, Ken 177
Ryder Cup (2010) 82–3
Ryder, Jack 223

Sackstein, Les 41
Saeed Ahmed 199
Saggers, Ron 145, 187
Salim Malik 120
Saqlain Mushtaq 212–13
Safraz Nawaz 119
Saville family 80
SCG see Sydney Cricket Ground
schools cricket 24
Schwarz, Reggie 141
Sellers, Brian 48
Selvey, Mike 172
Sharpe, Duncan 198
Shaw, George Bernard 51
Sheahan, Paul 104
Sheerlock, Rob 81
Sheffield Shield 6, 12, 18, 46, 127,
    140, 146, 154, 162–7, 182, 185–
    9, 191, 223, 225, 243, 255, 274
Shepherd, Barry 166
Sheppard, Rev. David 248

Shrewsbury, John 84
Sievers, Morris 195
Simons, Con 165
Simpson, Bob 146, 165, 202–3, 235
Simpson, Reg 144
Sincock, David 165
Skelding, Alex 68
Slade, Mr Justice 10
Slater, Keith 166
Slater, Michael 210, 227
Sledge, Percy 247
sledging 246–50
Sloan, Tom 4
Smith, Collie 237
Smith, Graeme 28, 264–5, 270
Smith, Mike 146
Smith, Peter 140
Smith, Sydney 242
Smith, Tom, New Cricket Umpiring and
    Scoring 21, 277
Snow, John 205, 207
Sobers, Sir Garfield 28, 61, 106, 108,
    113, 116, 119–20, 125, 162, 166,
    235
Solomon, Joe 235
Sonn, Percy 41
South Africa
    v Australia (1935–6) 224; (1949–50)
        145; (1952–3) 240, 242; (1957–8)
        250; (1997–8) 32–4; (1999) 261;
        World Cup 35; (2000) 35; (2005)
        270
    v England (1955) 250; (1960) 67;
        (1994–5) 174, 278; (1998)
        34;(2000) 39; (2003) 28–9, 260,
        264; (2004–5) 28, 29, 263–4, 266
    v India (2000) 35
    v Pakistan (2000) 35

v Sri Lanka (1998) 34
v West Indies (2005) 230
South African Cricket Board 242
South Australia, v Queensland (1977) 7
South Australian Cricket Association *see* SACA
Spiers and Pond 103
Spirit of Cricket 244–5
Spofforth, Fred 217–18, 220
Spooner, Reggie 48
Sporting Times 23
Sri Lanka
    v Australia (1995–6) 257; (2004) 28, 29
    v South Africa (1998) 34
Stackpole, Keith 205–6
Statham, Brian 122
Steele, David 251–2
Stephenson, H.H. 103–4
Stewart, Alec 176–7, 260, 265
Stollmeyer, Jeff 236–7
Strauss, Ray 171
Stuart, Moira 81–2
Subba Row, Raman 202
The Sun 15, 67–8, 157, 165, 201
Sunset + Vine 75, 81
Sussex, v Australia (1961) 101
Sutcliffe, Bert 158
Sutcliffe, Herbert 66, 110
Sutherland, James 221, 243
Suttle, Ken 256
Swanton, Jim 14, 16
Sydney Cricket Ground (SCG) 3, 7, 11, 13, 26, 46–9, 80, 87, 112–3, 118, 126–7, 132, 140, 144–5, 147, 154, 156, 164–6, 179, 182–9, 213–4, 219, 229, 240, 257, 269

Sydney Morning Herald 49, 128
Sydney *Sunday Telegraph* 49
Symcox, Pat 33, 40
Symonds, Andrew 268

Tallon, Don 145, 168, 187
Tasmania
    Bellerive Oval 214
    v Queensland 259
Tate, Maurice 30
Tattersall, Roy 140
Tayfield, Hughie 127
Taylor, Bill 13
Taylor, Johnny 47
Taylor, Mark 33, 54, 76, 176, 208–12, 225, 243, 269
Telegraph newspapers 93
television
    see also Channel Four; Channel Nine
    anti-siphoning list 13–14
    colour TV 9, 11
    commentating 15–17, 93
    commercial TV 11
    coverage of cricket 78–92
    commentators 78–9
    fees 7, 10
    Pay Television 13–14
    televising Australian sport 12–13
Tendulkar, Sachin, 108, 115–6, 125
Tests
    see also World Series Cricket
    Bodyline Series 38, 105, 122, 223
    Centenary Test 7, 172–3, 228
    first Test 216
    Test match double 274
    Tied Test 7, 8, 113, 114, 124, 161, 229, 261

third umpire 64, 76

Thomas, Grahame 163

Thoms, George 189

Thomson, Ian 101

Thomson, Jeff 61, 115, 122, 231, 251, 258

Thorpe, Graham 177, 264

Tied Test 7, 8, 113, 114, 124, 161, 229, 261

Titmus, Fred 30

Toshack, Ernie 154, 183

Treanor, Jack 156

Trengove, Wim 42

Trescothick, Marcus 29, 260

Tribe, George 142

Trimble, Sam 256

Trueman, Fred 86, 108, 122–3, 170–1, 182, 249, 251

Trumble, Hugh 221, 226

Trumper, Victor 46–7, 108–9, 124, 217, 219–20

Turner, C.T.B. 133

Tyson, Frank 122

UCBSA *see* United Cricket Board of South Africa

Ulyett, George 218

umpiring 21, 34, 62–77
  third umpire 64, 76
  walking decisions 98–102

Underwood, Derek 172

United Cricket Board of South Africa (UCBSA) 36–7, 41–2

V & G Insurance 256

Valentine, Alf 55, 189, 234, 237

Vaughan, Michael 29–30, 260, 265

VCA *see* Victorian Cricket Association

Vernon, Dudley 16

Victoria
  v New South Wales (1933–4) 48; (1956) 6–76

Victorian Cricket Association, TV fees 7

Vincent, Major 'Beau' 48

Voce, Bill 122

Vogler, Ernie 141

Wade, Herbie 224

Waight, Denis 233

Wakelam, Teddy 16

Walcott, Sir Clyde 236–7

Walker, Alan 183–4, 187

Walker, Max 231, 251

Walsh, Courtney 210–11

Walsh, Jack 140

Waqar Younis 95

Ward, Frank 112, 140, 195

Wardle, Johnny 65, 140

Warne, Shane 28–9, 38, 85, 106–8, 116, 120–3, 125–7, 137, 139–42, 160, 173, 175–6, 209, 211, 213, 219, 259, 261, 269
  wickets 126, 141–2, 173, 175–6, 209, 259

Warner, Sir Pelham 48, 223

Wasim Akram 95, 214

Wasim Bari, 120

Watson, Graeme 206

Watson, Willie 109

Waugh, Mark 32–4, 38, 176, 209–11, 213, 214, 261

Waugh, Steve 28, 35, 54, 105, 176, 208–12, 225, 227, 231, 261

Webb, Syd 201

Webber, Roy 278

Weekes, Sir Everton 109, 236–7

West Indian Players' Association 230, 238

West Indies
  v Australia (1951–2) 188–9, 229, 236, 239–40; (1955) 88, 153, 236; (1960) 7, 8; (1961) Tied Test 7, 8, 113–14, 124, 161, 229, 234–6; (1975–6) 9, 12, 115, 231–2; (1978) 13; (1991) 87; (1995) 210–12; (2004) 230; (2005) 238
  v England (1963) 5, 14, 170; (1976) 116, 233; (1984) 258–9; (1994) 113; (2004) 28–9
  v South Africa (2005) 230

West Indies Board 20, 238

West, Peter 5, 13–15, 68, 78, 85

White, Craig 177

White, Gordon 141

Whitington, R.S. 'Dick' 219

Willes, Christine 21

Willes, John 21

Willey, Peter 172

Williams, Charles 66

Williams, Henry 41

Williams, Stuart 212

Willis, Bob 118, 172–4, 208, 258

Wimbush, Wendy 277

Wisden 48, 52, 55, 64, 100, 106, 203, 234, 278

Wood, Barry 251

Wood, Graeme 174

Woodfull, Bill 48, 221, 223

Woolmer, Bob 172

World Cup 257–8; (1975) 9, 12; (1996) 257; (1999) 25, 257; (2003) 98, 257, 260; (2007) 229, 230

World Cup U-19 (2004) 64

World Series Cricket 10–12, 23, 52, 126, 233, 257

Worrell, Sir Frank 8, 67, 108, 113–4, 124–5, 161, 189, 234–8
  Frank Worrell Memorial Address 208
  Frank Worrell Trophy 209, 211–12, 229

Wright, Doug 112, 140, 142

Wrigley, Arthur 278

Zaheer Abbas 119–20

ZCU (Zimbabwe Cricket Union), international players 20

Zimbabwe 19–20

Zimbabwe Cricket Union *see* ZCU